Research Reports ESPRIT

Subseries
Project 322 · CAD Interfaces (CAD*I)
Volume 4

Subseries Editors:
I. Bey, Kernforschungszentrum Karlsruhe GmbH
J. Leuridan, Leuven Measurement and Systems

Edited in cooperation with
the Commission of the European Communities

R. Schuster D. Trippner M. Endres

CAD*I Drafting Model

Springer-Verlag
Berlin Heidelberg New York
London Paris Tokyo Hong Kong

Authors

Richard Schuster
Dietmar Trippner
Michael Endres
Bayerische Motorenwerke AG
Petuelring 130, D-8000 München 40, FRG

ESPRIT Project 322: CAD Interfaces (CAD*I) belongs to the Research and Development area "Computer-Aided Design and Engineering (CAD / CAE)" within the Subprogramme 5 "Computer-Integrated Manufacturing (CIM)" of the ESPRIT Programme (European Strategic Programme for Research and Development in Information Technology) supported by the European Communities.

ESPRIT Project 322 has been established to define the most important interfaces in CAD / CAM systems for data exchange, data base, finite element analysis, experimental analysis, and advanced modelling. The definitions of these interfaces are being elaborated in harmony with international standardization efforts in this field.

Partners in the project are:
Bayerische Motorenwerke AG / FRG · CISIGRAPH / France · Cranfield Institute of Technology / UK · Danmarks Tekniske Højskole / Denmark · Estudios y Realizaciones en Diseño Informatizado SA (ERDISA) /Spain · Gesellschaft für Strukturanalyse (GfS) mbH / FRG · Katholieke Universiteit Leuven / Belgium · Kernforschungszentrum Karlsruhe GmbH / FRG · Leuven Measurement and Systems / Belgium · NEH Consulting Engineers ApS / Denmark · Rutherford Appleton Laboratory / UK · Universität Karlsruhe / FRG.

ISBN 3-540-52051-1 Springer-Verlag Berlin Heidelberg New York
ISBN 0-387-52051-1 Springer-Verlag New York Berlin Heidelberg

Publication No. EUR 12762 of the
Commission of the European Communities,
Scientific and Technical Communication Unit,
Directorate-General Telecommunications, Information Industries and Innovation,
Luxembourg

Printed in Germany

Printing and Binding: Weihert-Druck GmbH, Darmstadt
2145/3140 – 543210 – Printed on acid-free paper

Acknowledgements

To begin with, the authors would like to thank the members of the respective drafting groups of the organizations DIN 96.4, ISO/TC184/SC4/WG1 and ESPRIT Project 322 (CAD*I) for the discussion contributing to this book. Especially the ideas and contributions of Mr. R. Korff and Mr. H. Scheder (BMW AG) should be pointed out.

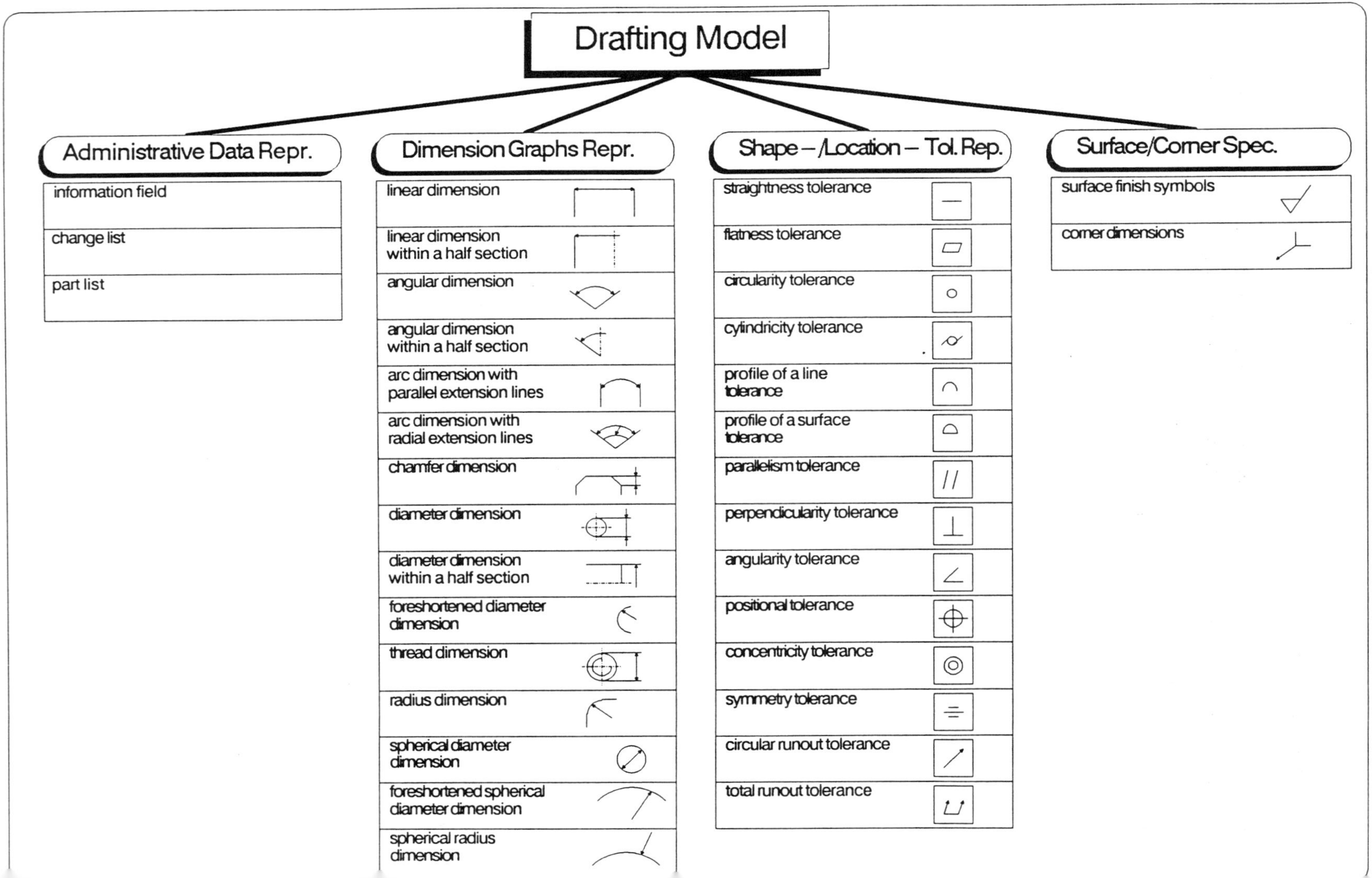

Drafting Model
Administrative Data Repr.
information field
change list
part list
Dimension Graphs Repr.
linear dimension
linear dimension within a half section
angular dimension
angular dimension within a half section
arc dimension with parallel extension lines
arc dimension with radial extension lines
chamfer dimension
diameter dimension
diameter dimension within a half section
foreshortened diameter dimension
thread dimension
radius dimension
spherical diameter dimension
foreshortened spherical diameter dimension
spherical radius dimension
Shape – /Location – Tol. Rep.
straightness tolerance
flatness tolerance
circularity tolerance
cylindricity tolerance
profile of a line tolerance
profile of a surface tolerance
parallelism tolerance
perpendicularity tolerance
angularity tolerance
positional tolerance
concentricity tolerance
symmetry tolerance
circular runout tolerance
total runout tolerance
Surface/Corner Spec.
surface finish symbols
corner dimensions

Summary

The content of this book is an information model for technical drawings, the so-called "Drafting Model". The Drafting Model is a part of a complex information model describing product definition data, their applications and their representations. The definition of the information model is a central component of the development of STEP, a future international standard for the exchange of product definition data.

Here the Drafting Model particularly encloses descriptions for the representations of organizational drawing data, tolerances, dimensions and surface attributes such as surface finish symbols (a survey of the whole content is shown in the figure above). Additional to that requirements for the Presentation Model concerning the representation of geometry as well as the integration process for both the Drafting and the Presentation Models are formulated. The extent of the Drafting Model is restricted to the application area "Mechanical Engineering".

Within the Drafting Model the annotation representations are described on the one hand informally and on the other hand formally using a high level language for information modeling, EXPRESS. Principally the representations of the annotation are described according to the international drawing standards. Thus the semantics pertinent to the specific graphical appearance are maintained. The data structures provide formal descriptions of annotations at a high generation level, which means that a "way" is defined how to generate these annotations. Further it is possible to describe single annotation graphs as well as complex configurations of several annotation graphs. The required associativity of the annotation representation to the product definition data is realized by referring to the representation of the geometry that itself refers to the geometry description of the product definition data.

This book is part of a series presenting the results of ESPRIT Project 322 "CAD Interfaces" (CAD*I). This volume concentrates on the Drafting Model as described above.

It is intended as a guideline for readers interested in:

- CAD-System development,
- Computer internal representation of technical drawings,
- Implementation of interface processors for CAD-Systems,
- Standardization of technical drawings created by CAD-Systems.

Project Overview

During the past 25 years computers have been introduced in industry to perform technical tasks such as drafting, design, process planning, data acquisition, process control and quality assurance. Computer-based solutions, however, are still in most cases single isolated devices within a manufacturing plant.

Computer technology is evolving rapidly, and the life cycle of today's products and production methods is shortening, with continuously increasing requirements from customers, and a trend to market interrelations between companies at a national and international level. This forces a growing need for efficient storage, retrieval and exchange of information. Integration of information is urgent within companies to interconnect departments which used to work more or less on their own. On the other hand direct communication with outside customers, suppliers and partner institutions will often determine the position of an enterprise among its competitors. In this sense, Computer Integrated Manufacturing (CIM) is the key of today for the competitiveness of tomorrow. But the realization of a future-oriented CIM concept is not possible without powerful, widely accepted and standardized interfaces. They are the vital issue on the way to CIM. They will contribute to harmonizing data structures and information flows and will play a major role in open CIM systems. Standardized interfaces allow for:

- Access to data produced and archived on computing equipment which is no longer in active use;
- Communication between hardware and software from different vendors;
- Paperless exchange of information.

ESPRIT Project 322 "CAD Interfaces" (CAD*I) started in 1984 is a five-year research and development programme on CAD interfaces with the aim of defining some missing interface specifications in the environment of computer aided design (CAD) systems for mechanical engineering. Parts design and CAD are the starting point in the design and manufacturing process, and can also be considered a starting point for information generation and data exchange.

Based on the results and using the experiences of former national standardization initiatives like IGES, VDAFS or SET, the CAD*I project team aimed from early in the project to contribute to the first international standard for product data exchange, because only an internationally accepted standard interface will fulfill the requirements of European industry.

The standardization work in CAD data exchange at international level is performed through ISO/TC184/SC4 under the name of STEP: Standard for the Exchange of Product Model Data. CAD*I has had a large influence on the STEP definitions especially for the exchange of geometry and shape information (curves, surfaces and solid models), the interface to Finite Element Analysis programmes and drafting information.

This report is one of a series of similar books which summarize the wealth of results achieved during the five years of ESPRIT project CAD*I.

CAD Interfaces

Main results are:

- Vendor independent interfaces consisting of a neutral file specification and corresponding pre- and post-processors for many commercial CAD systems have been defined, developed and tested. The CAD*I specifications for geometry and shape representation (curves, surfaces and solids) are clearly visible in the first international draft proposal standard. The processors are in practical use in several European and national projects. European system vendors have begun to integrate these results into their products.

- A general standard specification of a neutral file for exchanging finite element data has been developed and implemented. Tests have been performed with the interface processors for several FEM packages available on the market. In addition CAD models were transferred to finite element systems using the CAD*I neutral file. The results of this work have already appeared on the European market.

- New and improved data acquisition and analytical procedures for dynamic structural analysis have been specified and tested on complex real structures. Also, powerful tools for the intelligent integration (link) of experimental and analytical results in structural design have been developed, tested and merged into software products now available on the market. These results are visible in recent commercial products.

- Some new methods have been developed to enhance the communication interface in CAD/CAE systems. Future users of this kind of system will be able to enter information to the systems by handsketching input or by using technical terms from design language instead of via formal geometrical descriptions. First implementations have been successful; they are based on levels of internal interfaces using a product model.

- A neutral database interface based on the CAD*I neutral file format has been developed to handle archiving and retrieval of product information in a database. A set of standard access routines has been written and tested with existing CAD systems and a widely used commercial relational database management system. The introduction of these results into marketable products is on the way.

- An information model for the description of technical drawings has been developed: the CAD*I drafting model. This information model represents the highest level of sophistication within the level concept of the drafting model of the STEP specification.

A total of about 150 person-years of research and development effort has been spent on the project. The CAD*I project involved 12 partners in 6 countries of the European Community.

As project manager since 1985 I would like to express my appreciation to the co-manager J. Leuridan and the fifty or more people working in and on the project for their engagement to reach the originally stated goals. In addition I would like to pay special tribute to Mrs. P. MacConaill and R. Zimmermann from the Commission of the European Communities and to the reviewers G. Enderle(†), E.A. Warman and H. Nowacki for their cooperative support. Special acknowledgement is due also to Mrs. U. Frey for running the administrative part of the project and for her contributions to forming the spirit of the CAD*I team.

I. Bey, CAD*I project manager

Table of Contents

1. Introduction

1.1. Interfaces for the Exchange of Product Definition Data

The recent years involved a great increase in the use of CAD-Systems by industrial organizations for the development and manufacturing processes of technical products. In the beginning the creation of technical drawings was the main task of those systems. Meanwhile they are used to support the development and manufacturing process with several different applications. Therefore a more precise description of the technical product meeting the technical requirements of the specific application became imperative. This fact as well as economic and regional aspects caused the development of several different and mostly incompatible CAD-Systems being more or less adjusted to a specific application. The incompatibility is manifested - leaving out differences in hardware configurations - by different file formats, partially different information contents and different ways to describe the information contents. Those differences result from efforts to optimize the software with regard to the need of storage, running time of the functions of the system and the integrity of its data.

For the integration of applications necessary for the development and the manufacturing respectively of a technical product, it is necessary to make data - or portions of them - that are provided by one CAD-System available for a second CAD-System. Four solutions for the transfer of the data are conceivable:

- The first one is to reedit the data in the second system. This possibility obviously takes a lot of time and errors during the reediting cannot be excluded.

- Secondly a standardization of the file formats of all the systems is conceivable, but the pressure for optimizing the system does not allow this solution.

- The third possibility is to realize the data transfer by a direct connection of both the systems. The connection supports a direct conversion of the file format of the sending system into the file format of the receiving system. When considering the variety of the existing different CAD-Systems, this solution does not seem to be an appropriate solution for an extensive integration concept, because an interface for every connection of two systems has to be designated.

- The fourth and most practicable solution is to exchange data with the help of a neutral file format (a so-called "standardized interface"). There the data of the sending system are converted to the neutral file format and after that from the neutral format to the file format of the receiving format. Far less efforts are required when integrating the CAD-Systems with this concept, because only one connection becomes necessary for every different system. A further advantage of the neutral file format is the possibility of long-time storage of product definition data.

Existing standardized interfaces like IGES (Initial Graphics Exchange Specification), VDAFS (VDA-Flächenschnittstelle), SET (Standard d'Exchange et de Transfert), etc. up to now are restricted substantially to descriptions of geometry and definetely do not meet the requirement for an almost complete description of the product. A specification of a more complete product definition is intended for the first international standardized interface STEP (Standard for the Exchange of Product Model Data) the development of which is still going on. Besides the support of exchanging product model data STEP is intended to specify

- which information is neccessary to determine a technical product and to represent it where required and
- how a structure of the information contents could be achieved.

One of the main tasks of the European ESPRIT-Project CAD*I (CAD-Interfaces) was to support the development of STEP.

For the transfer of product definition data from a specific file format of a CAD-System to the neutral file format and vice versa it is of utmost importance to preserve the semantic assigned to the data by different ways (e. g.: By attributes or by the context the data are involved in). Thus, the data of the neutral format have to have the same information content as the data of the sending system. Consequently the specification of a neutral data format ideally has the same functionality as all conceivable specific file formats of the CAD-Systems. Functionality in this context means that the semantic of data elements is preserved during a data transfer from a specific CAD-System to the neutral file.

1.2. Approach to Classify Information Models

All data generated or manipulated by CAD-Systems contribute to the description of technical products and - in a broad sense - even technical processes (e. g.: Cutter paths). Different applications supported by CAD-Systems make different "views" at the product (or more accurate: Information models of the product) necessary to meet the requirements of those specific applications. For example a FEM-Analysis needs a geometry described by a mesh and the definition of cutter paths of a milling process needs a geometry described by surfaces.

Generally the information models supported by CAD-Systems can be subdivided into two classes with regard to their information content:

- Information models of the first class contain descriptions on a high level of abstraction - that means not adjusted to a specific application - of product information. That is geometrical, organizational, functional and technological information. In STEP terminology this information model is called the "**Core Model**". There the "Core Model" is characterized as containing "... the basic information that is required to define the shape of a product, plus other information that is likely to be common across many applications" (see /1/, 4.1).
- The information models containing information adjusted to a specific application are classed within another category. This category may comprise parts of the content of the "Core Model" namely geometrical, organizational, functional or technological information, but described under the aspect of one specific application (e. g.: For a FEM-Analysis the geometry of the product is described by a mesh that is an approximation of the theoretical geometry). Within the STEP specification these application oriented models are named "**Topical Information Models**".

The only logical relation between those two classes of information models is that the "Topical Information Model" can be derived from the "Core Model" to a certain extent. A mechanism in the reverse order seems to be absurd.

Actually the occurrence of an information model is not only influenced by the application, but also by the abilities of the CAD-System (e. g.: the description of the geometry depends on the modeller of the system, i. e. two- or three-dimensional wireframe, surfaces or solids) and the skill of the designer.

1.3. The Information Model for Technical Drawings

One of the information models classed with the "Topical Information Models" is the model containing descriptions of external representations - due to human interpretation - of product information. The common medium for the external representations are technical drawings.

Technical drawings generally consist of graphical representations of geometry, texts, symbols and tables that have to be described internally for an output device, e. g. a plotter or screen.

Partially the information contents of a technical drawing may be derived from an existing "Core Model" that internally describes the technical product. Derived may be for example representations of geometry, dimensional and tolerance values.

Additional to that further information being relevant only for the description of technical drawings is necessary, for instance: The definitions of views and sections concerning geometry representation, the descriptions of graphical appearances of dimensions and tolerances, the number of drawing sheets and their format, etc.

Within the STEP environment the descriptions of technical drawings are divided up into two models, the delimitation of which still is vague. The first is the Presentation Model dealing with the problems of physically representing lines, curves, fields and symbols, the representation of the geometry within views and sections and finally the text styles. Secondly there is the Drafting Model defining appearances of dimensions, tolerances and further geometry related attributes as well as administrative information. In the chapters 4. and 8.1. a possible adaption of both the models is outlined.

2. The Drafting Model

2.1. Requirements for the Development of the Drafting Model

The Drafting Model encloses unambiguous descriptions of representations on technical drawings. The extent of the various representations is restricted to the application area of "Mechanical Engineering" and only annotation representations are supported that are in accordance with the international drafting standards (the relevant standards are shown in figure 2.1). Thus there are descriptions of representations of drawing organization data, dimension graphs, tolerances and surface attributes. Descriptions of representations of the projected geometry are not integrated in the Drafting Model, but by describing necessary geometry appearances requirements are formulated for the responsible information models, especially the Presentation Model.

Principally it should be possible to integrate the developed Drafting Model into the STEP-Specification (for the current version of the STEP/IPIM see /1/; IPIM: Integrated Product Information Model). Therefore the following fundamental requirements derived from the STEP-Philosophy have been taken into consideration:

1. Guaranteed functionality is the first main requirement. Functionality means that the data describing an item may only be applied in the semantic scope of the item. The effect on the data structures is that the structures of one application schema consist of nothing but entity definitions of this specific application schema with the advantage that data of different schemas can be separated for different applications, e. g.: It should not be allowed to describe the extension lines of a dimension graph by geometry shape lines. For a further automatic processing of a set of those data, it would be impossible to distinguish between geometry representations and the representation of annotations. Only if there is a functional relation between two application schemas, a possibility of referencing data of the other schema should be provided and so support a valid description of this relation (e. g.: The representation of form and location tolerances partly depends on the representation of dimensions. Thus a possibilty for pointing from the tolerance representations schema to the dimension schema has to be granted.).

2. Another basic requirement is to distinguish between product information and the representation of this product information. For instance, the description of the geometry and not the description of the representation of dimensions originally contains the dimensions of the geometry. An unambiguous distinction, however, is not always

possible, e. g.: In a specific arrangement of dimension representations information about a sequence and direction of a manufacturing process may be inherent.

3. A further requirement is to avoid the description of redundant information. This step prevents the creation of contradictionary information contents in case of a succeeding manipulation of the data set.

4. The associativity of the represented annotation to the represented geometry has to be supported, which means that a represented element of the drafting schema is linked with a selected part of the representation of the geometry. Therefore a manipulation of the geometry model from which the representation of the geometry is derived (see /1/, 4.12, p.337), causes changes in the representation of the referring annotation. The drafting resource schema contains a list of entities describing interpretations of represented geometry - only an informal description is provided, because those descriptions should not be part of the Drafting Model - which are referenced by the entities describing dimension graphs. Inherent or formal constraints conduct to a correct associativity (e. g. a chamfer dimension may only reference a pictorial representation of a chamfer).

5. The language for the formal description of the data structures is EXPRESS as documented in /2/. The information modeling language EXPRESS has the aim to describe information contents at a high level of abstraction and is not designed with the purpose of creating structures with regard to a particular data base.

ISO	ISO/DIN	DIN
128	1011	406
129	1302	2300
	2692	7167
	5459	7168
	7083	7184
		7182

Fig. 2.1: Relevant drafting standards for the development of the CAD*I Drafting Model

2.2. Systematical Approach to the Drafting Model

At first an analysis of conventional drawings and current drafting standards with regard to the manifold possibilities of the representation of technical information is necessary. An analysis of technical drawings designed with the help of CAD-Systems makes no sense at this point, because this procedure would reduce the possibilities of the representations to the functions of the examined specific CAD-Systems.

Thereafter the manifold representation possibilities being described in the current drafting standards have to be checked with regard to their compatibility with CAD drafting applications. Several possibilities - mostly foreshortened representations - can be omitted, because they are provided for the only purpose to reduce the expense of the manual drafting procedure.

The result of the selection is a limited number of possibilities of the representation of technical information that have to be described in a so-called "logical model". The "logical model" requires unambigous informal descriptions of the annotation representations leaving out weak expressions like "to save time and space ...", "... similar to the examples shown in figures ...", "... provided that no ambiguity can arise ..." and "... in certain cases ..." (all the examples cited before are extracted from the drafting standard ISO 128). By using the "logical model" it must definetely be clear, if an annotation graph is approved or not. The "logical model" is included in the informal descriptions of the data structures and an extract is contained in the attachement to /4/, the statement catalog. Another function of the "logical model" is to lay down the rules and assumptions that are inherent in the formal description of the data structures. The rules and assumptions characterize the performance of the structures and may serve as a basis for a discussion about the Drafting Model. The formal descriptions on the other hand are much more difficult to criticize, because of the lacking in evidence of inherent rules and assumptions.

The informal specifications within the "logical model" may now be described by the formal EXPRESS language. The rules and assumptions as defined before can be principally integrated into the EXPRESS-Specification in two ways: They may be inherent in the data structure in such a manner that no instance of data according to the structure can violate those constraints. The other way for integrating constraints into the data structures is to define explicitely the constraints by so-called "WHERE-Clauses" provided by EXPRESS.

Finally the Drafting Model has to be integrated into the scope of the other application models, especially the Presentation Model. Here only a concept for the integration process is outlined.

A survey of the approach to the Drafting Model is shown in picture 2.2.

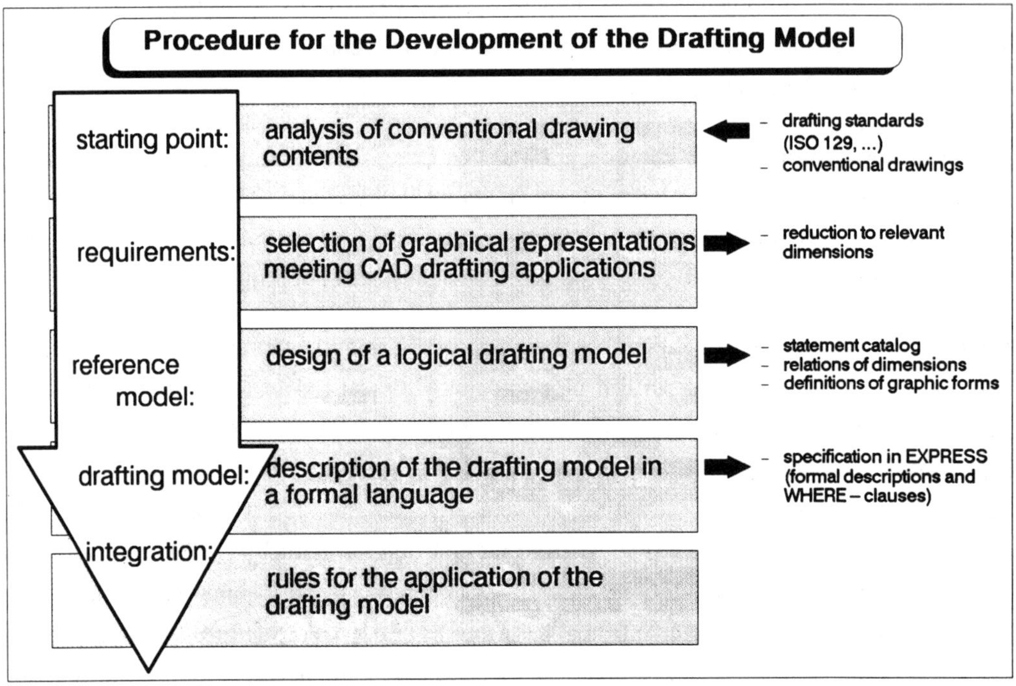

Fig. 2.2. Approach to the Drafting Model

2.3. The Basic Principles of the Drafting Model

There are three criteria for the classification of the Drafting Model: Aggregation, generation and association.

The grade of **aggregation** determines wether "complex" or "simple" graphs of annotation may be described by the data structures. "Complex" graphs of annotation consist of at least two "simple" graphs. A "complex" graph for example may be several dimension graphs combined to a dimension chain or a combination of a dimension graph with a surface finish symbol or a geometry tolerance frame, whereas a single dimension graph or a surface finish symbol are classified to "simple" graphs.

Characteristics of the Drafting Models

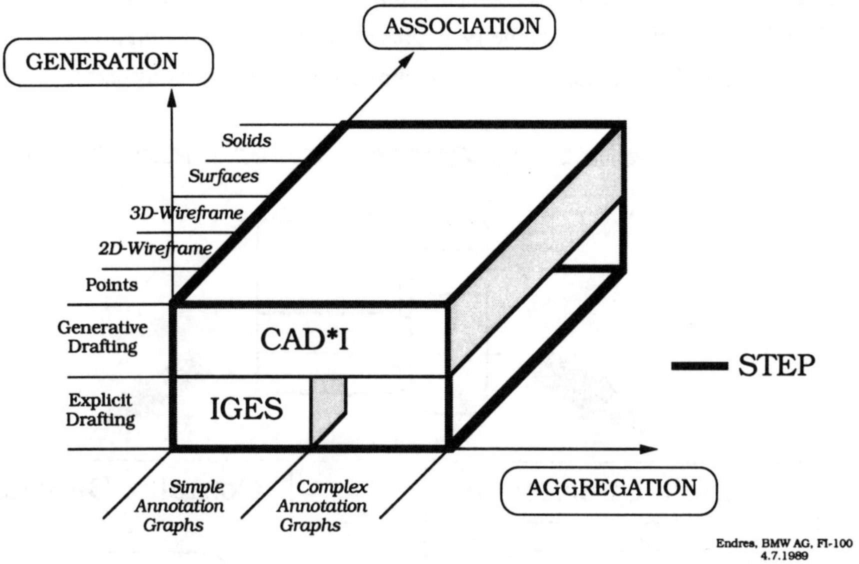

Fig. 2.3: Characteristics of the CAD*I Drafting Model

The criterion **generation** characterizes the way the annotation graphs are described. Explicitely described graphs consist of their components being combined within the structure, e. g.: A linear dimension may consist of the components extension lines, dimension line, dimension note and termination symbols. In this case the descriptions of the components mutually have no relations. Therefore constraints restricting the various possibilities of the combination of such components have to be formulated to guarantee appearances according to the drafting standards. Otherwise a decline in semantic content has to be accepted, e. g.: A graph with extension lines that are not parallel to each other may not be called linear dimension. Generative annotation graphs on the other hand are described by parameters, with which it is possible to generate the graph. The components no longer exist explicitely. For example it is sufficient for the description of a linear dimension to determine the direction of the dimension line, the starting point of the extension lines and the position of the dimension note to generate the graph. The advantage of generative descriptions is - contrary to explicit descriptions - that there are no redundant data. Explained with the example linear dimension again: An explicitely described linear dimension contains the directions of its components extension lines and dimension line, whereas within the generative linear dimension the direction of the extension lines may be derived as being perpendicular to the dimension line.

Finally **association** is the classification of a Drafting Model with regard to its links to the description of the geometry of the product definition data. Here several different geometry modeller have to be taken into consideration like 2D- or 3D-Wireframes, Surface- and Solid-Modeller. No link to the geometry is preserved where the annotation graphs are described relative to positions defined within a coordinate system of a drawing sheet.

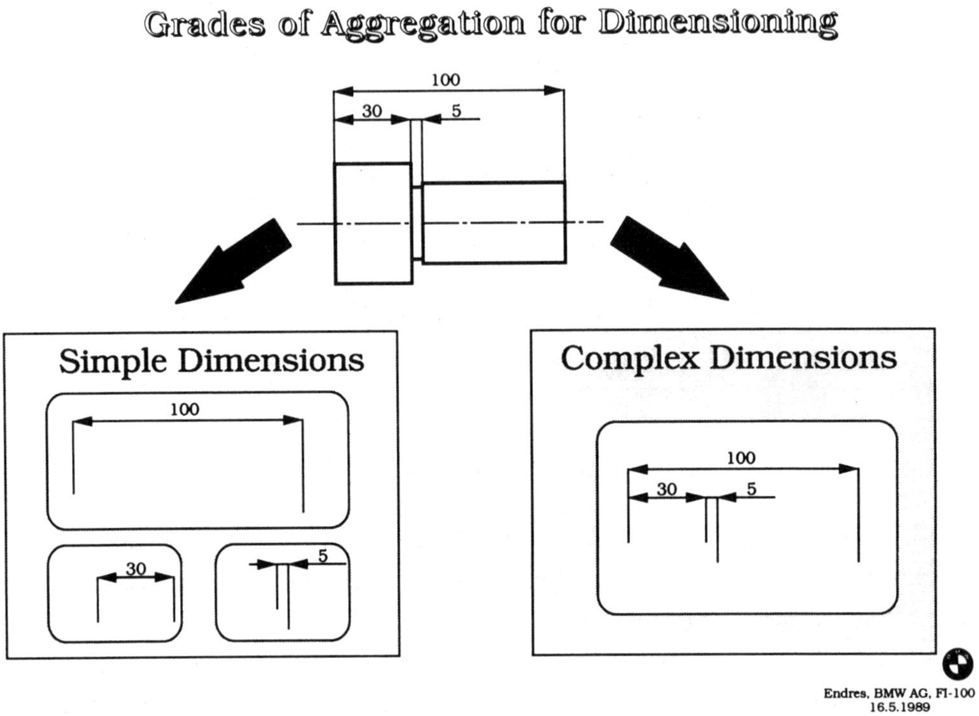

Fig. 2.4: Capabilities of the CAD*I Drafting Model in terms of aggregation (exemplary for dimensioning)

The characteristics of the CAD*I Drafting Model in comparison to other standards like IGES and the intended STEP specification are shown in figure 2.3. The CAD*I Drafting Model describes both complex and simple annotation graphs, the graphs are described in a generative way and the graphs may be linked either with the represented geometry - being projected from wireframes, surfaces or solids - or with points relative to a drawing sheet coordinate system (see figures 2.4, 2.5., 2.6.). A further explanation of the link between annotation and geometry can be found in chapter 8.1.

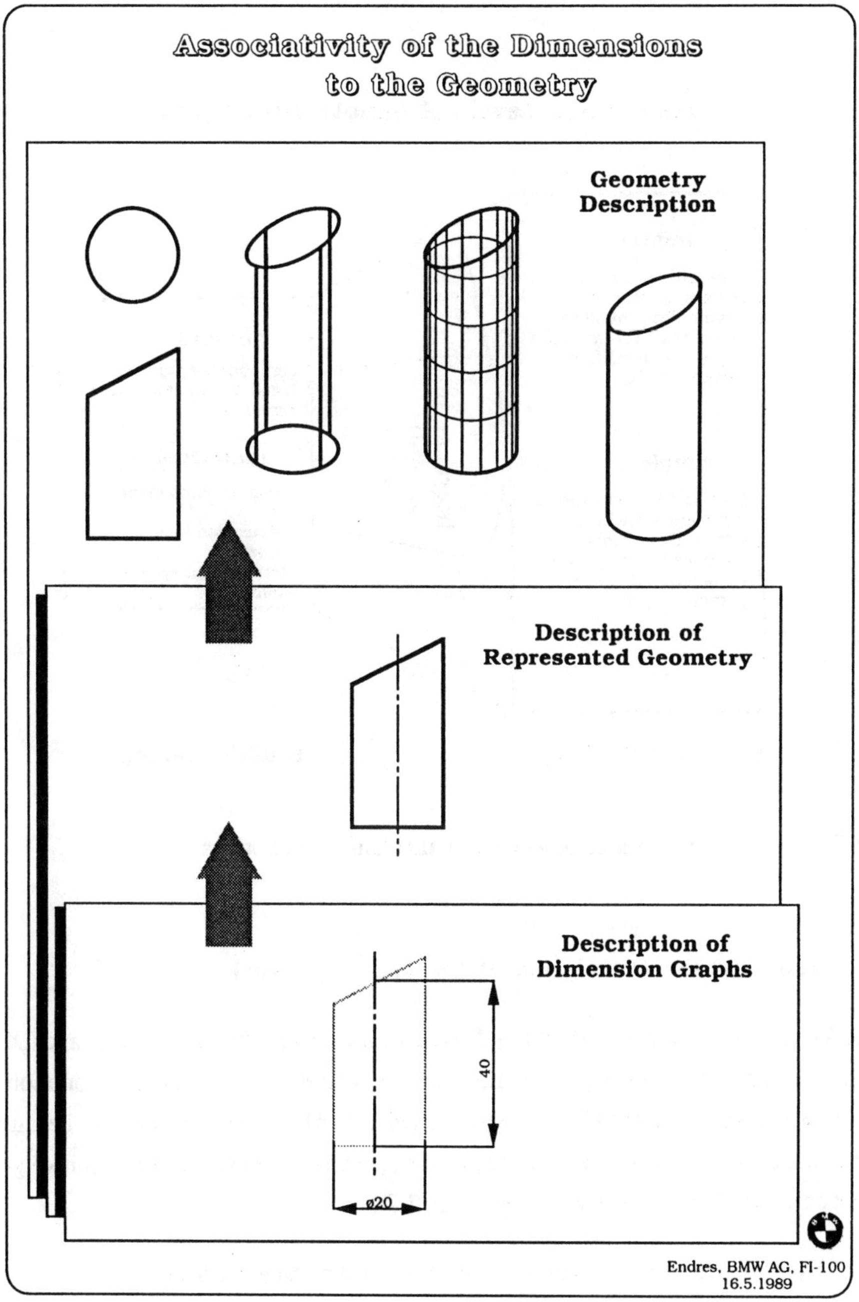

Fig. 2.6: The associativity of the CAD*I Drafting Model to the geometry (exemplary for dimensioning)

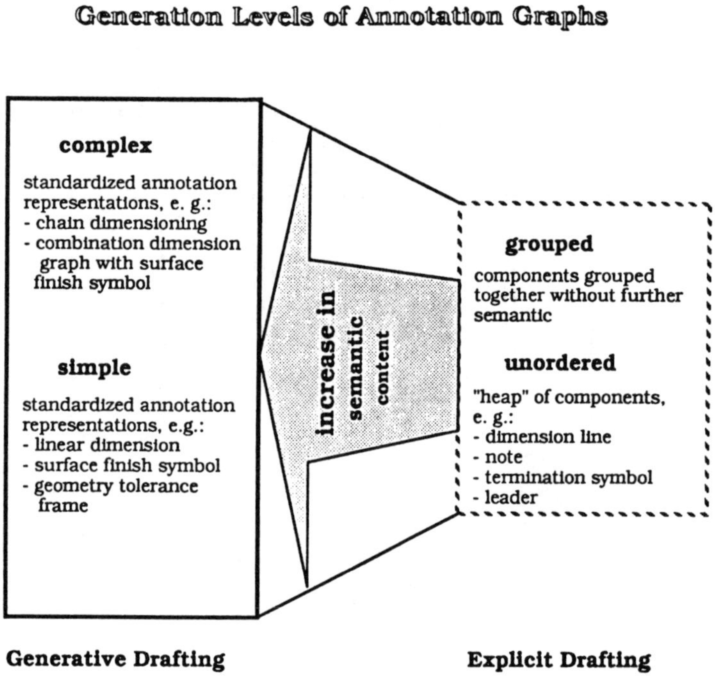

Fig. 2.5: Different level of generation of annotation descriptions

2.4. Tools for the Description of the Drafting Model

For the formal description of the Drafting Model the information modelling language EXPRESS (see /2/) is used. A pictorial representation of the structures with the help of common formal graphical notations like IDEF1X (see /8/) or EXPRESSAM (see /9/) is omitted, because these notations are too complex. A partial survey of the structures is provided by a primitive graphical notation obeying the following rules (see figure 2.7):

- Every represented entity type is placed within a rectangular frame.
- The keywords of the entity types are written in capital letters and placed at the top of the frame.

- The names of the attributes are written in lower case letters and listed beneath the keyword of the entity type.
- Where an attribute references another entity type, the frame of the entity type is connected with the attribute by a polyline. The values at the starting point of the line denote the minimal (left value) and the maximal (right value) number of entities that may be referenced. A "#" means an arbitrary value.
- Subtypes of an entity type are placed beneath the attributes of the supertype in shaded frames.
- Entity types that are not represented completely (i. e. missing attributes or subtypes) are marked by points being placed beneath the name of the entity type instead of the missing elements.

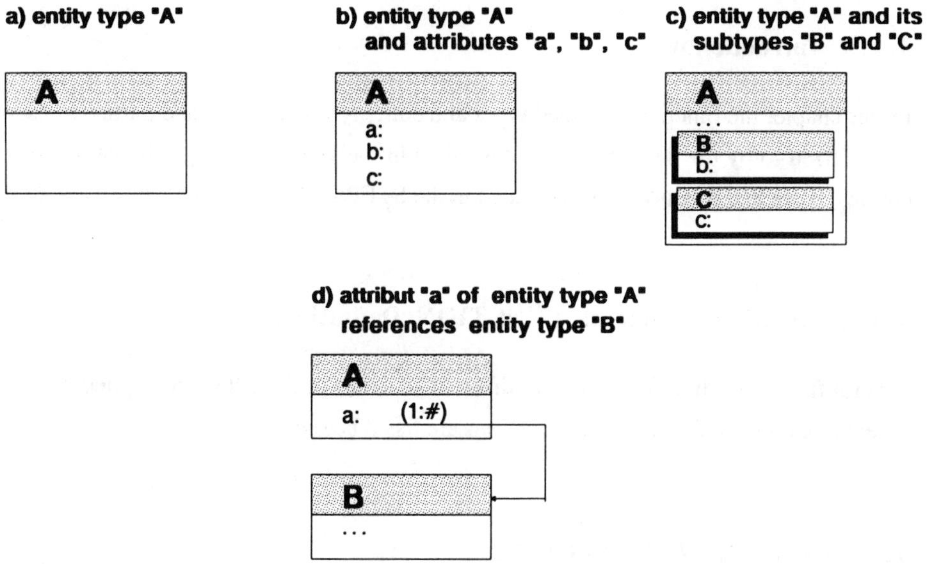

Fig. 2.7: Rules for the graphical representation of the data structures

3. Drafting Resources

```
*)
SCHEMA  drafting_schema;
   EXPORT  EVERYTHING;
   ASSUME  (ipim_resources_schema,  ipim_geometry_schema,
   ipim_presentation_schema,  ipim_tolerances_schema);
(*
```

```
*)
SCHEMA  drafting_resources_schema;
   EXPORT  EVERYTHING;
(*
```

3.1. Introduction

In this chapter the functions, defined types and entity types are listed and partially described that are referred to by the data structures described in the whole drafting schema. Further applied entities, types and functions are contained in the STEP/IPIM (see /1/).

3.2. Drafting Resources FUNCTION Definitions

Several functions already defined in different schemas of the IPIM are applied by the drafting schema. Additional definitions of functions are listed below:

3.2.1. ANGLE BETWEEN VECTORS

The function ANGLE_BETWEEN_VECTORS calculates the angle between two vectors. The third argument determines the measuring direction of the angle.

```
*)
FUNCTION angle_between_vectors (arg_1, arg_2: vector;
                          arg_3: rotational_direction):
                          REAL;
   LOCAL
      angle                 : REAL;
      k                     : REAL;
   END_LOCAL;
   k =  dot_product (arg_1, arg_2) / (vector_magnitude
      (arg_1) * (vector_magnitude (arg_2));
   angle = ACOS (k);
   CASE arg_3 OF
      "clockwise"           :  RETURN (-angle);
      "counterclockwise"    :  RETURN (angle);
   END_CASE;
END_FUNCTION;
(*
```

3.2.2. ARC CALC

The function ARC_CALC returns a value of type ARC_SEGMENT. The arc is derived from start and end point of the segment and the direction of the tangent in the end point of the segment.

```
*)
FUNCTION arc_calc (arg_1, arg_2: view_position; arg_3:
                          vector): arc_segment;
   (* There is no formal description of the code to
   determine the arc up to now, but an informal
   description can be offered: On principle the center
   point of the arc lies on a line perpendicular to the
   tangent in the end point of the arc. Relative to the
   tangent the center point is located on the same side
   as the start point. A further condition is that there
   is an equal distance (i. e. the radius) between center
```

```
   point and start point and between center point and end
   point. Both the connotation "start point" respectively
   "end point" and the direction in the end point
   determines the part of the arc being defined. *)
END_FUNCTION;
(*
```

3.2.3. CREATE LIST

This function is used to introduce an attribute type GENERIC_LIST based on an attribute type GENERIC that becomes the first element of the established list.

```
*)
FUNCTION create_list (arg: GENERIC): generic_list;
   LOCAL
      list                  : generic_list;
                               -- see /1/, 4.3.1.1.1
   END_LOCAL;
   list[1] = arg;
   RETURN (list);
END_FUNCTION;
(*
```

3.2.4. CREATE VECTOR

The function CREATE_VECTOR returns a vector that has the direction and length of an assumed line limited by two points defined by the two arguments of type VIEW_POSITION.

```
*)
FUNCTION create_vector (arg_1, arg_2: view_position):
                           vector_with_magnitude;
```

```
   LOCAL
      k                            : vector_with_magnitude;
                                     -- see /1/, 4.5.3.11
   END_LOCAL;
   IF distance (arg_1, arg_2) = 0 THEN
      RETURN (NULL);
   ELSE
      BEGIN
      k = arg_2 - arg_1;
      RETURN (k);
      END;
   END_IF;
END_FUNCTION;
(*
```

3.2.5. EXTEND LIST

The function EXTEND_LIST adds an entity of type GENERIC to an existing list of type GENERIC_LIST.

```
*)
FUNCTION extend_list (arg_1: generic_list, arg_2:
                              GENERIC): generic_list;
   LOCAL
      n                            : INTEGER;
   END_LOCAL;
   n = sizeof (arg_1);
   arg_1[n+1] = arg_2;
   RETURN (arg_1);
END_FUNCTION;
(*
```

3.2.6. ID

The function ID returns the value of its argument.

```
*)
FUNCTION id (arg: GENERIC): GENERIC;
END_FUNCTION;
(*
```

3.2.7. IS PERPENDICULAR TO

The function IS_PERPENDICULAR_TO returns a vector that is perpendicular to the tangent in a specified point of any given curve.

```
*)
FUNCTION is_perpendicular_to (arg_1: curve; arg_2:
                             view_position): vector;
   (* There is no formal description of the code to
   determine a perpendicular vector to a given two
   dimensional curve up to now. One possible procedure to
   determine such a vector would be to construct a
   tangent to a point of the curve (indicated by arg_1;
   the entity type CURVE is described in /1/, 4.5.3.16),
   to which that vector has to be perpendicular to. *)
END_FUNCTION;
(*
```

3.2.8. LAST TRUE REFERENCE

The function LAST_TRUE_REFERENCE returns the last entity of type DIM_PREDECESSOR of a composed dimension description comprised in a list of type LIST_OF_DIM_PREDECESSOR where the value of the attribute named "reference" of type LOGICAL is true.

```
*)
FUNCTION  last_true_reference  (arg:
                        list_of_dim_predecessor):
                        dim_predecessor;
   LOCAL
      list_length          : INTEGER;
      i                    : INTEGER;
   END_LOCAL;
   list_length  :=  sizeof  (arg);
   REPEAT  i:=  list_length  TO  1;
      UNTIL  arg[i].reference;
   END_REPEAT;
   RETURN  (arg[i]);
END_FUNCTION;
(*
```

3.2.9. RADIUS

The function RADIUS calculates the radius of an arc determined by its argument of type ARC_SEGMENT.

```
*)
FUNCTION  radius  (arg:  arc_segment):  POSITIVE_REAL;
   LOCAL
      k                          : REAL;
   END_LOCAL;
   k  =  distance  (arg.start_point,  arg.center);
   RETURN  (k);
END_FUNCTION;
(*
```

3.3. Drafting Resources ENTITY Definitions

The entity types listed here describe positions, basic two dimensional geometry elements and two dimensional appearances of three dimensional geometric features. These entity types serve as references for the generation of the representations of annotation information that is described relatively to them. Moreover the two dimensional geometry elements and features preserve the associativity of the "annotation graphs" to the product definition data, because they may be derived from the product definition data by rules defined within the presentation model (see /1/, 4.12). Up to now, the entity types describing two dimensional geometry elements and features have no formal EXPRESS specification.. The definitions of those entities only consist of an informal description that has the intention to formulate requirements for a formal description of "represented geometry" within the presentation model. Thus the following entity type definitions have a preliminary status.

3.3.1. DRAWING POSITION

The structure DRAWING_POSITION describes a position on selected drawing sheets relative to the drawing sheet coordinate system that is placed in the lower right corner of the sheets. The positive y-axis of the drawing sheet coordinate system is directed vertically upwards and the positive x-axis is directed horizontally from the right to the left.

```
*)
ENTITY  drawing_position;
   pos_on_sheet           : sheet_position;
   sheet_number           : OPTIONAL LIST [1:#] OF UNIQUE
                            CHARACTER;
END_ENTITY;
(*
```

ATTRIBUTE DEFINITIONS:

pos_on_sheet : A position relative to the drawing sheet coordinate system.

sheet_number : The list contains all drawing sheets the position is relevant to. Where the attribute **sheet_number** is omitted, the position is relevant to all sheets of a drawing.

3.3.2. SHEET POSITION

The entity type SHEET_POSITION describes a position on a drawing sheet relative to the drawing sheet coordinate system that is placed in the lower right corner of the sheet. The positive y-axis of the drawing sheet coordinate system is directed vertically upwards and the positive x-axis is directed horizontally from the right to the left.

```
*)
ENTITY  sheet_position;
   x_value                 : POSITIVE_REAL;
   y_value                 : POSITIVE_REAL;
END_ENTITY;
(*
```

ATTRIBUTE DEFINITIONS:

x_value : The offset in the x-direction of the drawing sheet coordinate system.

y_value : The offset in the y-direction of the drawing sheet coordinate system.

3.3.3. VIEW POSITION

VIEW_POSITION is the specification of a position given either in view coordinates or relative to a description of represented geometry. Thus this entity type should be the supertype of subtypes describing a position by coordinates relative to a defined view coordinate system, at a geometry representation (e. g.: An intersection of represented edges) or derived from a geometry representation (e. g.: A center point derived from a representation of an arc).

3.3.4. SYMBOL POSITION

The position either at a dimension graph or at a geometry representation or at a leader, where symbols (e. g. surface finish symbol) can be placed at.

```
*)
ENTITY  symbol_position  SUPERTYPE  OF
                         (reference_term_point  XOR
                         point_at_leader);
   position                  : view_position;
END_ENTITY;
(*
```

ATTRIBUTE DEFINITIONS:

position : The placement of the symbol.

3.3.5. REFERENCE TERM POINT

A position either on a dimension graph or on a geometry representation.

```
*)
ENTITY  reference_term_point  SUPERTYPE  OF
                         (point_on_dimension_graph  XOR
                         point_on_geometry)
                         SUBTYPE  OF  (symbol_position);
END_ENTITY;
(*
```

3.3.6. POINT ON DIMENSION GRAPH

A position on a dimension graph.

```
*)
ENTITY  point_on_dimension_graph  SUBTYPE  OF
                         (reference_term_point);
   dimension_graph              : rep_geometry_dimension;
WHERE
   embedded  (position,  dimension_graph);
END_ENTITY;
(*
```

ATTRIBUTE DEFINITIONS:

dimension_graph : The reference to the description of a dimension graph where the symbol is placed. The placement defined by the attribute **position** of the supertype SYMBOL_POSITION has to be "embedded" in the domain of the referenced dimension graph.

3.3.7. POINT ON GEOMETRY

A position on any curve being part of a representation of geometry. POINT_ON_GEOMETRY may also be a subtype of VIEW_POSITION.

3.3.8. POINT AT LEADER

The position of a symbol (e. g. surface finish symbol) at a leader.

```
*)
ENTITY  point_at_leader  SUBTYPE  OF  (symbol_position);
   leader_rep              : OPTIONAL  LIST  [1:#]  OF  UNIQUE
                             view_position;
   pos_at_reference        : view_position;
END_ENTITY;
(*
```

ATTRIBUTE DEFINITIONS:

leader_rep	:	This attribute references positions defining the polyline of a leader where a symbol is placed at. The start point of the polyline is described by **position** within the supertype SYMBOL_POSITION and the terminating point is described by **pos_at_reference**. Therefore a straight line represents the leader where the attribute **leader_rep** is omitted.
pos_at_reference	:	The position where the leader terminates with an arrow at a geometry curve, with a point on a represented surface or without any termination symbol at a dimension graph.

3.3.9. ARC SEGMENT

A segment of a circle. Either an explicit or derived attribute (proposed name "center") should describe the center of the arc to be referred to by drafting entities.

3.3.10. CENTER LINE

The center line is the representation of either the axis of a surface of revolution or the plane of symmetry of a symmetrical part in a view. The entity type is referred to by descriptions of graphical appearances of annotation.

3.3.11. SURFACE APP

The entity type SURFACE_APP is the supertype of all descriptions of representations of any surfaces described by the proposed subtypes STRAIGHT_GEOMETRY_APP, SURF_OF_REV_APP and CURVE_APP. A formal description of the entity types of this structure is omitted, because such a definition is subject to the presentation model.

3.3.12. STRAIGHT GEOMETRY APP

STRAIGHT_GEOMETRY_APP is the description for the representations of geometry elements that can be represented by straight lines, e. g.: Planes, ruled surfaces, surfaces of revolution with a straight line as generating line, etc.

3.3.13. SURF OF REV APP

SURF_OF_REV_APP is the structure for the description of representations of any surfaces of revolution.

3.3.14. CURVE APP

Any bounded curve like a line, arc, polynom, etc. being the representation of any surface or three dimensional curve. All curves described by this entity type should be defined in a parametric form.

3.3.15. CHAMFER REPRESENTATION

The description of the representations of both kinds of chamfers with an angle of 45° : The internal as well as the external chamfer. Within the representation of the chamfers it should be possible to refer to several lines in order to derive a direction and two line intersections for the relative description of a chamfer dimension (see figure 3.1).

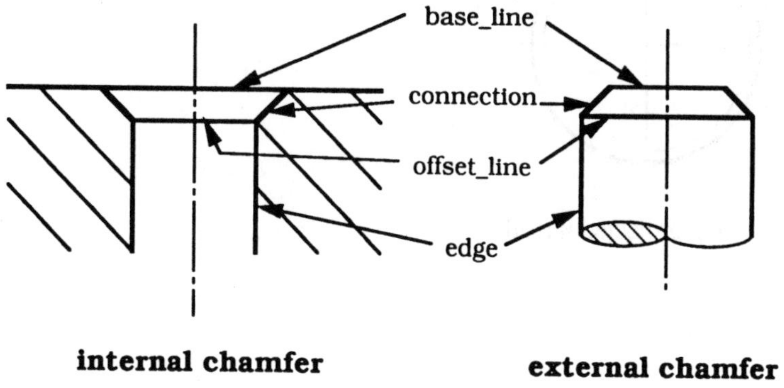

Fig. 3.1: Chamfer representations

3.3.16. SIDE PROJECTED THREAD

A side projection of a thread consists of straight lines representing the nominal diameter, the internal diameter and the center line (see figure 3.2). The description of a side projected thread is referred to by thread dimensionings.

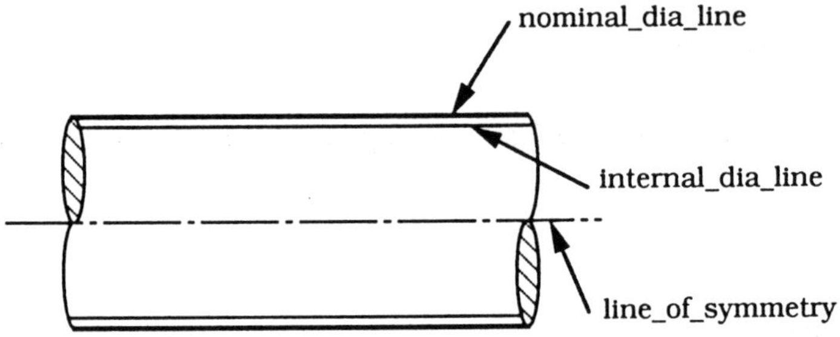

Fig. 3.2: Side projected thread

3.3.17. UP PROJECTED THREAD

An up projection of a thread consists of a circle and a segment of an arc representing the nominal diameter respectively the internal diameter and a point representing the center point (see figure 3.3). The description of an up projected thread is referred to by thread dimensionings.

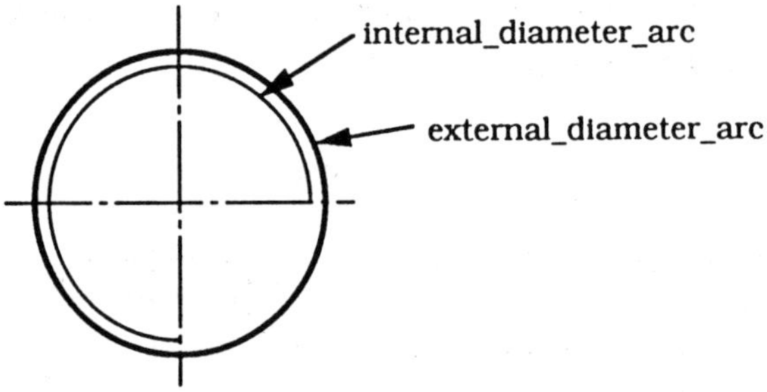

Fig. 3.3: Up projected thread

```
*)
END_SCHEMA;            -- end DRAFTING_RESOURCES_SCHEMA
(*
```

4. Drawing Organization

```
*)
SCHEMA  drawing_organization_schema;
   EXPORT  EVERYTHING;
   ASSUME  (drafting_resources_schema,
   dimensioning_schema,  tolerance_representation_schema,
   shape_attributes_representation_schema);
(*
```

4.1. Introduction

The entities listed in this schema describe representations of general product and administrative data, data being relevant to the layout of the drawing and data determining the rules applied for the representation of the product data. General product and administrative data describe for example release status, part number, change list, material, designer, supplier, etc. The layout of the drawing is determined by the usage of sheets, the size of the sheets, the positioning of views on the sheets, etc. The rules of representation of the product information contain the applied drafting standard with its projection rules, the line width usage, etc.
Principally descriptions of both the layout of the drawing and the rules of representation are contained in the IPIM_PRESENTATION_SCHEMA (see /1/, 4.12). Thus the information described in the IPIM_PRESENTATION_SCHEMA has to be integrated in the DRAWING_ORGANIZATION_SCHEMA. For an adequate integration of the data structures listed in the IPIM_PRESENTATION_SCHEMA it was necessary to make some changes in order to avoid redundancies. The changed data structures are documented within this chapter.

4.2. Drawing Organization TYPE Definitions

4.2.1. SEC CLASS

The defined type SEC_CLASS specifies the security classification applicable to a drawing. Enumerated are "confidential", "secret" and "top-secret".

```
*)
TYPE sec_class = ENUMERATION OF (confidential, secret,
                        top_secret);
END_TYPE;
(*
```

4.2.2. MASS DETERMINATION

MASS_DETERMINATION describes the way of determining the mass of a product. It may be a calculated or estimated nominal mass, the mass of a prototype or the average mass of a series.

```
*)
TYPE mass_determination = ENUMERATION OF (nominal_mass,
                        mass_of_prototype, average_mass);
END_TYPE;
(*
```

4.3. Changed ENTITY Definitions of IPIM_PRESENTATION_SCHEMA

Both the entity types PRESENTATION_SHEET and VIEW_WITH_ANNOTATION are defined in the IPIM_PRESENTATION_SCHEMA. For the informal description and attribute definitions see /1/, 4.12.10 .

Within the DRAWING_ORGANIZATION_SCHEMA several changes are proposed and documented below:

4.3.1. PRESENTATION SHEET

The entity PRESENTATION_SHEET is defined in the IPIM_PRESENTATION_SCHEMA (see /1/, 4.12.10.6, p.387). The attributes **annotation_on_sheet** and **sheet_admin_data** are omitted, because there are no definitions of the referred entity types.

Figure 4.1 shows the structure of the description of representations on a drawing sheet.

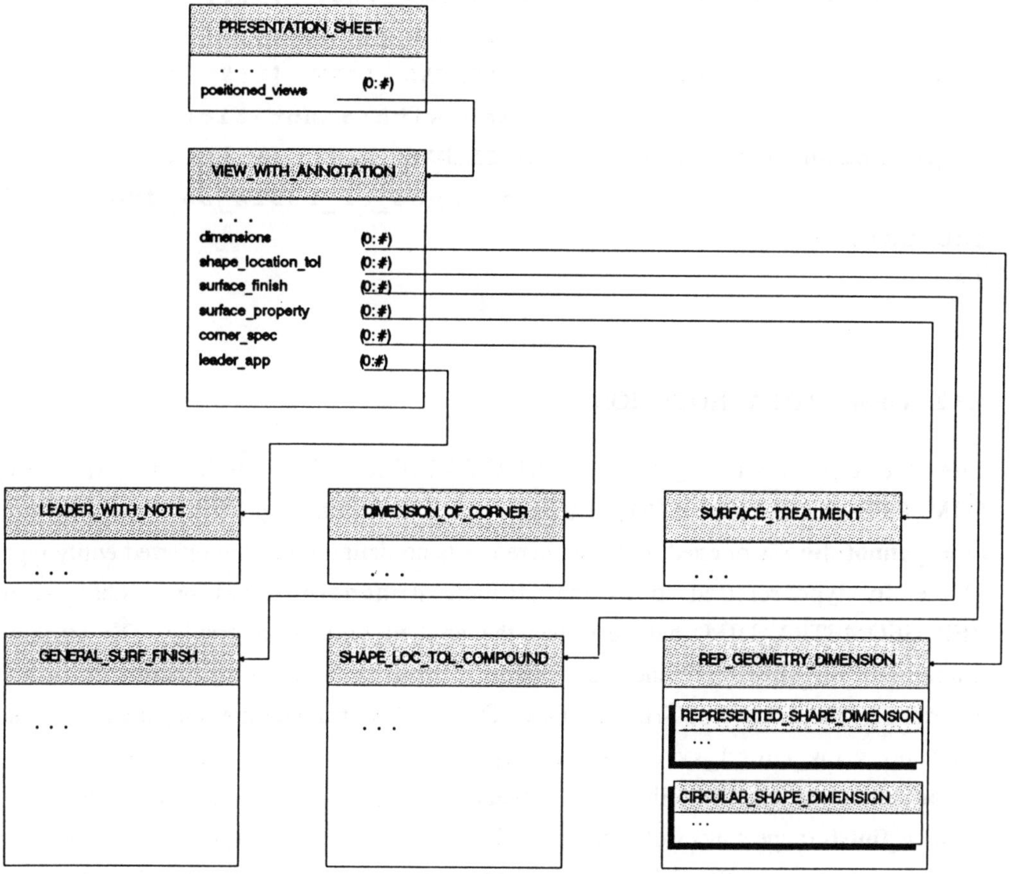

Fig. 4.1: The structure for the description of representations on a drawing sheet

```
*)
ENTITY  presentation_sheet;
   sheet_presentation_attr: OPTIONAL
                            general_presentation_
                            attributes;
```

```
   sheet_level_geometric_attr : OPTIONAL LIST [1:#] OF
                                change_geometry_related_
                                attributes;
   sheet_level_geometry     : OPTIONAL LIST [1:#] OF
                              tree_of_geometry;
   positioned_views         : OPTIONAL LIST [1:#] OF
                              view_with_annotation;
   positioned_tables        : OPTIONAL LIST [1:#] OF
                              instance_of_table_on_drawing;
END_ENTITY;
(*
```

4.3.2. VIEW WITH ANNOTATION

The entity VIEW_WITH_ANNOTATION is defined in the IPIM_PRESENTATION_SCHEMA (see /1/, 4.12.10.3, p.385). The attribute **other_annotation** is omitted, because there exists no definition of the referred entity type. The entity type referred to by the attribute **dimensions** has been changed to REP_GEOMETRY_DIM that describes the applied dimension graphs. The attribute **placement_on_sheet** references a position relative to the drawing coordinate system described by the entity type SHEET_POSITION. Further attributes are integrated, i. e.: The attributes **view_coord_syst_rep** (the representation of a view coordinate system), **shape_location_tol** (describing the appearances of shape and location_tolerances), **surface_finish** (appearances of surface finish symbols), **surface_property** (representation of surface treatment information), **corner_spec** (dimensions of corners) and **leader_app** (appearances of leaders) are added.

```
*)
ENTITY view_with_annotation;
   view_presentation_attr   : OPTIONAL
                              general_presentation_
                              attributes;
   selected_geometry        : tree_of_geometry;
```

```
   view_level_geometric_attr : OPTIONAL LIST [1:#] OF
                               change_geometry_related_
                               attributes;
   visible_layers         : OPTIONAL LIST [1:#] OF
                            INTEGER;
   incident_light         : OPTIONAL  light_resources;
   projection_geometry    : viewing_pipeline;
   view_limitation        : clipping;
   view_coord_syst_rep    : coord_syst_rep;
   dimensions             : OPTIONAL LIST [1:#] OF
                            rep_geometry_dimension;
   shape_location_tol     : OPTIONAL LIST [1:#] OF
                            shape_loc_tol_compound;
   surface_finish         : OPTIONAL LIST [1:#] OF
                            general_surf_finish;
   surface_property       : OPTIONAL LIST [1:#] OF
                            surface_treatment;
   corner_spec            : OPTIONAL LIST [1:#] OF
                            dimension_of_corner;
   leader_app             : OPTIONAL LIST [1:#] OF
                            leader_with_note;
   area_fill              : OPTIONAL LIST [1:#] OF
                            area_pattern_styles;
   rotation_on_sheet      : OPTIONAL  REAL;
   placement_on_sheet     : sheet_position;
END_ENTITY;
(*
```

4.4. Drawing Organization ENTITY Definitions

4.4.1. DRAWING

All data concerning exactly one drawing are comprised in this entity type. Partially the comprised data have their origin in different schemas, i. e.

IPIM_PRESENTATION_SCHEMA, DRAFTING_SCHEMA or TOLERANCING_SCHEMA and have to be referenced.
For a survey of the structure describing a drawing see figure 4.2.

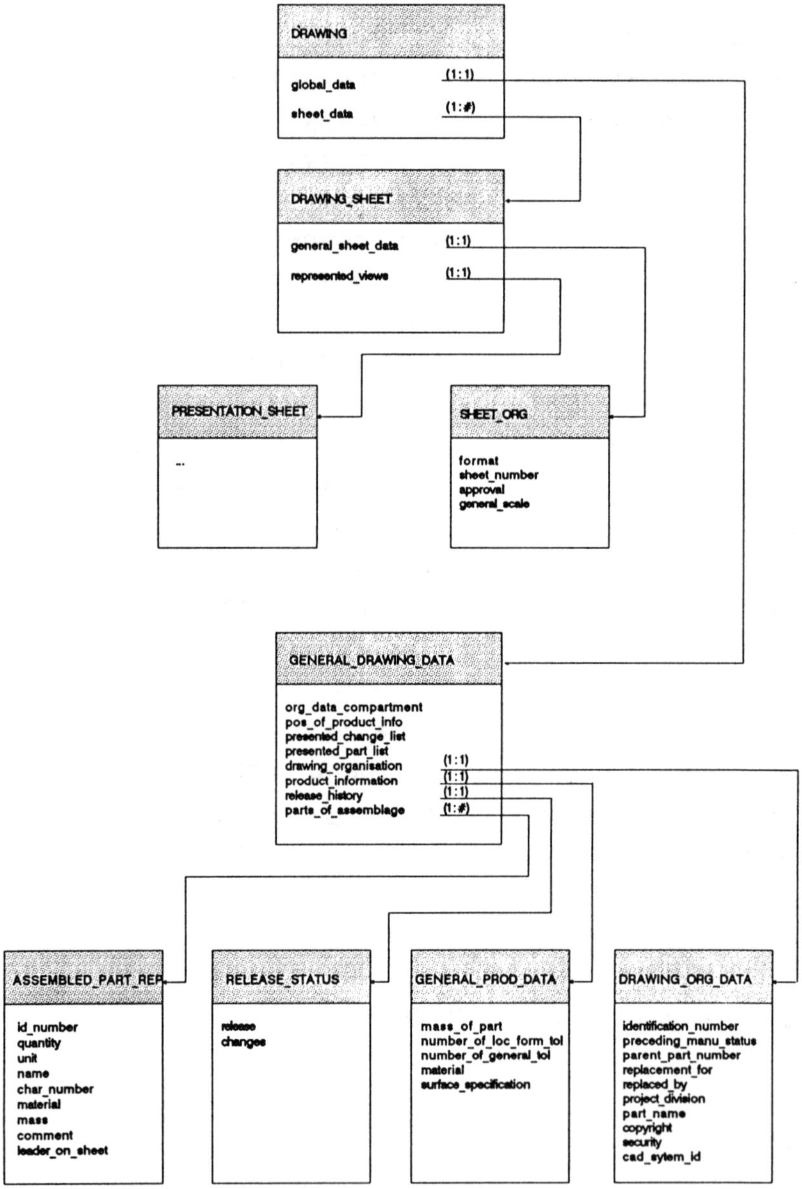

Fig. 4.2: Survey of the structure describing a drawing

The following assumptions with regard to a logical model for a drawing are considered:

- A drawing consists of at least one drawing sheet.

- A drawing owns exactly one drawing number

```
*)
ENTITY  drawing;
   global_data                    : general_drawing_data;
   sheet_data                     : LIST  [1:#]  OF  UNIQUE
                                    drawing_sheet;
END_ENTITY;
(*
```

ATTRIBUTE DEFINITIONS:

global_data : The attribute **global_data** references data describing the contents and appearance of the information field, the release status, etc. These data are valid for the whole drawing consisting of several sheets.

sheet_data : This attribute references all the sheets belonging to the specified drawing.

4.4.2. GENERAL DRAWING DATA

The structure GENERAL_DRAWING_DATA describes the appearance of the information field, the part list and the change list as well as their contents. The representation of this part of product information is placed on every single sheet belonging to the drawing.
The graphical appearance of the information field is described in the IPIM_PRESENTATION_SCHEMA (see /1/, 4.12.8.4.1 entity type TABLE_ON_DRAWING).
The following assumptions are considered concerning the information field:
- The data contained in an information field can be subdivided in three categories:
  i) Organizational drawing data such as the drawing number, the part name, the project the drawing is attached to, etc.

ii) Data describing general rules of representation of product information like the generally applied scale, the projection method (first angle or third angle projection method), etc.
iii) Data representing general product information, e. g.: Applied standards for general tolerances as well as shape and location tolerances, the mass of the product, the standard being used for the representation of the surface finish symbols, etc.

- The lower right corner of the information field is placed in the origin of the drawing sheet coordinate system that itself is placed in the lower right corner of the drawing sheet (see informal description of entity type DRAWING_SHEET).
- The actual appearance of the information field depends on the rules defined by the enterprise where the drawing was designed.
- The information field is represented on all sheets being part of a drawing.

```
*)
ENTITY  general_drawing_data;
   org_data_compartment    : org_data_appearance;
   pos_of_product_info     : gen_prod_data_appearance;
   presented_change_list      : change_list_appearance;
   presented_part_list     : OPTIONAL  part_list_appearance;
   drawing_organization    : drawing_org_data;
   product_information     : general_product_data;
   release_history         : release_status;
   parts_of_assemblage     : OPTIONAL  LIST  [1:#]  OF
                             assembled_part_rep;
WHERE
   (* a *)   ( (presented_part_list  =  NULL)  AND
   (parts_of_assemblage  =  NULL)  )  OR  (
   (presented_part_list  <>  NULL)  AND  (parts_of_assemblage
   <>  NULL)  );
END_ENTITY;
(*
```

ATTRIBUTE DEFINITIONS:

org_data_compartment : The placement and arrangement of the organizational drawing data in the information field. There is a subdivision in the

		description of the information field: **org_data_compartment** describes the representation of organizational drawing data and **pos_of_product_info** describes the representation of general product data within the information field.
pos_of_product_info	:	The placement and arrangement of the general product data in the information field.
presented_change_list	:	The appearance and the subdivision of the columns within the change list.
presented_part_list	:	The appearance and the subdivision of the columns within the part list.
drawing_organization	:	The referenced entity type DRAWING_ORG_DATA contains general organizational drawing (e. g.: The drawing number, the project the drawing belongs to, a copyright specification, the part name, etc.).
product_information	:	The representation of general product information that partially might be derived from the product model (e. g.: The mass of the part, the numbers of applied tolerance standards, the used materials, etc.).
release_history	:	A chronological list of the states of release and the changes made within this drawing.
parts_of_assemblage	:	A list of all parts whose assemblage is represented on this drawing.

PROPOSITIONS:

a. Either the attribute values of both **presented_part_list** and **parts_of_assemblage** are omitted or both are not omitted.

4.4.3. ORG DATA APPEARANCE

This is the structure describing the placement of the organizational drawing data in the information field. Corresponding to this structure the entity type DRAWING_ORG_DATA contains the descriptions of the organizational drawing data. Additional to that four positions are given concerning drawing sheet data, namely the positions for the placement of the representation of the sheet number, the sheet format, the revision documentation and the representation of the general scale applied.

The following rules determining the application of this structure together with the structure of DRAWING_ORG_DATA have to be considered:

- If a placement is described within the entity type ORG_DATA_APPEARANCE and there is no corresponding data in the entity type DRAWING_ORG_DATA, the field denoted by the specified placement is represented blankly.

```
*)
ENTITY  org_data_appearance;
   positions_of_org_data    : LIST  [14:14]  OF  UNIQUE
                              drawing_position;
WHERE
   (*  a  *)    (positions_of_org_data[i].sheet_number  =
   NULL);
END_ENTITY;
(*
```

ATTRIBUTE DEFINITIONS:

positions_of_org_data	: **positions_of_org_data** is a list of positions for organizational drawing data described relative to the drawing sheet coordinate systems on every drawing sheet belonging to a drawing. The sequence of the positions corresponds to the sequence of the information contents described by the entity types DRAWING_ORG_DATA and SHEET_ORG. Therefore **positions_of_org_data**[1] to **positions_of_org_data**[10] are the positions of the information contents of DRAWING_ORG_DATA and **positions_of_org_data**[11] to **positions_of_org_data**[14] are the positions of the information contents described by SHEET_ORG.

PROPOSITIONS:

a. The attributes **sheet_number** of the referenced entity types DRAWING_POSITION have to be omitted. That means: The positions are relevant to all sheets of the drawing.

4.4.4. DRAWING ORG DATA

The structure DRAWING_ORG_DATA contains data specifying the organization and administration of a drawing. The representations of these data are placed in the information field as described by the entity type ORG_DATA_APPEARANCE.

```
*)
ENTITY  drawing_org_data;
   identification_number  : drawing_number;
   preceding_manu_status  : OPTIONAL  drawing_number;
   parent_part_number     : OPTIONAL  drawing_number;
   replacement_for        : OPTIONAL  drawing_number;
   replaced_by            : OPTIONAL  drawing_number;
   project_division       : STRING;
   part_name              : STRING;
   copyright              : copyright_spec;
   security               : OPTIONAL  security_
                            classification;
   cad_system_id          : STRING;
UNIQUE
   identification_number,  preceding_manu_status,
   parent_part_number,  replacement_for,  replaced_by;
END_ENTITY;
(*
```

ATTRIBUTE DEFINITIONS:

identification_number : The number assigned to the drawing.

preceding_manu_status	:	The number identifying the drawing where a preceding manufacturing status of the same part is represented.
parent_part_number	:	The number of a drawing representing a part of a hierarchical higher level. E. g.: A drawing of a hierarchical higher level might be an assembly representation constituted - among other parts - by the part represented within this drawing.
replacement_for	:	This attribute contains the number of the drawing that has been replaced by the drawing described within this structure.
replaced_by	:	The number of the drawing replacing the drawing described within this structure.
project_division	:	The attribute **project_division** designates the project and its subdivision to which the drawing belongs to.
part_name	:	The name and possibly a further denotation of the part.
copyright	:	The holder of the copyright and further specifications concerning the copyright.
security	:	The security classification being assigned to this drawing. If the value is omitted, the drawing is subject to no security regulations.
cad_system_id	:	The identification of the CAD-System by which the drawing has been designed.

4.4.5. DRAWING NUMBER

The entity type DRAWING_NUMBER describes the number or array of signs necessary for identifying a drawing.

The described number or array of signs is subject to the propositions listed below:

- The definition of the number identifying a drawing depends on organizational characteristics determined by the specific enterprise or company.
- In case of subdividing the drawing sheets into sections for microfilming the number specified by DRAWING_NUMBER is not only represented in the information field, but also has to be placed in every section.

```
*)
ENTITY  drawing_number;
   number                        : STRING;
END_ENTITY;
(*
```

ATTRIBUTE DEFINITIONS:

number	:	The attribute **number** is constituted under the aspect of both the organizations of drawings and parts.

4.4.6. COPYRIGHT SPEC

The entity type COPYRIGHT_SPEC contains data describing the holder of the copyright and the regulations how to deal with the copyright.

```
*)
ENTITY  copyright_spec;
   name_of_holder                : STRING;
   text_of_statute               : STRING;
END_ENTITY;
(*
```

ATTRIBUTE DEFINITIONS:

name_of_holder	:	This attribute denotes the holder of the copyright. It might be the name of an enterprise, but also the name of a person.
text_of_statute	:	The specification of the regulations how to deal with the copyright.

4.4.7. SECURITY CLASSIFICATION

This entity type specifies the class of security applied for the drawing and the classifying person.

```
*)
ENTITY  security_classification;
   classification              : sec_class;
   classified_by               : signature;
END_ENTITY;
(*
```

ATTRIBUTE DEFINITIONS:

classification	:	**classification** references the defined type SEC_CLASS where the following security classes are enumerated: Confidential, secret and top secret.
classified_by	:	There is the signature of the person responsible for the classification.

4.4.8. GEN PROD DATA APPEARANCE

GEN_PROD_DATA_APPEARANCE is the structure describing the placement of the general product data in the information field. Corresponding to this structure the entity type GENERAL_PRODUCT_DATA contains the descriptions of the general product data.
The following rules determining the application of this structure together with the structure of GENEREAL_PRODUCT_DATA have to be considered:

- If a placement is described within the entity type GEN_PROD_DATA_APPEARANCE and there is no corresponding data in the entity type GENERAL_PRODUCT_DATA, the field denoted by the specified placement is represented blankly.

```
*)
ENTITY  gen_prod_data_appearance;
   pos_mass_of_part        : OPTIONAL  drawing_position;
```

```
   pos_loc_form_tol          : drawing_position;
   pos_gen_tol               : drawing_position;
   pos_product_mat           : drawing_position;
   pos_surface_spec          : OPTIONAL drawing_position;
WHERE
   (* a *)   ( (pos_mass_of_part = NULL) OR (
   (pos_mass_of_part <> NULL) AND
   (pos_mass_of_part.sheet_number = NULL) ) ) AND
   (pos_loc_form_tol.sheet_number = NULL) AND
   (pos_gen_tol.sheet_number = NULL) AND
   (pos_product_mat.sheet_number = NULL) AND (
   (pos_surface_spec = NULL) OR ( (pos_surface_spec <>
   NULL) AND (pos_surface_spec.sheet_number = NULL) ) );
END_ENTITY;
(*
```

ATTRIBUTE DEFINITIONS:

pos_... : Every attribute denotes a position relative to the drawing sheet coordinate systems on every drawing sheet belonging to a drawing. The sequence of the positions corresponds to the sequence of the information contents described by GENERAL_PRODUCT_DATA.

PROPOSITIONS:

a. The attributes **sheet_number** of the referenced entity types DRAWING_POSITION have to be omitted. That means: The positions are relevant to all sheets of the drawing.

4.4.9. GENERAL PRODUCT DATA

GENERAL_PRODUCT_DATA is the structure of the description of the data containing general information about the product model. The representations of these data are placed in the information field as described by the entity type GEN_PROD_DATA_APPEARANCE.

```
*)
ENTITY  general_product_data;
    mass_of_part              : OPTIONAL  mass;
    number_of_loc_form_tol    : STRING;
    number_of_general_tol     : STRING;
    material                  : LIST  [1:#]  OF  product_mat;
    surface_specification     : OPTIONAL  STRING;
END_ENTITY;
(*
```

ATTRIBUTE DEFINITIONS:

mass_of_part	:	This attribute specifies the kind (nominal, average or mass of prototype) and value of the determined mass of the product.
number_of_loc_form_tol	:	**number_of_loc_form_tol** contains the number of the standard according to which the tolerances of form and location are determined on the drawing (e. g.: ISO 1101).
number_of_general_tol	:	The number of the standard specifying the general tolerances to which all dimensions without an explicitly given tolerance are subject to (e. g.: DIN 7168).
material	:	A list of the applied materials.
surface_specification	:	The reference to the standard the surface finish specifications of the drawing are subject to (e. g.: ISO 1302).

4.4.10. MASS

This structure provides information about the mass and the method for determining the mass of the product.

```
*)
ENTITY  mass;
   mass_category           : mass_determination;
   unit                    : scaled_mass_unit;
                                -- see /1/, 4.4.2.5
```

```
   value                    : POSITIVE_REAL;
END_ENTITY;
(*
```

ATTRIBUTE DEFINITIONS:

mass_category	:	This attribute denotes the method of determining the mass of the product. Enumerated possibilities are: The nominal mass, the mass of a prototype and the average mass of a series.
unit	:	The unit specified for the declaration of the mass.
value	:	The value of the mass.

4.4.11. PRODUCT MAT

PRODUCT_MAT is the structure specifying the applied material, its identification number and its supplier.

```
*)
ENTITY  product_mat;
   material                 : STRING;
   number_of_material       : OPTIONAL  STRING;
   supplier                 : OPTIONAL  STRING;
END_ENTITY;
(*
```

ATTRIBUTE DEFINITIONS:

material	:	Here the abbreviaton for identifying the material is required.
number_of_material	:	The number of the material according to a table of listed materials.
supplier	:	The name of the supplier of the material.

4.4.12. CHANGE LIST APPEARANCE

CHANGE_LIST_APPEARANCE is the structure describing the placement of the data contained in the structure RELEASE_STATUS in the change list. The change list is represented on every sheet of a drawing.

```
*)
ENTITY  change_list_appearance;
   origin                      : drawing_position;
   column_offsets              : LIST  [5:6]  OF  POSITIVE_REAL;
WHERE
   (*  a  *)    column_offsets[i]  >  column_offsets[i+1];
   (*  b  *)   origin.sheet_number  =  NULL;
END_ENTITY;
(*
```

ATTRIBUTE DEFINITIONS:

origin : **origin** denotes a position relative to the drawing sheet coordinate systems on every sheet belonging to a drawing. The specified position is the lower right corner of the change list.

column_offsets : The offsets determine the columns of the change list relative to **origin**. The values are measured in the positive x-direction of the drawing sheet coordinate systems. The content of the columns is described by the entity types RELEASE_STATUS, RELEASE_SIGN and CHANGED_ITEM. **column_offsets**[1] is the offset for the release number, **column_offsets**[2] for the index, **column_offsets**[3] for the change number, **column_offsets**[4] for the specification of the changes, **column_offsets**[5] for the sign of the authority responsible for the giving of releases and **column_offsets**[6] for a sign indicating the microfilm status.

PROPOSITIONS:

a. The sequence of the columns of the change list from left to right is as follows: Column for the release number, column for the index, column for the change number, column for the specification, column for the authority and column for the flag for microfilming.

b. The attribute **sheet_number** of the referenced entity type DRAWING_POSITION has to be omitted. That means: The position is relevant to all sheets of the drawing.

4.4.13. RELEASE STATUS

The structure RELEASE_STATUS contains data describing the current states of release of the product as well as the documentation of the changes made during the process of approaching the production release for the product. The appearance of the change list is described in the structure CHANGE_LIST_APPEARANCE.

Concerning the change list the following constraints have to be considered:

- The change list is represented on every sheet of a drawing.
- The status of release is identical for all sheets of a drawing.
- In the change list all states of release (chronological order: Test release, planning release, production release and declaration of invalidity) as well as all new releases occuring together with changes are listed.
- The items listed in the change list are arranged in a chronological sequence: The oldest item is placed at the bottom of the list and the newest item is placed on top of the list.
- A listed changed item contains the following data: An index identifying the changes, the total number of changes indicated by this index, a short description of the changes, the number of the new release, the signature of the person responsible for the new release and a sign whether the current status of the drawing has been microfilmed or not. The indices (an index is a small letter; the list of indices starts with an "a") are attached to the changes in a chronological sequence.

```
*)
ENTITY  release_status;
   release                    : LIST  [1:4]  OF  UNIQUE
                                release_sign;
```

```
   changes                    : OPTIONAL LIST [1:#] OF UNIQUE
                                changed_item;
END_ENTITY;
(*
```

ATTRIBUTE DEFINITIONS:

release : This attribute contains all states of release given to the drawing. **release**[1] means test release, **release**[2] planning release, **release**[3] production release and **release**[4] declaration of invalidity.

changes : This is a chronological list of the changes made within a drawing.

4.4.14. CHANGED ITEM

CHANGED_ITEM is the structure containing information about the execution of a change in the drawing. The information is represented in the change list. There is no reference to a description of a changed appearance, because even the omission of an appearance may be listed. The changed item may affect more than one sheet of the drawing: Therefore the information contents of an instance of CHANGED_ITEM are represented in every change list of a drawing.

```
*)
ENTITY changed_item;
   new_release                : release_sign;
   number_of_changes          : INTEGER;
   specification              : STRING;
   symbol_placement           : LIST [1:#] OF
                                drawing_position;
DERIVE
   number_of_changes          : INTEGER := sizeof
                                (symbol_placement);
END_ENTITY;
(*
```

ATTRIBUTE DEFINITIONS:

new_release	:	The number of the new release after an execution of changes.
specification	:	A short description of the changes.
symbol_placement	:	**symbol_placement** describes the placement of the identifying index on the sheets where the changes are made. An identifying index is given to every instance of the entity type CHANGED_ITEM.
number_of_changes	:	The total number of changes described within this instance of CHANGED_ITEM. **number_of_changes** corresponds to the number of identifying indices placed on the sheets of a drawing.

4.4.15. RELEASE SIGN

RELEASE_SIGN is the structure comprising data that contain administrative information about release procedure and status and every changed item.

```
*)
ENTITY   release_sign;
   release_number          : STRING;
   authorized_by           : singature;
   index                   : CHARACTER;
   microfilmed             : LOGICAL;
END_ENTITY;
(*
```

ATTRIBUTE DEFINITIONS:

release_number	:	The attribute release_number contains the adminstrative number of a new release concerning a changed item or a release status of the drawing.
authorized_by	:	This attribute denotes the person who is responsible for the giving of releases.

index : The **index** is the identifying sign of the representation of the entity type **release_status** in the change list.

microfilmed : This flag gives evidence, if this status of the drawing already has been microfilmed.

4.4.16. PART LIST APPEARANCE

The structure PART_LIST_APPEARANCE describes the appearance of a table where information about all parts being relevant to the drawing is listed. The information being listed in this table is contained in the structure ASSEMBLED_PART_REP.

The following assumptions concerning the appearance of a part list are made:

- The part list is represented on a seperated sheet that does not belong to the group of drawing sheets; an information field is represented on it.
- The sheet format is the smallest sheet size available for a drawing sheet as defined within the structure SHEET_ORG.
- The frame of the table is aligned to the frame of the information field.
- The lines of the table are filled from bottom to top.
- Where a column is described within the entity type PART_LIST_APPEARANCE and there is no corresponding information content described within the structure ASSEMBLED_PART_REP, the column is represented blankly.

```
*)
ENTITY  part_list_appearance;
   column_offsets           : LIST  [8:8]  OF  POSITIVE_REAL;
WHERE
   (* a *)   column_offsets[i]  >  column_offsets[i+1];
END_ENTITY;
(*
```

ATTRIBUTE DEFINITIONS:

column_offsets : **column_offsets** specifies the horizontal distances of the columns of the part list from the right upper corner of the information field. In the columns the information contained in the entity type ASSEMBLED_PART_REP is represented. **column_offsets**[1] is the offset for the identification numbers, **column_offsets**[2] is the offset for the declarations of quantities, **column_offsets**[3] is the offset for the units, **column_offsets**[4] is the offset for the names, **column_offsets**[5] is the offset for the characteristic numbers, **column_offsets**[6] is the offset for the materials, **column_offsets**[7] is the offset for the masses of the parts and **column_offsets**[8] is the offset for the comments.

PROPOSITIONS:

a. The sequence of the columns of the part list from left to right is as follows: Column for the identification number, column for the quantity, column for the unit, column for the name, column for the characteristic number, column for the material, column for the mass and column for the comment.

4.4.17. ASSEMBLED PART REP

ASSEMBLED_PART_REP is the structure containing information of a part belonging to the drawing as well as a description of a leader pointing at the representation of this part on a drawing sheet. The information contents are represented in the part list described by the entity type PART_LIST_APPEARANCE.
The following assumptions are made:

- Leaders with identification numbers as their note point at the representations of assembled parts or items on a drawing sheet of the drawing.
- The information concerning the assembled parts or items is represented in a part list.

```
*)
ENTITY  assembled_part_rep;
   id_number                 : CHARACTER;
   quantity                  : INTEGER;
   unit                      : STRING;
   name                      : STRING;
```

```
   char_number          : STRING;
   material             : OPTIONAL  STRING;
   mass                 : OPTIONAL  STRING;
   comment              : OPTIONAL  STRING;
   leader_on_sheet      : leader_with_note;
END_ENTITY;
*)
```

ATTRIBUTE DEFINITIONS:

id_number	:	A sequential identification number for a part or item of the assembly.
quantity	:	A quantitative information of the item being described by this identification number (e. g.: The volume of a fluid, the number of pieces, ...).
unit	:	The unit for the quantitative information.
name	:	The name of the part or item.
char_number	:	The characteristic number of the part/item (e. g.: The number of a standard containing further information about the part/item).
material	:	A specification of the material of the part/item.
mass	:	The mass of the part/item.
comment	:	Further information concerning the part/item.
leader_on_sheet	:	This attribute describes a leader that points to a representation of the part/item on a drawing sheet.

4.4.18. DRAWING SHEET

In the structure DRAWING_SHEET all data concerning one sheet of the drawing like the possibly different layout of the sheets, the administrative data belonging to only one of the sheets, etc. are comprised.

The following assumptions concerning the data that belong to a drawing sheet are made:

- Every sheet of a drawing may have a different size.
- Every sheet has its own drawing sheet coordinate system.

- The origin of the drawing sheet coordinate system is placed in the lower right corner of the drawing sheet. The positive y-axis is directed vertically upwards and the positive x-axis is directed horizontally from the right to the left. Evidently only positive values make sense in this case.
- All sheets of a drawing have an identical drawing number, but different sheet numbers.
- An information field and a change list has to be represented on every sheet. A part list may be represented.

```
*)
ENTITY  drawing_sheet;
   general_sheet_data     : sheet_org;
   represented_views      : presentation_sheet;
END_ENTITY;
(*
```

ATTRIBUTE DEFINITIONS:

general_sheet_data	:	The data comprised here contain general organizational information about this drawing sheet (e. g.: The format of the sheet, the sheet number, the general scale applied within the sheet, etc.).
represented_views	:	This attribute references an entity type of the IPIM_PRESENTATION_SCHEMA describing views with annotation positioned on the sheet and attributes determining the presentation of the geometry.

4.4.19. SHEET ORG

The data comprised in this structure describe organizational information about this drawing sheet. The positions of these data on the sheets of the drawing are described within the entity type ORG_DATA_APPEARANCE.

```
*)
ENTITY  sheet_org;
   format                    : sheet_format;
   sheet_number              : INTEGER;
   approval                  : drawing_sheet_approval;
   general_scale             : REAL;
END_ENTITY;
(*
```

ATTRIBUTE DEFINITIONS:

format	:	The attribute **format** determines the size of the sheet. It may either be a standard format or an oversize format.
sheet_number	:	The number of the sheet that has to be different to the numbers of all the other sheets belonging to this drawing.
approval	:	Information about the revision of the drawing sheet.
general_scale	:	The scale mainly used for the representation of the geometry within this sheet. The value of this attribute might be derived from the information contained in the entity type VIEW_WITH_ANNOTATION that is referenced by PRESENTATION_SHEET that again is referenced by DRAWING_SHEET.

4.4.20. SHEET FORMAT

The entity type SHEET_FORMAT is the supertype of entity types describing the size of the drawing sheet. The size may either be a standard format as determined in current drafting standards or an oversize format exceeding the largest standard format.

```
*)
ENTITY  sheet_format  SUPERTYPE  OF  (standard_format  XOR
                                      oversize_format);
END_ENTITY;
(*
```

4.4.21. STANDARD FORMAT

This is the structure enumerating sheet formats determined by current drafting standards.

```
*)
ENTITY  standard_format  SUBTYPE  OF  (sheet_format);
   format_selection          : std_sheet_size;
                               -- see /1/, 4.15.1.4.5
END_ENTITY;
(*
```

ATTRIBUTE DEFINITIONS:

format_selection : The attribute **format_selection** references a defined type where standard sheet formats according to ISO, ANSI, DIN, etc. are enumerated (e. g.: A, B, ..., A0, A1, ...).

4.4.22. OVERSIZE FORMAT

OVERSIZE_FORMAT is the structure for the description of the size of a sheet exceeding the largest standard format.

```
*)
ENTITY  oversize_format  SUBTYPE  OF  (sheet_format);
   horizontal_elongation     : OPTIONAL  POSITIVE_REAL;
   vertical_elongation       : OPTIONAL  POSITIVE_REAL;
   micro_screening           : OPTIONAL  micro_section;
WHERE
   (* a *)   (vertical_elongation <> NULL) OR
   (horizontal_elongation  <>  NULL)  ;
END_ENTITY;
(*
```

ATTRIBUTE DEFINITIONS:

horizontal_elongation	:	The elongation of the largest standard format in the horizontal direction.
vertical_elongation	:	The elongation of the largest standard format in the vertical direction.
micro_screening	:	The subdivision of the drawing sheet in sections according to the format of the microfilm.

PROPOSITIONS:

a. There is at least one elongation in either horizontal or vertical direction.

4.4.23. MICRO SECTION

MICRO_SECTION is the structure of the specification of the subdivision of the drawing sheet into sections. The extent of the sections depends on the format of the microfilm.
The following assumptions are taken into consideration concerning the microfilming of technical drawings:

- Standard formats for drawing sheets do not exceed the extent of the microfilm format. Thus it is not necessary to subdivide those formats into sections.
- In case of microfilming the oversize formats need overlay marks (placed at the edge of the sheet) signifying the border and the overlay of two neighbouring sections. Overlay marks consist of two short lines indicating the joint border of two sections.
- The drawing number, the sheet number and the number of the section have to be represented in every section of the sheet.
- The vertical borders of a column of sections and the horizontal borders of a row of sections are aligned.
- The first row of sections is numbered from the lower right corner to the lower left corner. The row above is numbered from left to right and the next row but one again is numbered from the right to the left and so on.

```
*)
ENTITY  micro_section;
   micro_section_length     : POSITIVE_REAL;
```

```
   micro_section_height      : POSITIVE_REAL;
   overlay                   : POSITIVE_REAL;
   rel_pos_section_number    : POSITIVE_REAL;
END_ENTITY;
(*
```

ATTRIBUTE DEFINITIONS:

micro_section_length	:	The attribute **micro_section_length** determines the horizontal length of a section.
micro_section_height	:	The attribute **micro_section_height** determines the vertical height of a section.
overlay	:	The overlay length of the borders of two neighbouring sections.
rel_pos_section_number	:	The offset of the representation of the drawing number, the sheet number and the number of the section relative to the joint border with the preceding section.

4.4.24. DRAWING SHEET APPROVAL

The data contained in this structure document the procedure of the revision of the drawing sheet. Several instances have to give their approval to the drawing sheet. These instances are divided into two groups: The first group checks the representations within the drawing sheet and the second one checks the part being represented in the drawing sheet.

```
*)
ENTITY  drawing_sheet_approval;
   sheet_revision     : LIST  [1:4]  OF  UNIQUE  signature;
   part_check         : LIST  [1:3]  OF  OPTIONAL  signature;
END_ENTITY;
(*
```

ATTRIBUTE DEFINITIONS:

sheet_revision	:	This attribute contains a list of signatures of the instances responsible for the checking of the drawing sheet: **sheet_revision**[1] is the signature of the draftsman, **sheet_revision**[2] denotes the checking person, **sheet_revision**[3] is the person checking the sheet with regard to the standards and **sheet_revision**[4] is the person who is responsible for the sheet.
part_check	:	**part_check**[1] denotes the person checking the functionality of the part, **part_check**[2] identifies the person being responsible for the manufacturing of the part and **part_check**[3] is the responsible person in the workshop.

4.4.25. SIGNATURE

This entity type contains information about a signature documented on the drawing.

```
*)
ENTITY  signature;
   date                       : date;    -- see /1/,  4.4.1.2
   sign                       : STRING;
END_ENTITY;
(*
```

ATTRIBUTE DEFINITIONS:

date	:	The date of the signature.
sign	:	The abbreviation of the signer's name.

```
*)
END_SCHEMA;          --    end  DRAWING_ORGANIZATION_SCHEMA
(*
```

5. Dimensioning

```
*)
SCHEMA  dimensioning_schema;
   EXPORT  EVERYTHING;
   ASSUME  (drafting_resource_schema,
   tolerance_representation_schema);
(*
```

5.1. Introduction

This section contains a collection of entities describing dimension graphs. The actual classification of the dimension entities in supertypes and subtypes was - among other criteria - designed under the aspect that selected subgroups of those entities might be referenced by other entities even of other schemas.
Up to now there are no data structures designed for coordinate dimensioning in tabular form and coordinate dimensioning without dimension lines. In accordance to the rejections made to reduce the quantity of dimension representations, graphs with oblique extension lines (i. e. the extension lines are not perpendicular to the dimension line), foreshortening and not to scale dimension representations are not supported by this schema.

5.2. Dimensioning TYPE Definitions

5.2.1. LIST OF DIM PREDECESSOR

The definition of the list type is provided for use as argument type in subsequent function definitions.

```
*)
TYPE  list_of_dim_predecessor  =  LIST  [1:#]  OF
                                  dim_predecessor;
END_TYPE;
(*
```

5.2.2. REL DIR

The defined type REL_DIR provides a choice between different directions relative to a basis direction. Enumerated are "parallel", "horizontal" and "vertical".

```
*)
TYPE rel_dir = ENUMERATION OF (parallel, horizontal,
                              vertical);
END_TYPE;
(*
```

5.2.3. THREAD SPEC

THREAD_SPEC specifies the kind of a thread. The following possibilities are enumerated in succession: "Metric", "Fine Pitch", "Whitworth", "Trapezoid" and "Sawtooth".

```
*)
TYPE thread_spec = ENUMERATION OF (m, fp, w, tr, s);
END_TYPE;
(*
```

5.3. Dimensioning ENTITY Definitions

5.3.1. REP GEOMETRY DIMENSION

REP_GEOMETRY_DIMENSION is the supertype of the two subtypes REPRESENTED_SHAPE_DIMENSION and CIRCULAR_SHAPE_DIMENSION. Both describe certain instances of dimension graphs dimensioning representations of geometry.
This entity is referred to by the entity type VIEW_WITH_ANNOTATION (belongs to the scope of the DRAWING_ORGANIZATION_SCHEMA) in which all data describing a view of a drawing sheet are comprised.

```
*)
ENTITY  rep_geometry_dimension  SUPERTYPE  OF
                              (represented_shape_dimension  XOR
                              circular_shape_dimension);
END_ENTITY;
(*
```

5.3.2. REPRESENTED SHAPE DIMENSION

REPRESENTED_SHAPE_DIMENSION is the supertype of all entity types describing dimension graphs with the exception of graphs dimensioning the diameter or radius of represented circles or the nominal diameter of up projected threads (see figure 5.1). Limitations in valid combinations with pictorial representations of form and location tolerances are the reason for subdividing description of dimension graphs in different categories.

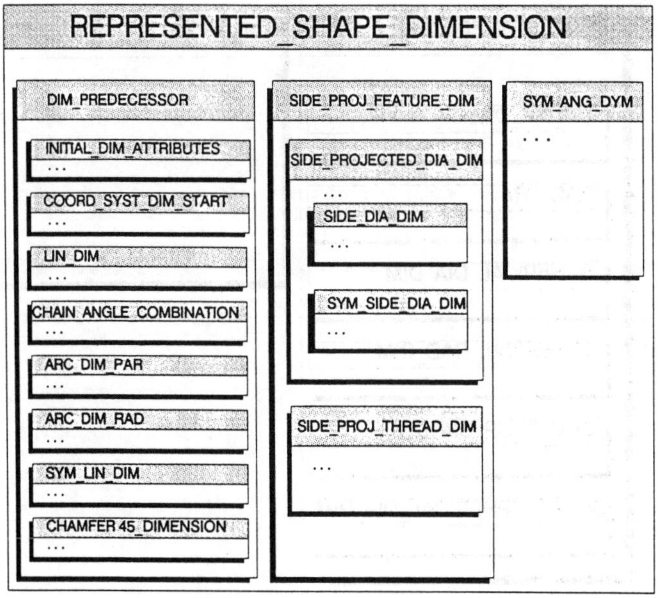

Fig. 5.1: Descriptions of dimension graphs (linear, angular, arc, chamfer and dimensions of side projected features)

```
*)
ENTITY  represented_shape_dimension  SUPERTYPE  OF
                              (dim_predecessor  XOR
```

```
                         side_projected_feature_dim  XOR
                         sym_ang_dim)
                         SUBTYPE  OF
                         (rep_geometry_dimension);
END_ENTITY;
(*
```

5.3.3. CIRCULAR SHAPE DIMENSION

The supertype CIRCULAR_SHAPE_DIMENSION contains all subtypes for the description of dimension graphs dimensioning circular representations of geometry including up projected threads (see figure 5.2).

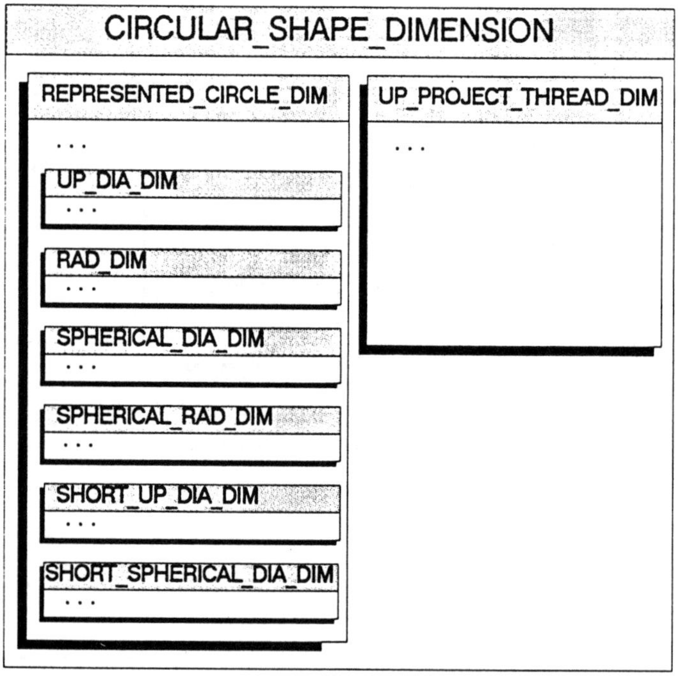

Fig. 5.2: Descriptions of dimension graphs (diameter and radius dimensions for circle representations)

```
*)
ENTITY  circular_shape_dimension  SUPERTYPE  OF
                              (represented_circle_dimension  XOR
                              up_projected_thread_dim)
                              SUBTYPE  OF
                              (rep_geometry_dimension);
END_ENTITY;
(*
```

5.3.4. DIM PREDECESSOR

The entity DIM_PREDECESSOR is the supertype of all constituents describing a dimension graph being composed by either one single dimension (e. g. a linear dimension) or several dimensions of possibly different types that form a dimension chain.
The concept of developing a dimension chain by using subtypes of DIM_PREDECESSOR is that every single dimension description points either to its preceding dimension description or to the entity types INITIAL_DIM_ATTRIBUTES or COORD_SYST_DIM_START. The succeeding single dimension description adopts some attributes from its predecessor, e. g.: The attribute **next_dir** of the predecessor is the starting direction of the dimension line of the successor (Remark: The attribute **next_dir** of the predecessor need not be identical with the attribute **next_dir** of the successor, e. g.: An angular dimension graph has a circular dimension line, the "ending direction" of which differs from the "starting direction" that is defined within the structure of the predecessor). Thus, several attributes that are not required for a complete description of an entity are derived and listed, because they serve as referenced data needed by other entities even of different subschemas to establish a valid relation between both entities.
The subtypes INITIAL_DIM_ATTRIBUTES, COORD_SYST_DIM_START, SYM_LIN_DIM and CHAMFER45°_DIMENSION cannot refer to a DIM_PREDECESSOR, whereas all other subtypes have to refer to exactly one DIM_PREDECESSOR. Therefore, the constructs described by subtypes referring to no DIM_PREDECESSOR serve as a start construct for a dimension graph. Mapping to the physical file structure, it must be realized that one of those subtypes referring to no DIM_PREDECESSOR terminates a preceding list of DIM_PREDECESSOR, because a basic requirement for STEP development is to permit nothing but back pointers.

```
*)
ENTITY  dim_predecessor  SUPERTYPE  OF
                         (initial_dim_attributes  XOR
                         coord_syst_dim_start  XOR  lin_dim
                         XOR  chain_angle_combination  XOR
                         arc_dim_par  XOR  arc_dim_rad  XOR
                         sym_lin_dim  XOR
                         chamfer45°_dimension)
                         SUBTYPE  OF
                         (represented_shape_dimension);
END_ENTITY;
(*
```

5.3.5. INITIAL DIM ATTRIBUTES

One of those subtypes of DIM_PREDECESSOR that cannot refer to a preceding DIM_PREDECESSOR is the entity INITIAL_DIM_ATTRIBUTES. The construct described by this entity serves as a starting point for succeeding constructs described by other subtypes of the supertype DIM_PREDECESSOR.

```
*)
ENTITY  initial_dim_attributes  SUBTYPE  OF
                         (dim_predecessor);
   next_dir              : direction;      --   see   /1/,
                           4.5.3.7
   determinator          : view_position;
DERIVE
   pre_list              : list_of_dim_predecessor  :=
                           create_list
                           (initial_dim_attributes);
   reference             : LOGICAL  :=  .T.;
WHERE
   (* a *)   coordinate_space  (next_dir)  =  2;
END_ENTITY;
(*
```

ATTRIBUTE DEFINITIONS:

next_dir : The direction defining the start direction of the dimension line described by a subtype of the entity type DIM_PREDECESSOR that references INITIAL_DIM_ATTRIBUTES. If the immediate successor has a false **reference** flag, all succeeding descriptions of dimensions up to and inclusively the first dimension with a true **reference** flag adopt this direction as the start direction of their dimension lines.

determinator : The **determinator** is the position where either a dimension line parallel to **next_dir** or an extension line perpendicular to **next_dir** has its origin. The existence and length of an extension line at this point is determined by the succeeding subtypes of DIM_PREDECESSOR relating to this very instance of INITIAL_DIM_ATTRIBUTES. A relation is established by either referring to this instance or referring to a subtype of DIM_PREDECESSOR that itself refers to this instance and has a false **reference** flag. Then an extension line exists, if one of those subtypes relating to the instance of INITIAL_DIM_ATTRIBUTES have an attribute **offset** that is not equal to zero.

pre_list : All subtypes of entity type DIM_PREDECESSOR integrated in the physical data structure describing a dimension graph up to this point are contained in the **pre_list**. This list is referred to by the succeeding DIM_PREDECESSOR to find the last entity of the preceding list of DIM_PREDECESSORs with a true **reference** flag.

reference : A successor of a list of DIM_PREDECESSORs searches with the function LAST_TRUE_REFERENCE applied by the attribute **pre_ref** for the last predecessor having a true **reference** flag. The start point of the new dimension line is either at the end point of the dimension line or at the extension line terminating the dimension line described by the last predecessor with a true **reference** flag. Here the **reference** flag is always true, because the structure INITIAL_DIM_ATTRIBUTES never has any predecessor.

PROPOSITIONS:

a. The dimensionality of **next_dir** has to have the value 2.

5.3.6. COORD SYST DIM START

Also COORD_SYST_DIM_START cannot refer to a preceding DIM_PREDECESSOR. So the construct described by this entity serves as a starting point for succeeding constructs described by other subtypes of the supertype DIM_PREDECESSOR. COORD_SYST_DIM_START is used as a starting point where a dimension graph is described relative to a local coordinate system represented like a grid.

```
*)
ENTITY  coord_syst_dim_start  SUBTYPE  OF
                              (dim_predecessor);
   referenced_syst        : coord_syst_rep;
   next_dir               : direction;      --    see   /1/,
                            4.5.3.7
   distance_from_zero     : REAL;
   syst_line_no           : INTEGER;
DERIVE
   pre_list               : list_of_dim_predecessor   :=
                            create_list
                            (coord_syst_dim_start);
   reference              : LOGICAL  :=  .T.;
   determinator           : view_position  :=  id
                            (vector_sum  (
                            skalar_times_vector
                            (referenced_syst.grid_offset  *
                            syst_line_no,  next_dir),
                            skalar_times_vector
                            (distance_from_zero,
                            perpendicular  (next_dir)  )  ));
```

```
WHERE
   (* a *)    coordinate_space (next_dir) = 2;
   (* b *)    (next_dir = perpendicular
   (referenced_syst.axis1_dir) ) XOR (next_dir =
   perpendicular (referenced_syst.axis2_dir) );
END_ENTITY;
(*
```

ATTRIBUTE DEFINITIONS:

referenced_syst	:	This is a reference to a representation of a coordinate system. The coordinate system is represented like a grid and the dimension line described by the successor(s) start at one of the lines of the grid.
next_dir	:	The direction defining the start direction of the dimension line described by a subtype of the entity type DIM_PREDECESSOR that references COORD_SYST_DIM_START. If the immediate successor has a false **reference** flag, all succeeding descriptions of dimensions up to and inclusively the first dimension with a true **reference** flag adopt this direction as the start direction of their dimension lines.
distance_from_zero	:	The distance of the point determined by **determinator** from the axis of the represented coordinate system being measured perpendicular to **next_dir**.
syst_line_no	:	The number of the line of the grid where **determinator** is placed.
pre_list	:	All subtypes of entity type DIM_PREDECESSOR integrated in the physical data structure describing a dimension graph up to this point are contained in the **pre_list**. This list is referred to by the succeeding DIM_PREDECESSOR to find the last entity of the preceding list of DIM_PREDECESSORs with a true **reference** flag.
reference	:	A successor of a list of DIM_PREDECESSORs searches with the function LAST_TRUE_REFERENCE applied by the

attribute **pre_ref** for the last predecessor having a true **reference** flag. The start point of the new dimension line is either at the end point of the dimension line or at the extension line terminating the dimension line described by the last predecessor with a true **reference** flag. Here the **reference** flag is always true, because COORD_SYST_DIM_START never has any predecessor.

determinator : The **determinator** is the position from where the distance of the start point of the dimension line described by the succeeding subtype of DIM_PREDECESSOR can be calculated easily: The distance is determined by the attribute **offset** of the successor. There is no need for a representation of an extension line.

PROPOSITIONS:

a. The dimensionality of **next_dir** has to have the value 2.

b. The starting direction **next_dir** of the dimension lines referring to this structure is parallel to one of the axes of the represented coordinate system.

5.3.7. LIN DIM

LIN_DIM is the structure of the descriptions of linear dimensions having no, one or two extension lines. The dimension that can be described according to this structure may stand alone or be contained in a combined dimension graph. For the representation of a linear dimension and the meaning of the attributes within the structure describing the representation see figure 5.3.

Even a superimposed running dimension - a special case of a dimension chain - may be represented, if a) all dimensions that descriptions are linked are linear dimensions and b) all **reference** flags of these linear dimensions are false and c) all **offsets** are zero or omitted.

In the structure following inherent constraints are considered:

- A linear dimension has one straight dimension line.
- The dimension line may be terminated by either 2 arrow heads or 2 circles or 1 arrow head and 1 circle.

- The length between the arrow heads or circles of a straight dimension line corresponds to the dimensional value with regard to the scale applied.
- Where a dimension line has 2 arrow heads they are oriented against each other.
- Linear dimensions have only straight extension lines.
- An extension line contacts the dimension line at the arrow head or circle.
- The extension line is directed perpendicular to the dimension line.
- Where a note is placed above a dimension line the direction of the note is parallel to the dimension line.

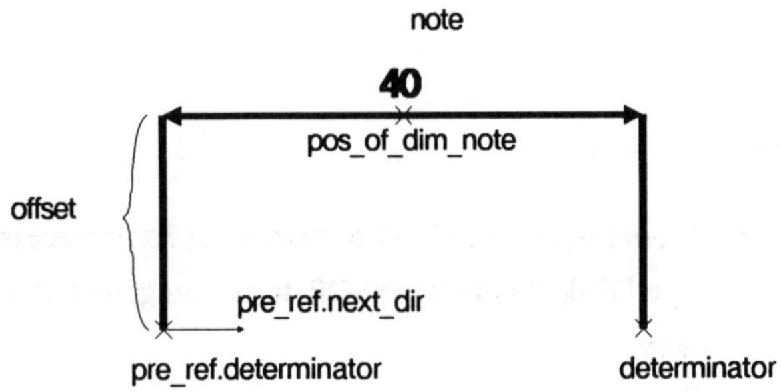

Fig. 5.3: A linear dimension described by the structure LIN_DIM

```
*)
ENTITY  lin_dim  SUBTYPE  OF  (dim_predecessor);
   first_attribute        : dim_predecessor;
   note                   : linear_length_notation;
   pos_of_dim_note        : dimension_note_position;
   terminator_inside      : LOGICAL;
   offset                 : OPTIONAL  REAL;
   determinator           : view_position;
   reference              : LOGICAL;
   DERIVE
   pre_list               : list_of_dim_predecessor  :=
   extend_list  (first_attribute.pre_list,  lin_dim);
```

```
   pre_ref                    : dim_predecessor  :=
   last_true_reference  (first_attribute.pre_list);
   next_dir                   : direction  :=  id
   (pre_ref.next_dir);
   dimension_value        : POSITIVE_REAL  :=  dot_product
   (create_vector  (pre_ref.determinator,  determinator),
   next_dir);
WHERE
   (* a *)    determinator <> pre_ref.determinator;
END_ENTITY;
(*
```

ATTRIBUTE DEFINITIONS:

first_attribute	:	There the entity LIN_DIM references its predecessor of entity type DIM_PREDECESSOR to be integrated in a dimension chain.
note	:	The dimension note of a linear dimension.
pos_of_dim_note	:	The position of the dimension note inclusive its direction given either implicitly in case of the attribute type is equal to DIM_NOTE_WITHOUT_LEADER or explicitly in case of the attribute type is equal to DIM_NOTE_WITH_LEADER. Both are subtypes of the entity type DIMENSION_NOTE_POSITION.
terminator_inside:		This flag determines the orientation of the applied arrow heads. It has no effect on a circle applied as a dimension line terminator. If the flag **terminator_inside** is true, both arrow heads point from the "middle" to the ends of the dimension line. If the flag **terminator_inside** is false, they point to the "middle" of the dimension line and a standard elongation of the dimension line beyond the represented outlines and/or

extension lines may be necessary. This depends on whether there is a preceding or a succeeding aligned dimension line. If two consecutive dimension descriptions have a false flag while the offset of the second is omitted or zero, the dimension lines have a circle instead of the arrow heads at their intersection.

offset : If the offset value is not omitted and not equal to zero, it follows that an extension line has to be created or an existing extension line has to be elongated at **pre_ref.determinator**. The **offset** is the distance - measured perpendicular to **pre_ref.next_dir** with regard to the sign of the value - between the dimension line and either the **determinator** (only if **first_attribute** is of entity type INITIAL_DIM_ATTRIBUTES or COORD_SYST_DIM_START) or the dimension line denoted by **first_attribute**. If **first_attribute** is of type ARC_DIM_PAR, the offset is measured from the arc center in a direction which is centrifugal and which points to the end point of the dimensioned arc.

determinator : The dimension line terminates either at the **determinator** or at an extension line that is defined by **determinator** and as being perpendicular to the dimension line.

reference : A successor of a list of DIM_PREDECESSORs searches with the function LAST_TRUE_REFERENCE applied by the attribute **pre_ref** for the last predecessor having a true **reference** flag. The start point of the new dimension line is either at the end point of the dimension line or at the extension line terminating the dimension line described by the last predecessor with a true **reference** flag.

pre_list : All subtypes of entity type DIM_PREDECESSOR integrated in the physical data structure describing a dimension graph up to this point are contained in the **pre_list**. This list is referred to by the succeeding DIM_PREDECESSOR to find the last entity of the preceding list of DIM_PREDECESSORs with a true **reference** flag.

pre_ref	:	**pre_ref** references the last predecessor having a true **reference** flag. The attributes **determinator** serving as origin of the dimension line or the extension line and **next_dir** serving as the start direction of the dimension line are adopted from the here selected entity of type DIM_PREDECESSOR.
next_dir	:	If a description of a linear dimension has a true **reference** flag, all succeeding dimensions having a false **reference** flag inclusively the first succeeding dimension having a true **reference** flag adopt this direction as the start direction of their dimension lines. In the event that there either is no successor or the **reference** flag is false, **next_dir** has no further application.
dimension_value	:	Here the **dimension_value** is derived. This value has the quality "desired size". It is not possible to derive a value having no basis in the geometry appearance, because otherwise problems with the requirement "associativity" would arise.

PROPOSITIONS:

a. Both the point denoted as **determinator** by this entity and the point denoted as **determinator** by the last predecessor having a true **reference** flag must not be identical.

5.3.8. SYM LIN DIM

The structure SYM_LIN_DIM is a description of a linear dimension dimensioning a symmetric object drawn as a fraction of a whole. Therefore not more than one extension line can be described. The dimension that can be described according to this structure may stand alone or be contained in a combined dimension graph where it serves as a starting construct for succeeding dimensions, because the entity type SYM_LIN_DIM cannot refer to a preceding DIM_PREDECESSOR. For the graphical appearance and the usage of the attributes of SYM_LIN_DIM see figure 5.4.

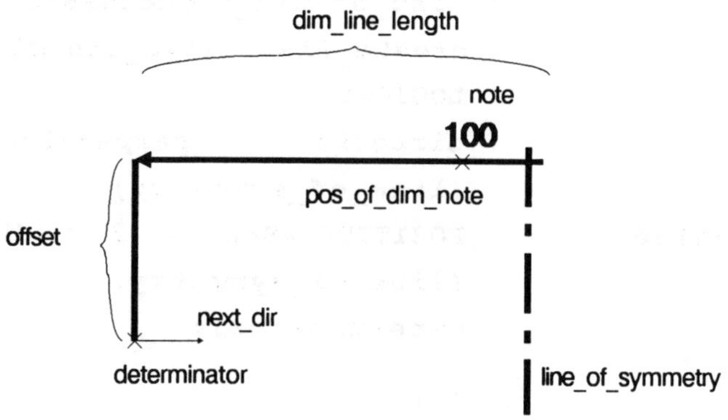

Fig. 5.4: A linear dimension for symmetric objects described by the structure SYM_LIN_DIM

In the structure the following inherent constraints are considered:

- A linear dimension of a symmetric object has one straight dimension line.
- The dimension line is terminated by one arrow head at the side of the extension line or represented geometry line and by the centerline on the other side.
- The double length between the terminating points of the dimension line corresponds to the dimensional value with regard to the scale applied.
- The arrow head is placed between the centerline and the extension line or represented geometry line.
- The straight extension line is directed perpendicular to the dimension line.
- Where a note is placed above a dimension line, the direction of the note is parallel to the dimension line.

```
*)
ENTITY  sym_lin_dim  SUBTYPE OF  (dim_predecessor);
   line_of_symmetry       : center_line;
   determinator           : view_position;
   note                   : dimension_note_position;
   offset                 : OPTIONAL  REAL;
```

```
   dim_line_length          : POSITIVE_REAL;
DERIVE
   pre_list                 : list_of_dim_predecessor  :=
                              create_list  (sym_lin_dim);
   reference                : LOGICAL  :=  .T.;
   next_dir                 : direction  :=  perpendicular
                              (line_of_symmetry);
   dimension_value          : POSITIVE_REAL  :=  2  *  distance
                              (line_of_symmetry,
                              determinator);
END_ENTITY;
(*
```

ATTRIBUTE DEFINITIONS:

line_of_symmetry : This is a reference to the centerline of the symmetrical object drawn as a fraction of a whole.

determinator : The dimension line terminates either at the **determinator** or at an extension line that is defined by **determinator** and as being perpendicular to the dimension line.

note : The dimension note of a linear dimension.

pos_of_dim_note : The position of the dimension note inclusive its direction given either implicitly in case of the attribute type is equal to DIM_NOTE_WITHOUT_LEADER or explicitly in case of the attribute type is equal to DIM_NOTE_WITH_LEADER. Both are subtypes of the entity type DIMENSION_NOTE_POSITION.

offset : If the offset value is not omitted and not equal to zero, it follows that an extension line has to be created connecting the **determinator** with the arrow head of the dimension line. The **offset** is the distance - measured perpendicular to **next_dir** with regard to the sign of the value - between the dimension line and the **determinator**.

dim_line_length : This is the length of the represented dimension line starting at the determinator or at the intersection of the dimension line and the extension line. The dimension line may exceed the centerline.

pre_list : All subtypes of entity type DIM_PREDECESSOR integrated in the physical data structure describing a dimension graph up to this point are contained in the **pre_list** (here the SYM_LIN_DIM occurence is the only element up to this point). This list is referred to by the succeeding DIM_PREDECESSOR to find the last entity of the preceding list of DIM_PREDECESSORs with a true **reference** flag.

reference : A successor of a list of DIM_PREDECESSORs searches with the function LAST_TRUE_REFERENCE applied by the attribute **pre_ref** for the last predecessor having a true **reference** flag. The start point of the new dimension line is either at the end point of the dimension line or at the extension line terminating the dimension line described by the last predecessor with a true **reference** flag. Here the **reference** flag is always true, because SYM_LIN_DIM never has any predecessor.

next_dir : The direction defining the direction of the dimension line of this SYM_LIN_DIM occurrence as well as the start direction of the dimension lines of succeeding dimension descriptions having a false **reference** flag and the first succeeding dimension having a true **reference** flag.

dimension_value : Here the **dimension_value** is derived. This value has the quality "desired size". It is not possible to derive a value having no basis in the geometry appearance, because otherwise problems with the requirement "associativity" would arise.

5.3.9. ANG DIM

ANG_DIM is the structure for the descriptions of angular dimensions. The two subtypes of ANG_DIM separate the descriptions of angular dimensions being integrated in a dimension chain described by entity types of DIM_PREDECESSOR and angular dimensions dimensioning chamfers of side projected rotational geometry (e. g. a hole) and either being combined with a diameter dimension or a thread dimension.

In the structure the following inherent constraints are considered (valid for both subtypes):

- An angular dimension has a circular dimension line.
- An extension line contacts the dimension line at a termination symbol.
- The extension lines of an angular dimension are straight and perpendicular to the tangents of the circular dimension line at its termination symbols.
- Where a dimension line has 2 arrow heads as its termination symbols, they are oriented against each other.
- Where a note is placed above a dimension line, the note is oriented concentrically to the dimension line.

```
*)
ENTITY  ang_dim  SUPERTYPE  OF  (chain_angle_combination  XOR
                              rotational_chamfer_dimension);
   note                        : planar_angle_notation;
   pos_of_dim_note             : dimension_note_position;
   develop_dir                 : rotational_direction;
                                 -- see /1/, 4.3.1.9
   terminator_inside           : LOGICAL;
   offset                      : OPTIONAL  REAL;
   determinator                : view_position;
   next_dir                    : direction;    --  see  /1/,
                                 4.5.3.7
WHERE
   (* a *)   coordinate_space (next_dir)  =  2;
END_ENTITY;
(*
```

ATTRIBUTE DEFINITIONS:

note	:	The dimension note of an angular dimension.
pos_of_dim_note	:	The position of the dimension note inclusive its direction given either implicitly in case of the attribute type is equal to DIM_NOTE_WITHOUT_LEADER or explicitly in case of the attribute type is equal to DIM_NOTE_WITH_LEADER. Both

are subtypes of the entity type DIMENSION_NOTE_POSITION.

develop_dir : The direction in which the dimension graph is developed: In a mathematical positive (i. e. counterclockwise) or in a mathematical negative direction (i. e. clockwise).

terminator_inside : This flag determines the orientation of the applied arrow heads. It has no effect on a circle applied as a dimension line terminator. If the flag **terminator_inside** is true, both arrow heads point from the "middle" to the ends of the dimension line. If the flag **terminator_inside** is false, they point to the "middle" of the dimension line and a standard elongation of the dimension line beyond the represented outlines and/or extension lines may be necessary. This depends on whether there is a preceding or a succeeding aligned dimension line. The following statement is applicable only in case of the description of the angular dimension is of type CHAIN_ANGLE_COMBINATION: If two consecutive dimension descriptions have a false flag while the offset of the second is omitted or zero, the dimension lines have a circle instead of the arrow heads at their intersection.

offset : If the offset value is not omitted and not equal to zero, it follows that an extension line has to be created or an existing extension line has to be elongated either at **pre_ref.determinator** in case of CHAIN_ANGLE_COMBINATION or at **first_attribute.determinator** in case of ROTATIONAL_CHAMFER_DIMENSION. The **offset** is the distance between the dimension line described here and the preceding dimension line along the created or existing extension line. If **first_attribute** is of type ARC_DIM_PAR, the offset is measured from the arc center in a direction which is centrifugal and which points to the end point of the dimensioned arc.

determinator : The dimension line terminates either at the **determinator** or at an extension line that is defined by **determinator** and as being perpendicular to the dimension line in its terminating point (i. e. perpendicular to **next_dir**).

next_dir : The direction of the cicular dimension line in its terminating point. If the subtype CHAIN_ANGLE_COMBINATION is applied and has a true **reference** flag, all succeeding dimensions having a false **reference** flag inclusively the first succeeding dimension having a true **reference** flag adopt this direction as the start direction of their dimension lines. In the event that there either is no successor or the **reference** flag is false, **next_dir** has no further application.

PROPOSITIONS:

a. The dimensionality of **next_dir** has to have the value 2.

5.3.10. CHAIN ANGLE COMBINATION

The angular dimension that can be described according to this structure may stand alone or be contained in a combined dimension graph developed by subtypes of DIM_PREDECESSOR. For the representation of an angular dimension and the meaning of the attributes within the structure describing the representation see figure 5.5. The pictorial appearance described by this structure may have zero, one or two extension lines.

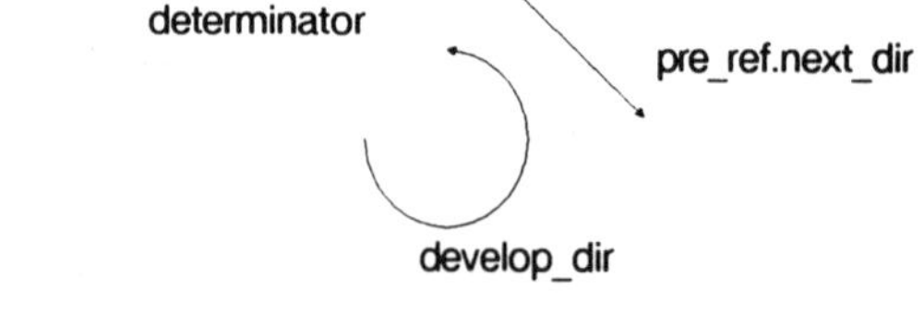

Fig. 5.5: An angular dimension described by the structure CHAIN_ANGLE_COMBINATION

In the structure the following inherent constraints are considered:

- The circular dimension line may be terminated by either 2 arrow heads or 2 circles or 1 arrow head and 1 circle.
- The circular dimension line may exceed the arrow heads, but not the circles.

```
*)
ENTITY chain_angle_combination SUBTYPE OF (ang_dim AND
                               dim_predecessor);
   first_attribute          : dim_predecessor;
   reference                : LOGICAL;
DERIVE
   pre_lis                  : list_of_dim_predecessor :=
                              extend_list
                              (first_attribute.pre_list,
                              chain_angle_combination);
   pre_ref                  : dim_predecessor :=
                              last_true_reference
                              (first_attribute.pre_list);
   dimension_value          : POSITIVE_REAL :=
                              angle_between_vectors
                              (next_dir, pre_ref.next_dir,
                              develop_dir);
END_ENTITY;
(*
```

ATTRIBUTE DEFINITIONS:

first_attribute	:	There the entity CHAIN_ANGLE_COMBINATION references its predecessor of entity type DIM_PREDECESSOR to be integrated in a dimension chain.
reference	:	A successor of a list of DIM_PREDECESSORs searches with the function LAST_TRUE_REFERENCE applied by the attribute **pre_ref** for the last predecessor having a true **reference** flag. The start point of the new dimension line is either at the end point of the dimension line or at the extension

		line terminating the dimension line described by the last predecessor with a true **reference** flag.
pre_list	:	All subtypes of entity type DIM_PREDECESSOR integrated in the physical data structure describing a dimension graph up to this point are contained in the **pre_list**. This list is referred to by the succeeding DIM_PREDECESSOR to find the last entity of the preceding list of DIM_PREDECESSORs with a true **reference** flag.
pre_ref	:	**pre_ref** references the last predecessor having a true **reference** flag. The attributes **determinator** serving as origin of the dimension line or the extension line and **next_dir** serving as the start direction of the dimension line are adopted from the here selected entity of type DIM_PREDECESSOR.
dimension_value	:	Here the **dimension_value** is derived. This value has the quality "desired size". It is not possible to derive a value having no basis in the geometry appearance, because otherwise problems with the requirement "associativity" would arise.

5.3.11. ROTATIONAL CHAMFER DIMENSION

The angular dimension that can be described according to this structure may only combined with a diameter or thread dimension graph dimensioning side projected circular objects. The dimension graph described by this structure resembles a dimension graph as described by the structure CHAIN_ANGLE_COMBINATION.

In the structure the following inherent constraints are considered:

- The circular dimension line is terminated by 2 arrow heads.
- The circular dimension line may exceed the arrow heads.
- The dimension graph may have one or two extension lines.

```
*)
ENTITY  rotational_chamfer_dimension  SUBTYPE  OF
                            (ang_dim);
   first_attribute        : side_projected_feature_dim;
```

```
DERIVE
   dimension_value          : POSITIVE_REAL  :=
                              angle_between_vectors
                              (next_dir,
                              first_attribute.next_dir,
                              develop_dir);
END_ENTITY;
(*
```

ATTRIBUTE DEFINITIONS:

first_attribute : **first_attribute** references either a thread dimension description of a side projected thread or a diameter dimension of a side projected circle. The angular dimension graph will be combined with the referenced dimension graph. The dimension graph described by ROTATIONAL_CHAMFER_DIMENSION contacts the extension line of the thread or diameter dimension that is placed on the same side of the centerline as the **determinator**.

dimension_value : Here the **dimension_value** is derived. This value has the quality "desired size". It is not possible to derive a value having no basis in the geometry appearance, because otherwise problems with the requirement "associativity" would arise.

5.3.12. ARC DIM PAR

ARC_DIM_PAR is the structure of descriptions of arc dimensions having two parallel extension lines and two further lines indicating the center ("center indication lines") of the dimensioned arc (each line connects one terminating point of the arc with the center of the arc). For a valid dimension graph the angle between the both lines indicating the center may not exceed 90°. The dimension that can be described according to this structure may stand alone or be contained in a dimension chain. A graphical appearance is shown in figure 5.6.

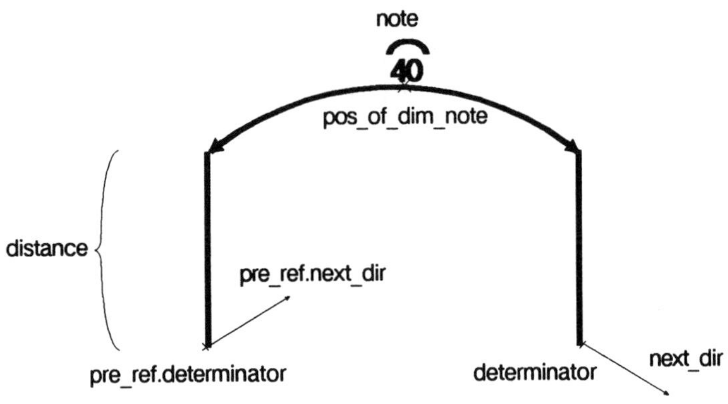

Fig. 5.6: An arc dimension described by the entity ARC_DIM_PAR

In the structure the following inherent constraints are considered:

- A dimension of an arc has one circular dimension line that is an offset curve of the arc, i. e. both the dimension line and the arc have the same radius.
- The dimension line is terminated by 2 arrow heads that are oriented against each other.
- The length of the dimension line between the arrow heads corresponds to the dimensional value with regard to the scale applied.
- The straight extension lines are perpendicular to the secant between both terminating points of the dimensioned arc and contact the dimension line at its arrow heads.
- Where a note is placed above a dimension line, the note is oriented concentrically to the dimension line.

```
*)
ENTITY  arc_dim_par  SUBTYPE  OF  (dim_predecessor);
   first_attribute          : dim_predecessor;
   note                     : linear_length_notation;
   pos_of_dim_note          : dimension_note_position;
```

```
   terminator_inside        : LOGICAL;
   distance                 : POSITIVE_REAL;
   determinator             : view_position;
   reference                : LOGICAL;
   next_dir                 : direction;   see /1/, 4.5.3.7
DERIVE
   pre_list                 : list_of_dim_predecessor  :=
                              extend_list
                              (first_attribute.pre_list,
                              arc_dim_par);
   pre_ref                  : dim_predecessor  :=
                              last_true_reference
                              (first_attribute.pre_list);
   determined_arc           : arc_segment  :=  arc_calc
                              (first_attribute.determinator,
                              determinator,  next_dir);
   dimension_value          : POSITIVE_REAL  :=  extent
                              (determined_arc);
WHERE
   (* a *)   coordinate_space  (next_dir)  =  2;
   (* b *)   extent  (determined_arc)  <=  π/2  *  radius
   (determined_arc);
   (* c *)   determinator  <>  pre_ref.determinator;
END_ENTITY;
(*
```

ATTRIBUTE DEFINITIONS:

first_attribute : There the entity ARC_DIM_PAR references its predecessor of entity type DIM_PREDECESSOR to be integrated in a dimension chain.

note : The dimension note of an arc dimension.

pos_of_dim_note : The position of the dimension note inclusive its direction given either implicitly in case of the attribute type is equal to DIM_NOTE_WITHOUT_LEADER or explicitly in case of the attribute type is equal to DIM_NOTE_WITH_LEADER. Both are subtypes of the entity type DIMENSION_NOTE_POSITION.

terminator_inside : This flag determines the orientation of the applied arrow heads. If the flag **terminator_inside** is true, both arrow heads point from the "middle" to the ends of the dimension line. If the flag **terminator_inside** is false, they point to the "middle" of the dimension line and a standard elongation of the dimension line beyond the represented extension lines is necessary.

distance : **distance** is the offset between the circular dimension line and the dimensioned arc.

determinator : The terminating point of the dimensioned arc described by **determinator** and the center of the arc are the terminating points of one of the "center indication lines".

reference : A successor of a list of DIM_PREDECESSORs searches with the function LAST_TRUE_REFERENCE applied by the attribute **pre_ref** for the last predecessor having a true **reference** flag. A true **reference** flag designates the "center indication line" through the **determinator** as start construct for succeeding dimension graphs having false **reference** flags inclusively the first successor having a true **reference** flag.

next_dir : If a description of an arc dimension has a true **reference** flag, all succeeding dimensions having a false **reference** flag inclusively the first succeeding dimension having a true **reference** flag adopt this direction as the start direction of their dimension lines. In the event that there either is no successor or the **reference** flag is false, **next_dir** has no further application.

pre_list : All subtypes of entity type DIM_PREDECESSOR integrated in the physical data structure describing a dimension graph up to this point are contained in the **pre_list**. This list is referred to by the succeeding DIM_PREDECESSOR to find the last entity of the preceding list of DIM_PREDECESSORs with a true **reference** flag.

pre_ref : **pre_ref** references the last predecessor having a true **reference** flag. The attributes **determinator** serving as origin of one extension line and **next_dir** serving as the start direction of the dimension line are adopted from the here selected entity of type DIM_PREDECESSOR.

determined_arc : The dimensioned arc derived from the two terminating points and a direction in one of these points. Obviously the procedure might have been designed vice versa.

dimension_value : Here the **dimension_value** is derived. This value has the quality "desired size". It is not possible to derive a value having no basis in the geometry appearance, because otherwise problems with the requirement "associativity" would arise.

PROPOSITIONS:

a. The dimensionality of **next_dir** has to have the value 2.

b. The angle between both "center indication lines" may not exceed 90°.

c. Both the point denoted as **determinator** by this entity and the point denoted as **determinator** by the last predecessor having a true reference flag must not be identical.

5.3.13. ARC DIM RAD

ARC_DIM_RAD is the structure of descriptions of arc dimensions having two extension lines through the center of the dimensioned arc. For a valid dimension graph the angle between the both extension lines has to exceed 90° (see figure 5.7). The dimension that can be described according to this structure may stand alone or be contained in a dimension chain.
In the structure the following inherent constraints are considered:

- A dimension of an arc has one circular dimension line that is concentric to the dimensioned arc.
- The dimension line is terminated by 2 arrow heads that are oriented against each other.
- The straight extension lines are perpendicular to the tangents of the circular dimension line in its terminating points.
- Where a note is placed above a dimension line, the note is oriented concentrically to the dimension line.

- A leader points from the dimension note to the dimensioned arc and terminates at the arc with an arrow as termination symbol.

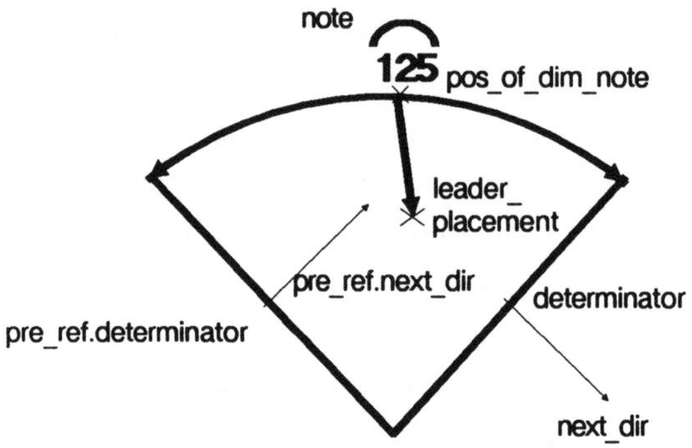

Fig. 5.7: An arc dimension described by the entity ARC_DIM_RAD

```
*)
ENTITY arc_dim_rad SUBTYPE OF (dim_predecessor);
   first_attribute        : dim_predecessor;
   note                   : linear_length_notation;
   pos_of_dim_note        : dimension_note_without_leader;
   terminator_inside      : LOGICAL;
   offset                 : view_position;
   next_dir               : direction;       -- see /1/,
                            4.5.3.7
   leader_placement       : POSITIVE_REAL;
DERIVE
   reference              : LOGICAL := .T.;
   pre_list               : list_of_dim_predecessor :=
                            extend_list
                            (first_attribute.pre_list,
                            arc_dim_rad);
```

```
  pre_ref                  : dim_predecessor  :=
                             last_true_reference
                             (first_attribute.pre_list);
  determined_arc           : arc_segment  :=  arc_calc
                             (first_attribute.determinator,
                             determinator,  next_dir);
  dimension_value          : POSITIVE_REAL  :=  extent
                             (determined_arc);
WHERE
  (* a *)   coordinate_space (next_dir) = 2;
  (* b *)   extent (determined_arc) > π/2 * radius
  (determined_arc);
END_ENTITY;
(*
```

ATTRIBUTE DEFINITIONS:

first_attribute : There the entity ARC_DIM_RAD references its predecessor of entity type DIM_PREDECESSOR to be integrated in a dimension chain.

note : The dimension note of an arc dimension.

pos_of_dim_note : The position of the dimension note inclusive its direction given implicitly as being oriented concentrically to the circular dimension line.

terminator_inside : This flag determines the orientation of the applied arrow heads. If the flag **terminator_inside** is true, both arrow heads point from the "middle" to the ends of the dimension line. If the flag **terminator_inside** is false, they point to the "middle" of the dimension line and a standard elongation of the dimension line beyond the represented extension lines is necessary.

offset : If the offset value is not omitted and not equal to zero, it follows that an extension line has to be created or an existing extension line has to be elongated at **pre_ref.determinator**. The **offset** is the distance - measured perpendicular to **pre_ref.next_dir** with regard to the sign of the value -

between the dimension line and either the **determinator** (only if **first_attribute** is of types INITIAL_DIM_ATTRIBUTES or COORD_SYST_DIM_START) or the dimension line denoted by **first_attribute**. If **first_attribute** is of type ARC_DIM_PAR, the offset is measured from the arc center in a direction which is centrifugal and which points to the end point of the arc dimensioned by ARC_DIM_PAR.

determinator : The dimension line terminates either at the determinator or at an extension line that is defined by determinator and as being perpendicular to the circular dimension line in its terminating point.

next_dir : If a description of an arc dimension has a true **reference** flag, all succeeding dimensions having a false **reference** flag inclusively the first succeeding dimension having a true **reference** flag adopt this direction as the start direction of their dimension lines. In the event that there is either no successor or the **reference** flag is false, **next_dir** has no further application.

leader_placement : There is a leader pointing from the dimension note to the dimensioned arc. The attribute **leader_placement** specifies the placement of the arrow head of the leader on the parametric arc being determined by **determined_arc**.

reference : A successor of a list of DIM_PREDECESSORs searches with the function LAST_TRUE_REFERENCE applied by the attribute **pre_ref** for the last predecessor having a true **reference** flag. The true **reference** flag designates the extension line at the **determinator** as start construct for succeeding dimension graphs having false **reference** flags inclusively the first successor having a true **reference** flag.

pre_list : All subtypes of entity type DIM_PREDECESSOR integrated in the physical data structure describing a dimension graph up to this point are contained in the **pre_list**. This list is referred to by the succeeding DIM_PREDECESSOR to find the last entity of the preceding list of DIM_PREDECESSORs with a true **reference** flag.

pre_ref : **pre_ref** references the last predecessor having a true **reference** flag. The attributes **determinator** serving as origin of one extension line and **next_dir** serving as the start direction of the dimension line are adopted from the here selected entity of type DIM_PREDECESSOR.

determined_arc : The dimensioned arc derived from the two terminating points and a direction in one of these points. Obviously the procedure might have been designed vice versa.

dimension_value : Here the **dimension_value** is derived. This value has the quality "desired size". It is not possible to derive a value having no basis in the geometry appearance, because otherwise problems with the requirement "associativity" would arise.

PROPOSITIONS:

a. The dimensionality of **next_dir** has to have the value 2.
b. The angle between both extension lines has to exceed 90°.

5.3.14. CHAMFER 45° DIMENSION

The structure CHAMFER45°_DIMENSION describes a combined dimension dimensioning a chamfer: It contains information of both the linear length and the angle (this kind of dimension representation is only applicable for 45° chamfers) of the chamfer. The pictorial appearance of the dimension graph is shown in figure 5.8. The dimension that can be described according to this structure may stand alone or be contained in a dimension chain where it serves as a starting construct for succeeding dimensions, because the entity type CHAMFER45°_DIMENSION has no reference to a preceding DIM_PREDECESSOR.
In the structure the following inherent constraints are considered:

- A dimension of a chamfer has one straight dimension line.
- The dimension line is terminated by 2 arrow heads that are pointing from the terminating points of the dimension line to the "middle" of the dimension line and are placed beyond the extension lines respectively geometry lines.
- The dimension line may be combined with straight extension lines.
- The extension lines are perpendicular to the straight dimension line.

- Where a dimension note is placed above a dimension line, the direction of the note is parallel to the dimension line.
- The dimension note is composed by the value of the linear length of the chamfer (here the value of the angle has to be equal to 45°). Both values are separated by an "x".

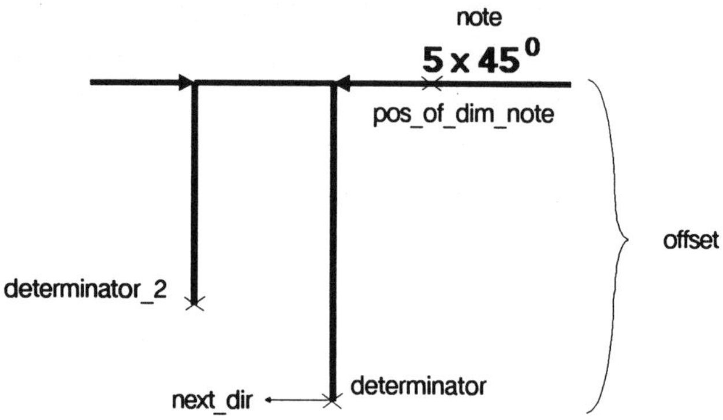

Fig. 5.8: A dimensioning of a 45°-chamfer according to CHAMFER45°_DIMENSION

```
*)
ENTITY  chamfer45°_dimension  SUBTYPE  OF
                        (dim_predecessor);
   geometry_appearance   : chamfer_representation;
   note                  : linear_length_notation;
   pos_of_dim_note       : dimension_note_position;
   offset                : OPTIONAL  REAL;
DERIVE
   reference             : LOGICAL  :=  .T.;
   pre_list              : list_of_dim_predecessor  :=
                           create_list
                           (chamfer45°_dimension);
```

```
   next_dir                 : direction  :=  perpendicular
                              (geometry_appearance.base_line
                              );
   determinator             : view_position  :=  intersect
                              (geometry_appearance.base_line
                              ,  geometry_appearance.edge  XOR
                              geometry_appearance.connection
                              );
   determinator_2           : view_position  :=  intersect
                              (geometry_appearance.offsetlin
                              e,  geometry_appearance.edge);
   dimension_value          : POSITIVE_REAL  :=  dot_product
                              (create_vector
                              (determinator_1,
                              determinator_2),  next_dir);
WHERE
   (* a *)   coordinate_space (next_dir) = 2;
END_ENTITY;
(*
```

ATTRIBUTE DEFINITIONS:

geometry_appearance : This is a reference to a part of the represented geometry identified as an appearance of a chamfer in order to guarantee an associative dimension representation.

note : The dimension note of a chamfer dimension. The string "x 45° " has to be placed to the right of the dimensional value.

pos_of_dim_note : The position of the dimension note inclusive its direction given either implicitly in case of the attribute type is equal to DIM_NOTE_WITHOUT_LEADER or explicitly in case of the attribute type is equal to DIM_NOTE_WITH_LEADER. Both are subtypes of the entity type DIMENSION_NOTE_POSITION.

offset : If the offset value is not omitted and not equal to zero, it follows that an extension line has to be created or an existing extension line has to be elongated at **determinator**. The

offset is the distance - measured perpendicular to **next_dir** with regard to the sign of the value - between the dimension line and the **determinator**.

reference : A successor of a list of DIM_PREDECESSORs searches with the function LAST_TRUE_REFERENCE applied by the attribute **pre_ref** for the last predecessor having a true **reference** flag. The start point of the dimension line of a successor is at the **determinator** respectively at the extension line belonging to **determinator**, because there is always a true **reference** flag at this point.

pre_list : All subtypes of entity type DIM_PREDECESSOR integrated in the physical data structure describing a dimension graph up to this point are contained in the **pre_list**. Here the only element is CHAMFER45°_DIMENSION. This list is referred to by the succeeding DIM_PREDECESSOR to find the last entity of the preceding list of DIM_PREDECESSORs with a true **reference** flag.

next_dir : All succeeding dimensions having a false **reference** flag inclusively the first succeeding dimension having a true **reference** flag adopt this direction as the start direction of their dimension lines. In the event that there is no successor, **next_dir** has no further application.

determinator : The dimension line terminates either at the **determinator** or at an extension line that is defined by **determinator** and as being perpendicular to the dimension line.

determinator_2 : The other defining point of the dimension line is either the **determinator_2** or a point on an extension line that is defined by **determinator_2** and as being perpendicular to the dimension line.

dimension_value : Here the **dimension_value** the linear extension of the chamfer is derived. This value has the quality "desired size". It is not possible to derive a value having no basis in the geometry appearance, because otherwise problems with the requirement "associativity" would arise.

PROPOSITIONS:

a. The dimensionality of **next_dir** has to have the value 2.

5.3.15. SYM ANG DIM

The structure SYM_ANG_DIM is a description of an angular dimension dimensioning a symmetric object drawn as a fraction of a whole (see figure 5.9). Therefore not more than one extension line can be described. No possibility to integrate this structure in a description of a dimension chain is provided.

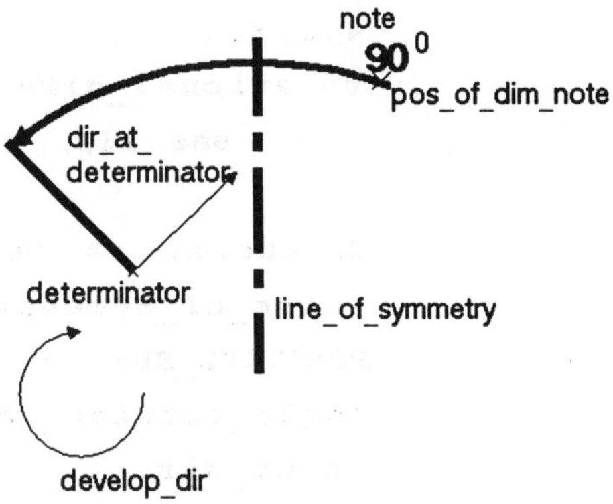

Fig. 5.9: An angular dimension according to SYM_ANG_DIM

In the structure the following inherent constraints are considered:

- An angular dimension of a symmetric object has one circular dimension line.
- The dimension line is terminated by 1 arrow head at the side of the extension line or represented geometry line and by the centerline on the other side.
- The arrow head is placed between the centerline and the extension line or represented geometry line.
- The extension line is perpendicular to the tangent of the circular dimension line at its arrow head.

- Where a **note** is placed above a dimension line, the **note** is oriented concentrically to the dimension line.

```
*)
ENTITY sym_ang_dim SUBTYPE OF
                         (represented_shape_dimension);
   line_of_symmetry      : center_line;
   determinator          : view_position;
   note                  : planar_angle_notation;
   pos_of_dim_note       : dimension_note_position;
   distance              : OPTIONAL POSITIVE_REAL;
   dir_at_determinator   : direction;    -- see /1/,
                           4.5.3.7
   develop_dir           : rotational_direction;
                              -- see /1/, 4.3.1.9
DERIVE
   next_dir              : direction := perpendicular
                           (line_of_symmetry);
   dimension_value       : POSITIVE_REAL := 2 *
                           angle_between_vectors
                           (next_dir,
                           dir_at_determinator,
                           develop_dir);
WHERE
   (* a *)   coordinate_space (dir_at_determinator) = 2;
   (* b *)   coordinate_space (next_dir) = 2;
END_ENTITY;
(*
```

ATTRIBUTE DEFINITIONS:

line_of_symmetry : This is a reference to the centerline of the symmetrical object drawn as a fraction of a whole.

determinator	:	The dimension line terminates either at the **determinator** or at an extension line that is defined by **determinator** and as being perpendicular to the dimension line at its arrow head (i. e. perpendicular to **next_dir**).
note	:	The dimension note of an angular dimension.
pos_of_dim_note	:	The position of the dimension note inclusive its direction given either implicitly in case of the attribute type is equal to DIM_NOTE_WITHOUT_LEADER or explicitly in case of the attribute type is equal to DIM_NOTE_WITH_LEADER. Both are subtypes of the entity type DIMENSION_NOTE_POSITION.
distance	:	The radius of the circular dimension line.
dir_at_determinator	:	The direction of the dimension line at the arrow head.
develop_dir	:	The direction in which the dimension graph is developed: In a mathematical positive (i. e. counterclockwise) or in a mathematical negative direction (i. e. clockwise).
next_dir	:	The direction of the dimension line at the center line.
dimension_value	:	Here the **dimension_value** is derived. This value has the quality "desired size". It is not possible to derive a value having no basis in the geometry appearance, because otherwise problems with the requirement "associativity" would arise.

PROPOSITIONS:

a. The dimensionality of **dir_at_determinator** has to have the value 2.
b. The dimensionality of **next_dir** has to have the value 2.

5.3.16. SIDE PROJECTED FEATURE DIM

SIDE_PROJECTED_FEATURE_DIM is the supertype of dimension descriptions dimensioning side projections of either threads or circles being derived from rotational surfaces such as cylinders, cones, etc. The subtypes of the structure SIDE_PROJECTED_FEATURE_DIM may be referenced by the entity type ROTATIONAL_CHAMFER_DIMENSION that describes the appearance of a dimension graph dimensioning the angle of a chamfer of a surface of revolution or a thread.

```
*)
ENTITY  side_projected_feature_dim  SUPERTYPE  OF
                                (side_projected_dia_dim  XOR
                                side_projected_thread_dim)
                                SUBTYPE  OF
                                (represented_shape_dimension);
END_ENTITY;
(*
```

5.3.17. SIDE PROJECTED DIA DIM

SIDE_PROJECTED_DIA_DIM is the structure of descriptions of diameter dimension graphs dimensioning side projected circles derived from surfaces of revolution. A side projected surface of revolution is represented by two curves that are symmetrical relative to a represented centerline. Where the rotational surface is drawn as a fraction of a whole one of the two curves is not represented. A section perpendicular to the centerline defines the dimensioned side projected circle.

In the structure the following inherent constraints are considered:

- Diameter dimensions of side projected circles have straight dimension lines.
- Diameter dimensions of side projected circles have straight extension lines.
- The extension lines are perpendicular to the dimension line.
- Where a dimension note is placed above a dimension line, the direction of the note is parallel to the dimension line.
- The character "ø" precedes the dimensional value.

```
*)
ENTITY  side_projected_dia_dim  SUPERTYPE  OF  (side_dia_dim
                                XOR  sym_side_dia_dim)
                                SUBTYPE  OF
                                (side_projected_feature_dim);
   line_of_symmetry         :  center_line;
```

```
   determinator          : view_position;
   note                  : linear_length_notation;
   pos_of_dim_note       : dimension_note_position;
   offset                : OPTIONAL  REAL;
DERIVE
   next_dir              : direction  :=  perpendicular
                             (line_of_symmetry);
   dimension_value       : POSITIVE_REAL  :=  2  *  distance
                             (line_of_symmetry,
                             determinator);
WHERE
   (* a *)   coordinate_space  (next_dir)  =  2;
END_ENTITY;
(*
```

ATTRIBUTE DEFINITIONS:

line_of_symmetry : This is a reference to the centerline of the side projected circle.

determinator : The dimension line terminates either at the **determinator** or at an extension line that is defined by **determinator** and as being perpendicular to the dimension line (i. e. perpendicular to **next_dir**). If the subtype SIDE_DIA_DIM is applied, the other terminating point of the dimension line is placed symmetrically to the first terminating point. If the subtype SYM_SIDE_DIA_DIM is applied, the dimension line ends at the **line_of_symmetry** without a termination symbol.

note : The dimension note of a linear dimension.

pos_of_dim_note : The position of the dimension note inclusive its direction given either implicitly in case of the attribute type is equal to DIM_NOTE_WITHOUT_LEADER or explicitly in case of the attribute type is equal to DIM_NOTE_WITH_LEADER. Both are subtypes of the entity type DIMENSION_NOTE_POSITION.

offset : The distance between the **determinator** and the dimension line measured perpendicular to **next_dir**.

next_dir : The direction of the dimension line and the starting direction of the dimension line of an angular dimension of entity type ROTATIONAL_CHAMFER_DIMENSION pointing at a subtype of SIDE_PROJECTED_DIA_DIM.

dimension_value : Here the **dimension_value** is derived. This value has the quality "desired size". It is not possible to derive a value having no basis in the geometry appearance, because otherwise problems with the requirement "associativity" would arise.

PROPOSITIONS:

a. The dimensionality of **next_dir** has to have the value 2.

5.3.18. SIDE DIA DIM

SIDE_DIA_DIM is the subtype of SIDE_PROJECTED_DIA_DIM describing diameter dimension graphs dimensioning side projected circles where no fractions of a whole geometry representation are drawn. A typical representation of such a diameter dimension is shown in figure 5.10.

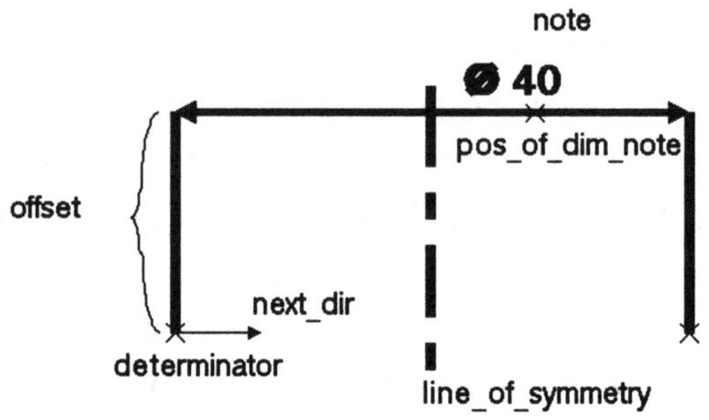

Fig. 5.10: A diameter dimension described by SIDE_DIA_DIM

In the structure the following inherent constraints are considered:
- The dimension line contacts zero, one or two extension lines.
- The dimension line has two arrow heads as termination symbols.

- The length between the arrow heads corresponds to the dimensional value with regard to the scale applied.

```
*)
ENTITY  side_dia_dim  SUBTYPE  OF  (side_projected_dia_dim);
   terminator_inside          : LOGICAL;
END_ENTITY;
(*
```

ATTRIBUTE DEFINITIONS:

terminator_inside : This flag determines the orientation of the applied arrow heads. If the flag **terminator_inside** is true, the arrow heads point from the "middle" of the dimension line to the intersection points between dimension line and either extension line or a point of the dimensioned circle appearance.

5.3.19. SYM SIDE DIA DIM

SYM_SIDE_DIA_DIM is the subtype of SIDE_PROJECTED_DIA_DIM describing diameter dimension graphs dimensioning side projected circles where fractions of a whole geometry representation are drawn.

In the structure the following inherent constraints are considered:

- The dimension line contacts zero or one extension line.
- The dimension line has one arrow head as termination symbol and exceeds the centerline without any symbol.
- The arrow head is placed between the centerline and either the extension line or the curve describing the outline of the rotational surface.
- The double length between the arrow head and the represented centerline corresponds to the dimensional value with regard to the scale applied.

```
*)
ENTITY  sym_side_dia_dim  SUBTYPE  OF
                         (side_projected_dia_dim);
   dim_line_length            : POSITIVE_REAL;
END_ENTITY;
(*
```

ATTRIBUTE DEFINITIONS:

dim_line_length : The length of the dimension line.

5.3.20. THREAD DIMENSIONING

THREAD_DIMENSIONING is the supertype for dimension descriptions dimensioning either side or up projected threads.

In the structure the following inherent constraints are considered:

- A thread dimension has a straight dimension line.
- A dimension line of a thread dimension has two arrow heads as termination symbols.
- The two arrow heads are oriented against each other.
- Where a dimension note is placed above a dimension line, the direction of the note is parallel to the dimension line.
- A character denoting the kind of the dimensioned thread precedes the dimensional value.
- The length between the arrow heads of the dimension line corresponds to the nominal diameter of the thread.
- An extension line is directed perpendicularly to the dimension line.

```
*)
ENTITY  thread_dimensioning  SUPERTYPE  OF
                         (up_projected_thread_dim  XOR
                         side_projected_thread_dim);
   terminator_inside     : LOGICAL;
   note                  : thread_notation;
   pos_of_dim_note       : dimension_note_position;
END_ENTITY;
(*
```

ATTRIBUTE DEFINITIONS:

terminator_inside : If the **terminator_inside** flag is true, the arrow heads are placed between the terminating points of the dimension line and point away from the "middle" of the dimension line. If the flag is false, the arrow heads point to the "middle" of the dimension line and the dimension line has to be elongated beyond the arrow heads.

note : The dimension note of a thread dimension.

pos_of_dim_note : The position of the dimension note inclusive its direction given either implicitly in case of the attribute type is equal to DIM_NOTE_WITHOUT_LEADER or explicitly in case of the attribute type is equal to DIM_NOTE_WITH_LEADER. Both are subtypes of the entity type DIMENSION_NOTE_POSITION.

5.3.21. SIDE PROJECTED THREAD DIM

The structure SIDE_PROJECTED_THREAD_DIM describes thread dimensions of side projected threads. Being a subtype - among others - of SIDE_PROJECTED_FEATURE_DIM the dimension graph described according to this structure may be combined with an angular dimension described by ROTATIONAL_CHAMFER_DIMENSION.
In the structure the following inherent constraints are considered:

- A thread dimension has zero, one or two straight extension lines.

```
*)
ENTITY side_projected_thread_dim SUBTYPE OF
                          (thread_dimensioning AND
                          side_projected_feature_dim);
   thread_appearance      : side_projected_thread;
   determinator           : view_position;
   offset                 : OPTIONAL REAL;
```

```
DERIVE
   next_dir              : direction  :=  perpendicular
                            (thread_appearance.
                            line_of_symmetry);
   dimension_value       : POSITIVE_REAL  :=  2  *  distance
                            (determinator,
                            thread_appearance.
                            line_of_symmetry);
WHERE
   (* a *)   coordinate_space (next_dir)  =  2;
   (* b *)   embedded (determinator, thread_appearance);
END_ENTITY;
(*
```

ATTRIBUTE DEFINITIONS:

thread_appearance : This attribute references an identified representation of a side projected thread. Some values of the attributes of this entity type can be derived from this appearance, e. g. the direction of the dimension line (see **next_dir**).

determinator : The determinator is a terminating point of the dimension line or the origin of an extension line that is directed perpendicular to **next_dir**.

offset : The distance between the **determinator** and the dimension line measured perpendicular to **next_dir**.

next_dir : The direction of the dimension line and the starting direction of the dimension line of an angular dimension of entity type ROTATIONAL_CHAMFER_DIMENSION pointing at SIDE_PROJECTED_THREAD_DIM.

dimension_value : Here the **dimension_value** is derived. This value has the quality "desired size". It is not possible to derive a value having no basis in the geometry appearance, because otherwise problems with the requirement "associativity" would arise. The **dimension_value** represents the nominal size of the thread.

PROPOSITIONS:

a. The dimensionality of **next_dir** has to have the value 2.

b. The point denoted by **determinator** has to lie on the represented outline of the thread.

5.3.22. UP PROJECTED THREAD DIM

The structure UP_PROJECTED_THREAD_DIM describes thread dimensions of up projected threads.
In the structure the following inherent constraints are considered:

- A thread dimension has zero or two straight extension lines.
- If the segment of a circle representing the nominal diameter of the thread does not extend to either one of the terminating points of the dimension line or one of the origins of the extension line, then the circle has to be extended to one of this point by a circular curve.

```
*)
ENTITY  up_projected_thread_dim  SUBTYPE  OF
                            (thread_dimensioning  AND
                            circular_shape_dimension);
   geometry_appearance    : up_projected_thread;
   dim_line_dir           : direction;       --    see   /1/,
                            4.5.3.7
   distance               : REAL;
DERIVE
   dimension_value        : POSITIVE_REAL  :=  2  *  radius
                            (geometry_appearance.
                            nominal_diameter_arc);
WHERE
   (*  a  *)   coordinate_space  (dim_line_dir)  =  2;
END_ENTITY;
(*
```

ATTRIBUTE DEFINITIONS:

thread_appearance	:	This attribute references an identified representation of an up projected thread.
dim_line_dir	:	The direction of the dimension line.
distance	:	The **distance** between the centerpoint of the thread and the dimension line measured perpendicular to **dim_line_dir**. Where **distance** is not equal to zero, two extension lines with a length equal to **distance** are established.
dimension_value	:	Here the **dimension_value** is derived. This value has the quality "desired size". It is not possible to derive a value having no basis in the geometry appearance, because otherwise problems with the requirement "associativity" would arise. The **dimension_value** represents the nominal size of the thread.

PROPOSITIONS:

a. The dimensionality of **dim_line_dir** has to have the value 2.

5.3.23. REPRESENTED CIRCLE DIMENSION

REPRESENTED_CIRCLE_DIMENSION is the supertype of descriptions of dimension graphs dimensioning apearances of circles that are projections of geometry like cylinders, spheres, etc. The pictorial representations of some dimensions described by different subtypes of REPRESENTED_CIRCLE_DIMENSION are identical with the exception of the character preceding the dimensional value. Nevertheless they are described by different structures, because they contain different information about the represented geometry. (E. g.: A diameter dimension graph of an up projected cylinder looks like a diameter dimension graph of a sphere. By using different types of dimension it is possible to draw conclusions about the geometry from which the represented circle projected.)

In the structure the following inherent constraints are considered:

- A radius or a diameter dimension of a represented circle has a straight dimension line.
- Where a dimension note is placed above a dimension line the direction of the note is parallel to the dimension line.

```
*)
ENTITY  represented_circle_dimension  SUPERTYPE  OF
                         (up_dia_dim  XOR  rad_dim  XOR
                         spherical_dia_dim  XOR
                         spherical_rad_dim  XOR
                         short_up_dia_dim  XOR
                         short_spherical_dia_dim)
                         SUBTYPE  OF
                         (circular_shape_dimension);
   geometry_appearance   : arc_segment;
   dim_line_dir          : direction;      --   see   /1/,
                           4.5.3.7
   note                  : linear_length_notation;
   pos_of_dim_note       : dimension_note_position;
WHERE
   (* a *)   coordinate_space (dim_line_dir) = 2;
END_ENTITY;
(*
```

ATTRIBUTE DEFINITIONS:

geometry_appearance	:	This attribute references a represented circle or a segment of it.
dim_line_dir	:	The direction of the dimension line.
note	:	The dimension note of the dimension graph.
pos_of_dim_note	:	The position of the dimension note inclusive its direction given either implicitly in case of the attribute type is equal to DIM_NOTE_WITHOUT_LEADER or explicitly in case of the attribute type is equal to DIM_NOTE_WITH_LEADER. Both are subtypes of the entity type DIMENSION_NOTE_POSITION.

PROPOSITIONS:

a. The dimensionality of **dim_line_dir** has to have the value 2.

5.3.24. UP DIA DIM

The structure UP_DIA_DIM describes a diameter dimension of a represented circle or segment of a circle (see figure 5.11).
In the structure the following inherent constraints are considered:

- The dimension line has two arrow heads as termination symbols.
- The arrow heads are oriented against each other.
- Zero or two extension lines contact the dimension line.
- An extension line is perpendicular to the dimension line.
- The character "ø" precedes the dimensional value.
- The length between the arrow heads of the dimension line corresponds to the dimensional value with regard to the scale applied.

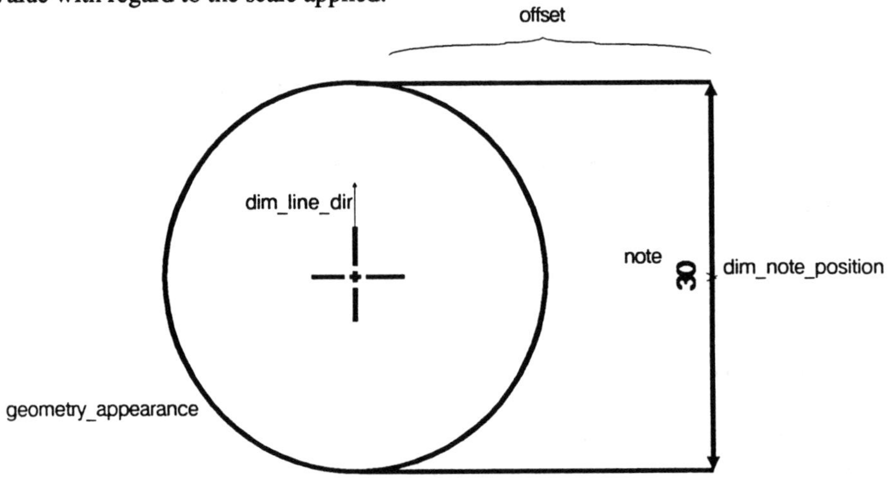

Fig. 5.11: A diameter dimension described by the structure UP_DIA_DIM

```
*)
ENTITY up_dia_dim SUBTYPE OF
(represented_circle_dimension);
   terminator_inside      : LOGICAL;
   distance               : REAL;
DERIVE
   dimension_value        : POSITIVE_REAL := 2 * radius
                              (geometry_appearance);
END_ENTITY;
(*
```

ATTRIBUTE DEFINITIONS:

terminator_inside : If the **terminator_inside** flag is true, the arrow heads are placed between the terminating points of the dimension line and point away from the "middle" of the dimension line. If the flag is false, the arrow heads point to the "middle" of the dimension line and the dimension line has to be elongated beyond the arrow heads.

distance : The **distance** between the centerpoint of the circle and the dimension line measured perpendicular to **dim_line_dir**. Where **distance** is not equal to zero, two extension lines with a length equal to **distance** are established.

dimension_value : Here the **dimension_value** is derived. This value has the quality "desired size". It is not possible to derive a value having no basis in the geometry appearance, because otherwise problems with the requirement "associativity" would arise.

5.3.25. RAD DIM

RAD_DIM is the structure describing a radius dimension of a represented circle or segment of a circle (see figure 5.12).

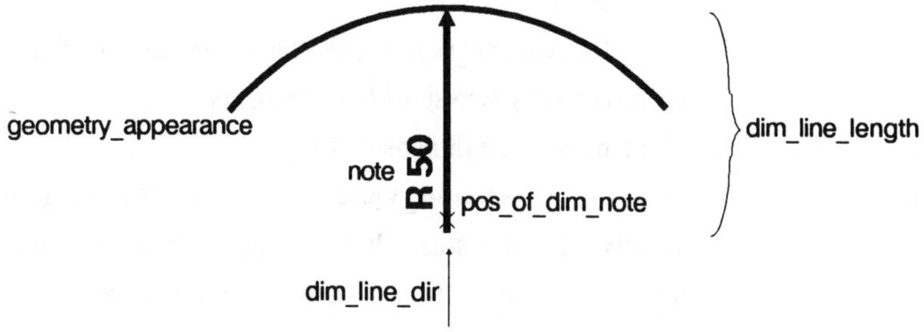

Fig. 5.12: A radius dimension according to RAD_DIM

In the structure the following inherent constraints are considered:

- The dimension line is terminates at the represented circle with an arrow head. On the other side the dimension line terminates without a symbol.
- The arrow head points to the circle.
- The character "R" precedes the dimensional value.

```
*)
ENTITY rad_dim SUBTYPE OF
(represented_circle_dimension);
   inside_flag              : LOGICAL;
   center_rep               : LOGICAL;
   dim_line_length          : POSITIVE_REAL;
DERIVE
   dimension_value          : POSITIVE_REAL := radius
                              (geometry_appearance);
END_ENTITY;
(*
```

ATTRIBUTE DEFINITIONS:

inside_flag	:	If the **inside_flag** is true, the dimension line is represented from the circle to and optionally beyond the centerpoint. If the **inside_flag** is false, the dimension line is represented "outside" of the circle.
center_rep	:	If the flag **center_rep** is true, the center point of the circle is represented by two short line segments.
dim_line_length	:	The length of the dimension line.
dimension_value	:	Here the **dimension_value** is derived. This value has the quality "desired size". It is not possible to derive a value having no basis in the geometry appearance, because otherwise problems with the requirement "associativity" would arise.

5.3.26. SPHERICAL DIA DIM

SPHERICAL_DIA_DIM describes a diameter dimension of a represented circle or segment of a circle projected from a sphere. The graphical appearance resembles the dimension graph described by the structure UP_DIA_DIM.

In the structure the following inherent constraints are considered:

- The dimension line has two arrow heads as termination symbols.
- The arrow heads are oriented against each other.
- Zero or two extension lines contact the dimension line.
- An extension line is perpendicular to the dimension line.
- The character "Sø" precedes the dimensional value.
- The length between the arrow heads of the dimension line corresponds to the dimensional value with regard to the scale applied.

```
*)
ENTITY spherical_dia_dim SUBTYPE OF
                         (represented_circle_dimension);
  terminator_inside       : LOGICAL;
  distance                : REAL;
DERIVE
  dimension_value         : POSITIVE_REAL := 2 * radius
                            (geometry_appearance);
END_ENTITY;
(*
```

ATTRIBUTE DEFINITIONS:

terminator_inside : If the **terminator_inside** flag is true, the arrow heads are placed between the terminating points of the dimension line and point away from the "middle" of the dimension line. If the flag is false, the arrow heads point to the "middle" of the dimension line and the dimension line has to be elongated beyond the arrow heads.

distance : The **distance** between the centerpoint of the circle and the dimension line measured perpendicular to **dim_line_dir**. Where **distance** is not equal to zero, two extension lines with a length equal to **distance** are established.

dimension_value : Here the **dimension_value** is derived. This value has the quality "desired size". It is not possible to derive a value having no basis in the geometry appearance, because otherwise problems with the requirement "associativity" would arise.

5.3.27. SPHERICAL RAD DIM

SPHERICAL_RAD_DIM is the structure describing a radius dimension (similar to the dimension graph described by the structure RAD_DIM) of a represented circle or segment of a circle projected from a sphere.

In the structure the following inherent constraints are considered:

- The dimension line is terminated on the side contacting the circle by one arrow head. On the other side the dimension line terminates without a symbol.
- The arrow head points to the circle.
- The character "SR" precedes the dimensional value.

```
*)
ENTITY spherical_rad_dim SUBTYPE OF
                          (represented_circle_dimension);
   inside_flag            : LOGICAL;
   center_rep             : LOGICAL;
   dim_line_length        : POSITIVE_REAL;
DERIVE
   dimension_value        : POSITIVE_REAL  :=  radius
                             (geometry_appearance);
END_ENTITY;
(*
```

ATTRIBUTE DEFINITIONS:

inside_flag : If the **inside_flag** is true, the dimension line is represented from the circle to and optionally beyond the centerpoint. If the **inside_flag** is false, the dimension line is represented "outside" of the circle.

center_rep : If the flag **center_rep** is true, the center point of the circle is represented by two short line segments.

dim_line_length : The length of the dimension line.

dimension_value : Here the **dimension_value** is derived. This value has the quality "desired size". It is not possible to derive a value having no basis in the geometry appearance, because otherwise problems with the requirement "associativity" would arise.

5.3.28. SHORT UP DIA DIM

SHORT_UP_DIA_DIM is the structure describing a diameter dimension of a represented segment of a circle. The dimension graph has no extension line and the length of the dimension line has no relation to the dimensional value. The dimension graph is similar to the graph described by the structure RAD_DIM.

In the structure the following inherent constraints are considered:

- The dimension line is represented between the circle and the centerpoint without contacting the centerpoint.
- The dimension line is terminated on the side contacting the circle by one arrow head. On the other side the dimension line terminates without a symbol.
- The arrow head points to the circle.
- The character "ø" precedes the dimensional value.

```
*)
ENTITY short_up_dia_dim SUBTYPE OF
                        (represented_circle_dimension);
   dim_line_length       : POSITIVE_REAL;
```

```
DERIVE
   dimension_value          : POSITIVE_REAL := 2 * radius
                               (geometry_appearance);
END_ENTITY;
(*
```

ATTRIBUTE DEFINITIONS:

dim_line_length : The length of the dimension line.

dimension_value : Here the **dimension_value** is derived. This value has the quality "desired size". It is not possible to derive a value having no basis in the geometry appearance, because otherwise problems with the requirement "associativity" would arise.

5.3.29. SHORT SPHERICAL DIA DIM

Within this structure a diameter dimension of a represented segment of a circle derived from a sphere is described. The dimension graph has no extension line and the length of the dimension line has no relation to the dimensional value (see entity type RAD_DIM).
In the structure the following inherent constraints are considered:

- The dimension line is represented between the circle and the centerpoint without contacting the centerpoint.
- The dimension line is terminated on the side contacting the circle by one arrow head. On the other side the dimension line terminates without a symbol.
- The arrow head points to the circle.
- The character "Sø" precedes the dimensional value.

```
*)
ENTITY  short_spherical_dia_dim  SUBTYPE  OF
                            (represented_circle_dimension);
   dim_line_length          : POSITIVE_REAL;
```

```
DERIVE
   dimension_value          : POSITIVE_REAL := 2 * radius
                                (geometry_appearance);
END_ENTITY;
(*
```

ATTRIBUTE DEFINITIONS:

dim_line_length : The length of the dimension line.

dimension_value : Here the **dimension_value** is derived. This value has the quality "desired size". It is not possible to derive a value having no basis in the geometry appearance, because otherwise problems with the requirement "associativity" would arise.

5.3.30. DIMENSION NOTE

The dimension note and its representation is described by the structure DIMENSION_NOTE. Different subtypes of DIMENSION_NOTE for the description of either linear length dimensions or planar angle dimensions are provided.
In the structure the following inherent constraints are considered:

- If the value is less than one unit, a zero precedes the decimal point.
- Where the dimension is a whole number, neither the decimal point nor a zero is shown.
- Where the dimension exceeds a whole number by a decimal fraction of one unit, the last digit to the right of the decimal point is not followed by a zero.

```
*)
ENTITY  dimension_note  SUPERTYPE  OF
                        (linear_length_notation  XOR
                        planar_angle_notation);
   kind_of_dimension     : dimension_characterization;
   text                  : OPTIONAL  STRING;
   precision             : INTEGER;
END_ENTITY;
(*
```

ATTRIBUTE DEFINITIONS:

kind_of_dimension	:	**kind_of_dimension** specifies the representation of the dimension note and the quality of the dimensional value.
text	:	Additional to a dimensional value there is the possibility to integrate a text relating to and preceding the value.
precision	:	The number of decimal digits of the dimensional value that are represented. The dimension value should not have more decimal digits than the dimension tolerance.

5.3.31. LINEAR LENGTH NOTATION

The structure according to LINEAR_LENGTH_NOTATION describes dimensions of linear length.

```
*)
ENTITY  linear_length_notation  SUBTYPE  OF
                                (dimension_note);
   unit_representation   : OPTIONAL  length_unit;
                                     -- see /1/,  4.4.2.2
END_ENTITY;
(*
```

ATTRIBUTE DEFINITIONS:

unit_representation	:	The length unit valid for the dimensional value, e.g. millimeter, meter, inch, etc. All but the unit millimeter are represented by an abbreviation behind the dimensional value.

5.3.32. PLANAR ANGLE NOTATION

The structure according to PLANAR_ANGLE_NOTATION describes dimensions of planar angle.

```
*)
ENTITY  planar_angle_notation  SUBTYPE  OF
                         (dimension_note);
   unit_representation   : plane_angle_unit;
                              -- see /1/, 4.4.2.16
END_ENTITY;
(*
```

ATTRIBUTE DEFINITIONS:

unit_representation	:	The angle unit valid for the dimensional value, e. g.: Second, minute, degree, etc.

5.3.33. THREAD NOTATION

THREAD_NOTATION is applied to describe dimension notes of threads.
In the structure the following inherent constraints are considered:

- If the value is less than one unit, a zero precedes the decimal point.
- Where the dimension is a whole number, neither the decimal point nor a zero is shown.
- If the dimensioned representation is a left handed thread, a "LH" succeeds the dimensional value.

```
*)
ENTITY  thread_notation;
   kind_of_thread        : thread_spec;
   applied_tolerance     : thread_fit_classes;
                              -- see /1/, 4.8.1.7.8
   pitch                 : POSITIVE_REAL;
   thread_hand           : hands;   -- see /1/, 4.8.1.7.7
   text                  : OPTIONAL  STRING;
END_ENTITY;
(*
```

ATTRIBUTE DEFINITIONS:

kind_of_thread	:	**kind_of_thread** specifies the kind of the dimensioned thread. An abbreviation of the kind precedes the dimensional value.
applied_tolerance	:	**applied_tolerance** is a reference to a library containing standardized fit classes for threads.
pitch	:	The pitch of the dimensioned thread. Where a standard thread is dimensioned, the **pitch** is a function of **kind_of_thread** and nominal diameter.
thread_hand	:	This attribute indicates, if there is a right or left handed thread. Where the attribute value is equal to LEFT_HAND, a "LH" succeeds the dimensional value.
text	:	An additional comment (e. g.: The number of a standard) may be placed to the right of the dimensional value.

5.3.34. DIMENSION CHARACTERIZATION

DIMENSION_CHARACTERIZATION is the supertype of the descriptions of the different qualities assigned to the dimensional values (see figure 5.13).

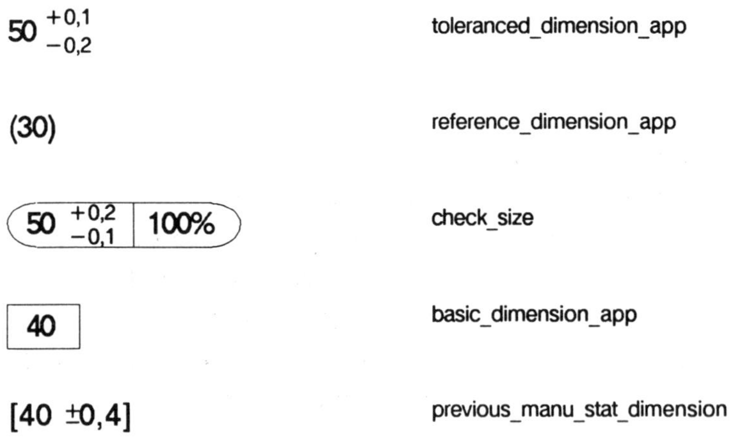

Fig. 5.13: Different qualities of the dimensional values

```
*)
ENTITY  dimension_characterization  SUPERTYPE  OF
                         (toleranced_dimension_app  XOR
                         reference_dimension_app  XOR
                         check_size  XOR  basic_dimension_app
                         XOR  previous_manu_stat_dimension);
END_ENTITY;
(*
```

5.3.35. TOLERANCED DIMENSION APP

TOLERANCED_DIMENSION_APP is the description of a toleranced dimensional value. The applied tolerances might be represented behind the dimensional value. If general tolerances - valid for the whole drawing sheet - are applied, there is no representation of tolerances at this appearance of a dimensional value.

In the structure the following inherent constraints are considered:

- The upper limit is placed above the lower limit.
- Where the magnitude of the upper limit is equal to the magnitude of the lower limit, only one value is represented with both positive and negative signs.

```
*)
ENTITY  toleranced_dimension_app  SUBTYPE  OF
                         (dimension_characterization);
   dimension_deviation      : OPTIONAL  dim_tolerance;
END_ENTITY;
(*
```

ATTRIBUTE DEFINITIONS:

dimension_deviation : A reference to the applied dimension tolerances consisting of upper and lower limits. If **dimension_deviation** is omitted, general tolerances are applied. The entity type DIM_TOLERANCE is specified in the tolerance representation schema.

5.3.36. REFERENCE DIMENSION APP

REFERENCE_DIMENSION_APP is the description of a representation of a dimensional value having the quality "temporary size". The dimensional value together with its optional dimension tolerances is represented between brackets. Tolerances may only be assigned to temporary size dimensions, if the technical drawing is drawn for construction purposes only.
In the structure the following inherent constraints are considered:

- The dimension tolerances are placed to the right of the dimensional value.
- The upper limit is placed above the lower limit.
- Where the magnitude of the upper limit is equal to the magnitude of the lower limit, only one value is represented with both positive and negative signs.

```
*)
ENTITY  reference_dimension_app  SUBTYPE  OF
                          (dimension_characterization);
   dimension_deviation      : OPTIONAL  dim_tolerance;
END_ENTITY;
(*
```

ATTRIBUTE DEFINITIONS:

dimension_deviation : A reference to the applied dimension tolerances consisting of upper and lower limits. If **dimension_deviation** is omitted, general tolerances are applied. The entity type DIM_TOLERANCE is specified in the tolerance representation schema.

5.3.37. CHECK SIZE

A dimensional value assigned with the quality "check size" is of special importance for the quality assurance. The dimensional value together with its tolerances and the amount of the inspected parts is represented in a frame.
In the structure the following inherent constraints are considered:

- The dimension tolerances are placed behind the dimensional value.

- The upper limit is placed above the lower limit.
- Where the magnitude of the upper limit is equal to the magnitude of the lower limit, only one value is represented with both positive and negative signs.
- The amount of the inspected parts out of a series is represented separated by a slash and behind the tolerances.

```
*)
ENTITY check_size SUBTYPE OF
                        (dimension_characterization);
   dimension_deviation   : dim_tolerance;
   inspection_spec       : OPTIONAL STRING;
END_ENTITY;
(*
```

ATTRIBUTE DEFINITIONS:

dimension_deviation	:	A reference to the applied dimension tolerances consisting of upper and lower limits. The entity type DIM_TOLERANCE is specified in the tolerance representation schema.
inspection_spec	:	The amount of inspected parts given as a total number or as a percentage.

5.3.38. BASIC DIMENSION APP

A dimensional value characterized as a "basic dimension" may not be toleranced and describes the exact size of a dimensioned length, angle, etc. The dimensional value is represented in a cornered frame.

```
*)
ENTITY basic_dimension_app SUBTYPE OF
                        (dimension_characterization);
END_ENTITY;
(*
```

5.3.39. PREVIOUS MANU STAT DIMENSION

This structure classifies a dimensional value as a dimension assigned to a geometry representation of a previous or succeeding manufacturing status. The dimensional value together with its dimension tolerances is placed between cornered brackets.
In the structure the following inherent constraints are considered:

- The dimension tolerances are placed behind the dimensional value.
- The upper limit is placed above the lower limit.
- Where the magnitude of the upper limit is equal to the magnitude of the lower limit, only one value is represented with both positive and negative signs.

```
*)
ENTITY  previous_manu_stat_dimension  SUBTYPE  OF
                          (dimension_characterization);
   dimension_deviation      : OPTIONAL  dim_tolerance;
END_ENTITY;
(*
```

ATTRIBUTE DEFINITIONS:

dimension_deviation : A reference to the applied dimension tolerances consisting of upper and lower limits. If **dimension_deviation** is omitted, general tolerances are applied. The entity type DIM_TOLERANCE is specified in the tolerance representation schema.

5.3.40. DIMENSION NOTE POSITION

DIMENSION_NOTE_POSITION is the supertype of descriptions of two different possible positions of the dimension note: Either above a dimension line with regard to the reading direction of the drawing or at a leader pointing to the dimension line.

```
*)
ENTITY  dimension_note_position  SUPERTYPE  OF
                        (dim_note_without_leader  XOR
                        dim_note_with_leader);
   pos_on_dim_line            : REAL;
END_ENTITY;
(*
```

ATTRIBUTE DEFINITIONS:

pos_on_dim_line : **pos_on_dim_line** denotes a point on the parametric dimension line. The specified point is either the start point of a leader or the origin of the dimension note. Attention should be paid to the fact that it is not allowed for a dimension note to cross an extension line of the described dimension graph.

5.3.41. DIM NOTE WITHOUT LEADER

DIM_NOTE_WITHOUT_LEADER is the description of a dimension note placed above and being parallel to the dimension line.

```
*)
ENTITY  dim_note_without_leader  SUBTYPE  OF
                        (dimension_note_position);
END_ENTITY;
(*
```

5.3.42. DIM NOTE WITH LEADER

DIM_NOTE_WITH_LEADER is the description of a dimension note placed at a leader that points to a dimension line. The leader is represented by a single straight line without a termination symbol.

```
*)
ENTITY  dim_note_with_leader  SUBTYPE  OF
                              (dimension_note_position);
   note_position          : view_position;
   direction              : rel_dir;
END_ENTITY;
(*
```

ATTRIBUTE DEFINITIONS:

note_position	:	**note_position** denotes the origin of the dimension note.
direction	:	The referenced defined type REL_DIR specifies the direction of the dimension note. The direction is given as being either horizontal or vertical relative to the reading direction of the drawing or as being parallel to the dimension line of the dimension graph.

5.3.43. COORD SYST REP

This structure describes the appearance of a coordinate system within a view. The coordinate system is represented by several grid lines. The view coordinate system need not be identical with the system desribed by COORD_SYST_REP.

```
*)
ENTITY  coord_syst_rep;
   placement              : view_position;
   axis1_dir              : direction;      --   see   /1/,
                            4.5.3.7
   axis2_dir              : direction;      --   see   /1/,
                            4.5.3.7
   grid_offset            : POSITIVE_REAL;
   axis1_name             : STRING;
   axis2_name             : STRING;
```

```
   area                          : polyline;       --    see   /1/,
                                  4.5.3.24
WHERE
   (* a *)   coordinate_space (axis1_dir) = 2;
   (* b *)   coordinate_space (axis2_dir) = 2;
   (* c *)   axis1_dir = perpendicular (axis2_dir);
   (* d *)   closed (area);
END_ENTITY;
(*
```

ATTRIBUTE DEFINITIONS:

placement	:	The position of the origin of a represented coordinate system relative to view coordinates.
axis1_dir	:	The direction of one of the axes of the represented coordinate system.
axis2_dir	:	The direction of the second axis of the represented coordinate system. Both axes have to be perpendicular to each other.
grid_offset	:	The offset of the grid lines.
axis1_name	:	The sign denoting all grid lines that are parallel to **axis1_dir**. The sign is represented at the intersection of the grid line and the border described by the attribute **area**.
axis2_name	:	The sign denoting all grid lines that are parallel to **axis2_dir**. The sign is represented at the intersection of the grid line and the border described by the attribute **area**.
area	:	The closed polygon described by the referenced entity type POLYLINE specifies an area within the view, where the grid lines of the coordinate system are represented.

PROPOSITIONS:

a. The dimensionality of **axis1_dir** has to have the value 2.

b. The dimensionality of **axis2_dir** has to have the value 2.

c. The direction defined by **axis1_dir** has to be perpendicular to the direction defined by **axis2_dir**.

d. The entity type POLYLINE has to specify a closed polygon that is the border of the area within which the coordinate system is represented.

```
*)
END_SCHEMA;           -- end DIMENSIONING_SCHEMA;
(*
```

6. Tolerance Representation

```
*)
SCHEMA  tolerance_representation_schema;
   EXPORT  EVERYTHING;
   ASSUME  (drafting_resources_schema,
   dimensioning_schema);
(*
```

6.1. Introduction

In the TOLERANCE_REPRESENTATION_SCHEMA entity types for the descriptions of dimension tolerances including fit classes as well as descriptions of graphical representations of shape and location tolerances are listed.
The dimension tolerances are represented in connection with dimensional values that are components of dimension graphs described in the DIMENSIONING_SCHEMA. Thus the entity types establishing a tolerance range are referenced by entity types describing the appearance of a dimension note within the description of a dimension graph.
Representations of shape and location tolerances and their datum feature symbols may be attached to representations of geometry and/or dimension graphs. The following facts are considered and contained either in the informal or in the formal description of the entity types.
The relative positioning of these tolerance symbols and their datum feature symbols to the geometry appearances and/or dimension graphs may contain further information, e. g.:

i) The leader of a circular runout tolerance pointing at a represented rotational surface determines the direction of the tolerance zone: Where the direction of the leader is dimensioned relative to the represented axis by an angular dimension, the direction of the leader is identical with the direction of the tolerance zone (see figure 6.1). Otherwise, if there is not such a dimension graph, the tolerance zone is perpendicular to every point of the rotational surface (see figure 6.2).

ii) Two parallel side projected planes are represented by two parallel lines and a line of symmetry. If the leader of a flatness tolerance points at one of these lines, the tolerance zone controls the deviation regarding flatness of this represented plane (see figure 6.3). But if the leader is aligned to the dimension line dimensioning the distance between the two planes, the flatness tolerance is relevant to both the planes (see figure 6.4).

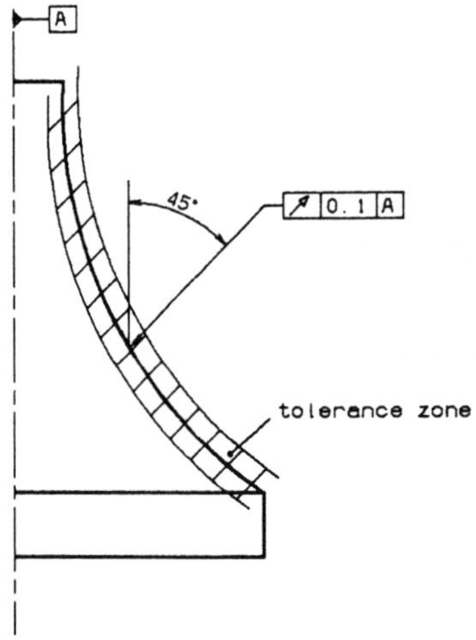

Fig. 6.1: Specified tolerance zone direction

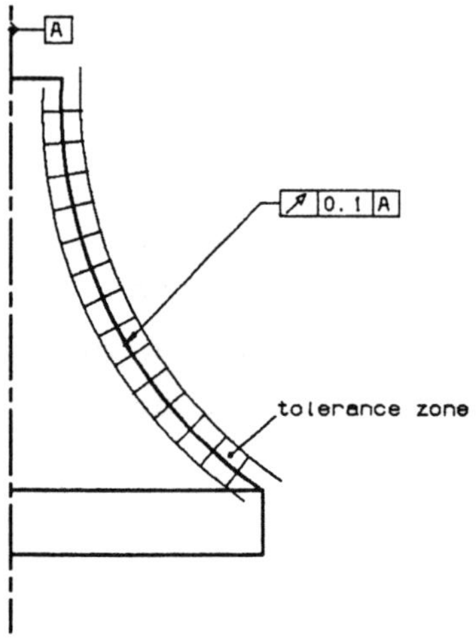

Fig. 6.2: Perpendicular tolerance zone

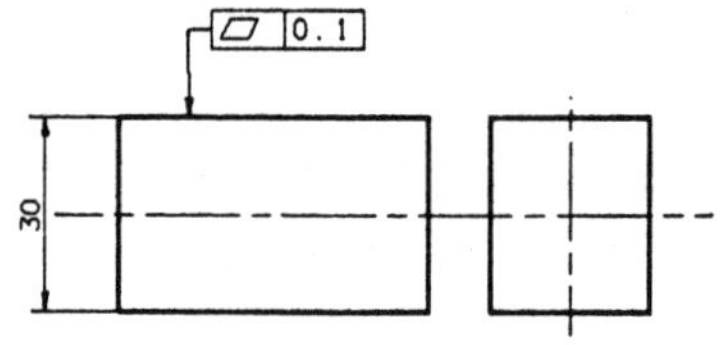

Fig. 6.3: Flatness tolerance relevant to one plane

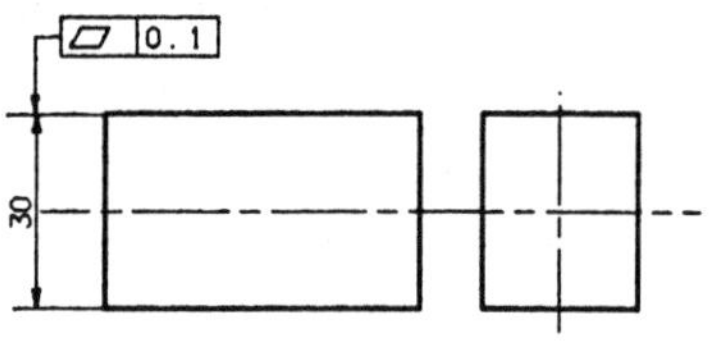

Fig. 6.4: Flatness tolerance relevant to both planes

Another fact contained in the formal description is that certain shape and location tolerances should only be applicable by certain geometry occurrences. For example it makes no sense to attach a flatness tolerance to a rotational surface.

Furthermore rules are established to guarantee that only valid datum features can be referenced by the descriptions of shape and location tolerances, e. g.: A parallelism tolerance being attached to an axis may either have another axis or one to two planes that are perpendicular to each other as datum features. Obviously the axis and the planes have different qualities (the term "valence" is proposed in this context) when being applied as datum features.

6.2. Tolerance Representations TYPE Definitions

6.2.1. AXIS DATUM VALENCE

The defined type AXIS_DATUM_VALENCE characterizes the rank of a represented axis being referred to as a datum of a profile, orientation, location or runout tolerance.

In contrast to a represented plane that can be referred to as a primary, secondary or tertiary datum an axis may only serve as a primary or secondary datum.

```
*)
TYPE  axis_datum_valence  =  ENUMERATION  OF  (primary,
                                  secondary);
END_TYPE;
(*
```

6.3. Tolerance Representation ENTITY Definitions

6.3.1. DIM TOLERANCE

DIM_TOLERANCE is the supertype of the two entity types that either describe a tolerance range or a fit class. According to this structure it is no longer possible to represent both a tolerance range and a fit class because of the difficulties arising with a redundant data set.

Concerning dimension tolerances the following statements have to be considered:

- The dimension tolerances are placed directly after the dimensional value.

```
*)
ENTITY  dim_tolerance  SUPERTYPE  OF  (size_tol_range  XOR
                                  fit_class_spec);
END_ENTITY;
(*
```

6.3.2. SIZE TOL RANGE

The entity type SIZE_TOL_RANGE determines the tolerated deviation of a specified dimension.

In the structure the following inherent constraints are considered:

- The tolerance values are represented in smaller letters than the dimensional value.
- Where the upper tolerance value is not equal to the lower tolerance value, the upper tolerance value is placed above and the lower tolerance value is placed beneath.
- A sign precedes every tolerance value.
- Where the upper tolerance value is equal to the lower tolerance value, only one value is represented aligned to the dimensional value with a preceding "±".
- The unit of the tolerance values is equal to the unit of the dimensional value.

```
*)
ENTITY  size_tol_range  SUBTYPE  OF  (dim_tolerance);
   upper_tolerance        : OPTIONAL  REAL;
   lower_tolerance        : OPTIONAL  REAL;
WHERE
   (* a *)   ( ( (upper_tolerance = NULL) AND
   (lower_tolerance <> NULL) AND (lower_tolerance < 0.0)
   ) OR ( (lower_tolerance = NULL) AND (upper_tolerance
   <> NULL) AND (upper_tolerance > 0.0) ) ) OR (
   (upper_tolerance <> NULL) AND (lower_tolerance <>
   NULL) AND (upper_tolerance > lower_tolerance) );
END_ENTITY;
(*
```

ATTRIBUTE DEFINITIONS:

upper_tolerance : The nominal size of the dimension plus the value of **upper_tolerance** determines the greatest permissible size.

lower_tolerance : The nominal size of the dimension minus the value of **lower_tolerance** determines the least permissible size.

PROPOSITIONS:

a. The rules listed below are described in the WHERE-Clauses:
   - Either **upper_tolerance** or **lower_tolerance** may be omitted, but not both of them.
   - Where the attribute **upper_tolerance** is omitted, the attribute **lower_tolerance** has to have a negative value.
   - Where the attribute **lower_tolerance** is omitted, the attribute **upper_tolerance** has to have a positive value.
   - If neither **upper_tolerance** nor **lower_tolerance** is omitted, the value of **upper_tolerance** has to be greater than the value of **lower_tolerance**.

6.3.3. FIT CLASS SPEC

The entity type FIT_CLASS_SPEC specifies the fit class of a represented part or form feature. The tolerance zone of a fit - determined by the placement of the tolerance zone relative to the nominal size and the quality of the tolerance zone - is specified in the ISO-Standards relevant to this subject. There the extent of the specified tolerance zones depends on the dimensional value. In the ISO-Standards several combinations of quality and placements of the zones are recommended.

In the structure the following inherent constraints are considered:

- The letters determining the placement of the tolerance range and the number determining the quality of the tolerance zone have a smaller representation than the dimensional value.
- Where the letter determining the placement of the tolerance range is written in upper case letters, the whole expression is placed above.
- Where the letter determining the placement of the tolerance range is written in lower case letters, the whole expression is placed beneath.

- The letter determining the placement of the tolerance zone precedes the number determining the quality of the tolerance zone.

```
*)
ENTITY fit_class_spec SUBTYPE OF (dim_tolerance);
   tol_zone_placement    : CHARACTER;
   quality               : CHARACTER;
   internal_or_external  : LOGICAL;
END_ENTITY;
(*
```

ATTRIBUTE DEFINITIONS:

tol_zone_placement	:	This attribute describes the placement of the tolerance zone relative to the nominal size. The attribute value is of type CHARACTER which in this case has to be part of the alphabet. It is controlled by the flag **internal_or_external,** whether the value is represented by upper case letters or by lower case letters.
quality	:	**quality** identifies the extent of the tolerance zone. The value of **quality** is a number in the range of: 01, 0, 1, 2, 3, ..., 18. "01" represents the smallest, "18" represents the largest extent of the tolerance zone.
internal_or_external	:	This flag has to become true, if the tolerance zone is applied by an external dimension, e.g. the diameter of a shaft. In this case the letter described by **tol_zone_placement** is represented by a lower case letter. On the other hand, if the flag is false, the tolerance zone is applied by inside dimensions like the inside diameter of a hole. Then the letter described by **tol_zone_placement** is represented by an upper case letter.

6.3.4. SHAPE LOC TOL COMPOUND

SHAPE_LOC_TOL_COMPOUND is the structure of the description of the placement of the geometry tolerance frame (ANSI-Terminology: "feature control frame") and its graphical linkage with the geometry appearances or dimension graphs (The size of the geometry tolerance frame is given relative to the line width by the drawing standards).
With this structure it is possible to combine more than one representation of shape and location tolerances that refer to exactly the same geometry appearance. In this case the geometry tolerance frames are placed one on top of the other.

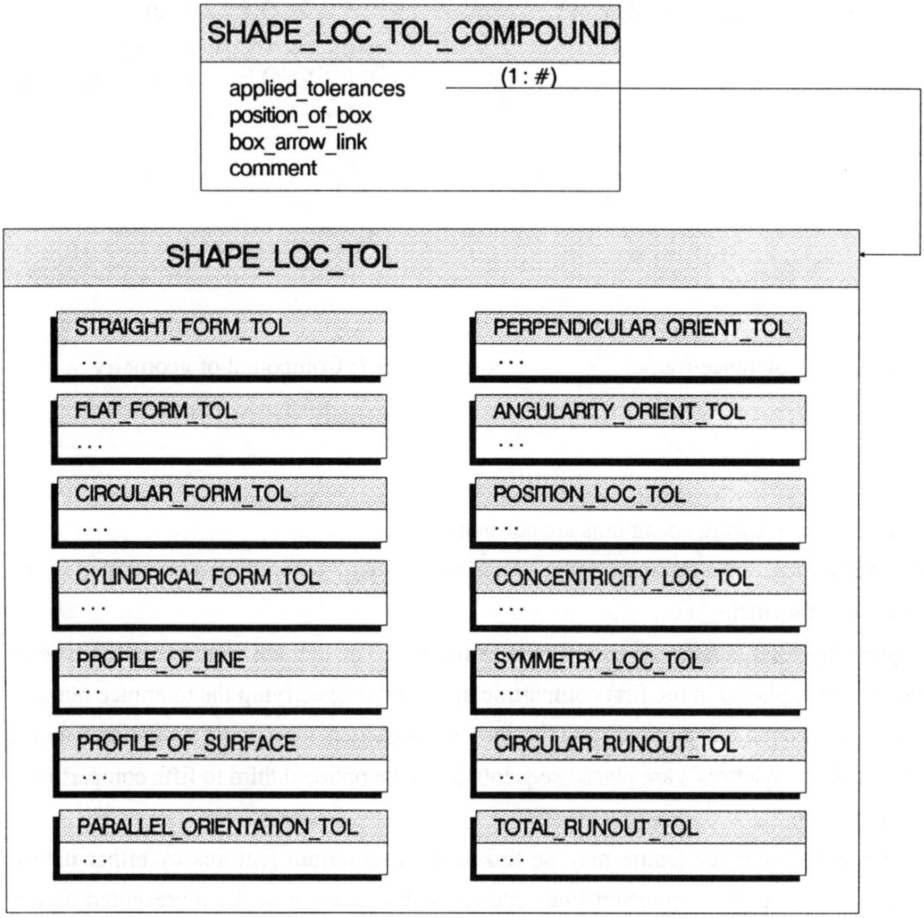

Fig. 6.5: Data structure for the description of representations of geometry tolerances

Another possibility is one shape and location tolerance referring to one or more geometry appearances. But according to the design of this structure it is not possible to represent several types of shape and location tolerances linked with more than one geometry element. An overview of the data structure describing the representation of geometry tolerances is given in figure 6.5.

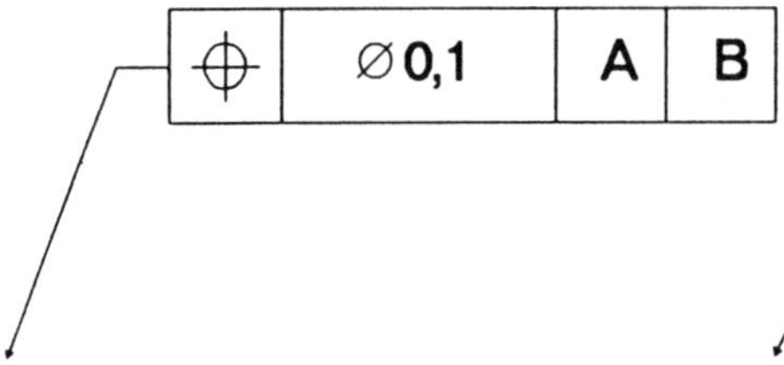

Fig. 6.6: Geometry tolerance frame

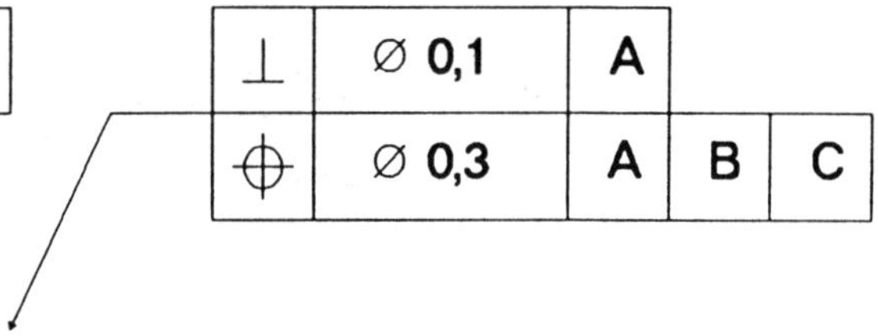

Fig. 6.7: Compound of geometry tolerance frames

In the structure the following constraints are considered:

- The geometry tolerance frames are placed horizontally with regard to the orientation of the drawing sheet format.
- The geometry tolerance frame is designed as follows: The symbol identifying the type of the tolerance is placed in the first compartment, the value specifying the tolerance range is placed in the second compartment and the zero to three letters identifying the datum features ("datum reference letters") are placed sequentially in the optional third to fifth compartment (see figure 6.6).
- The geometry tolerance frame may be linked with its datum features by either datum reference letters or by connected lines ending with a triangle at the represented datum feature or at a dimension graph that is connected with it.
- The leader connecting the geometry tolerance frame with the controlled geometry appearance starts in a horizontal direction in the middle of the left edge constituted by either one or more geometry tolerance frames.

- The leader may have more than one arrow as termination symbol placed at geometry appearances or directed perpendicular to an extension line or aligned to a dimension line of a dimension graph.
- The arrows of the leader and the starting line at the geometry tolerance frame are linked by either lines or an index letter being placed at both the arrow and the geometry tolerance frame.
- Where more than one geometry tolerance frames is placed one on top of the other, their edges on the left side are aligned (see figure 6.7).

```
*)
ENTITY  shape_loc_tol_compound;
   applied_tolerances      : SET  [1:#]  OF  shape_loc_tol;
   position_of_box         : view_position;
   box_arrow_link          : ref_to_geometry;
   comment                 : OPTIONAL  STRING;
WHERE
   (* a *)   ( (typeof  (applied_tolerances[i])  =  typeof
   (applied_tolerances[i+1])  )  AND
   (applied_tolerances[i].tolerance_value  =
   applied_tolerances[i+1].tolerance_value)
   (applied_tolerances[i].tol_geometry_app  <>
   applied_tolerances[i+1].tol_geometry_app)  )  XOR  (
   (typeof  (applied_tolerances[i])  )  <>  (typeof
   (applied_tolerances[i+1])  )  AND
   (applied_tolerances[i].tol_geometry_app  =
   applied_tolerances[i+1].tol_geometry_app)  );
   (* b *)   (sizeof  (applied_tolerances)  =1)  OR  (  (sizeof
   (applied_tolerances)  >  1)  AND  (is_parallel
   (applied_tolerances[i].arrow_direction,
   applied_tolerances[i+1].arrow_direction)  )  AND
   (applied_tolerances[i].arrow_position  =
   applied_tolerances[i+1].arrow_position)  );
END_ENTITY;
(*
```

ATTRIBUTE DEFINITIONS:

applied_tolerances	:	All shape and location tolerances that refer to the same geometry appearance are listed. Their geometry tolerance frames are placed one on top of the other.
position_of_box	:	This attribute determines the middle of the left edge constituted by either one or a combination of several geometry tolerance frames.
box_arrow_link	:	The entity type referenced by this attribute constitute the leader. Two possibilities for the appearance of the leader are described by the subtypes of the entity type REF_TO_GEOMETRY: The first one describes the lines connecting the compound of geometry tolerance frames with the representation of the geometry. The second possibility is to place the arrow(s) together with an index at the geometry appearances and an identical index at the line starting at the compound. Here the index replaces the line(s) connecting the arrow(s) with the compound. In both cases the first line starts at the point denoted by **position_of_box** in a horizontal direction and the line(s) terminating at a geometry appearance or a dimension graph have the direction specified by the attribute **arrow_direction** of the entity types referenced by **applied_tolerances**.
comment	:	If the applied tolerances are valid for more than one identically represented form feature, the shape and location tolerance may be represented once and an additional remark specifies the number of the identical form features. The remark is placed above the geometry tolerance frame.

PROPOSITIONS:

a. Where both the types and the values of the applied shape and location tolerances are identical and valid for more than one geometry element, different geometry appearances have to be referenced. But if the types of the applied shape and location tolerances are different, the tolerances have to refer to the same geometry element.

b. Where more than one geometry feature tolerance is represented in one compound, the arrow positions defined by each tolerance have to be the same and the direction of the arrows have to be parallel.

6.3.5. SHAPE LOC TOL

SHAPE_LOC_TOL is the supertype of all entity types describing shape and location tolerances. According to the ISO-Standard the category of shape and location tolerances can be sudivided in further types: Form, profile, orientation, location and runout tolerances (The keywords of the subtypes of SHAPE_LOC_TOL hint at this subdivision).

```
*)
ENTITY  shape_loc_tol  SUPERTYPE  OF  (straight_form_tol  XOR
                                       flat_form_tol  XOR
                                       circular_form_tol  XOR
                                       cylindrical_form_tol  XOR
                                       profile_of_line  XOR
                                       profile_of_surface  XOR
                                       parallel_orientation_tol  XOR
                                       perpendicular_orient_tol  XOR
                                       angularity_orient_tol  XOR
                                       position_loc_tol  XOR
                                       concentricity_loc_tol  XOR
                                       symmetry_loc_tol  XOR
                                       circular_runout_tol  XOR
                                       total_runout_tol);
END_ENTITY;
(*
```

6.3.6. STRAIGHT FORM TOL

The structure STRAIGHT_FORM_TOL describes the representation of a straightness tolerance that belongs to the type of form tolerances. Form tolerances must not have datum features, because the form of a geometry element does not depend on other geometry appearances.

In the structure the following inherent constraints are considered:

- The straightness tolerance must only be represented in a view, where the controlled geometry element is represented by a bounded line. The bounded line may be the projection of a plane, cylindrical or conical surface or ruled surface.
- If the represented straight line is part of the projection of a surface of revolution (e. g. centerline or shapeline), the tolerance zone may have a circular form.
- Where the tolerance zone has a circular form, a "ø" precedes the tolerance value.
- A unit length may be specified and placed to the right of the tolerance value, separated by a slash.
- Where a maximum material condition is applied, an "M" placed in a circle succeeds the tolerance value and the optional unit length.
- The arrow of the leader of the geometry tolerance frame is perpendicular to the representation of the controlled geometry elements.

```
*)
ENTITY straight_form_tol  SUBTYPE OF (shape_loc_tol);
   tol_geometry_app       : straight_geometry_app;
   tolerance_value        : REAL;
   per_unit_length        : OPTIONAL POSITIVE_REAL;
   circular_tol_zone      : LOGICAL;
   material_condition     : tol_mlsn;    see /1/, 4.10.1.2.9
   arrow_position         : reference_term_point;
DERIVE
   arrow_direction        : direction := perpendicular
                            (tol_geometry_app.
                            dir_of_geometry_app);
WHERE
   (* a *)   (tolerance_value > 0.0) OR ( (tolerance_value
   = 0.0) AND (material_condition = .maxmc.) );
   (* b *)   ( (typeof (arrow_position) =
   point_on_geometry) AND (embedded (tol_geometry_app,
   arrow_position) ) ) OR ( (typeof (arrow_position) =
   point_on_dimension_graph) AND ( TYPEOF
   (arrow_position.dimension_graph)  =
   represented_shape_dimension) AND (is_parallel
```

```
   (arrow_direction,
   arrow_position.dimension_graph.next_dir)  )  );
END_ENTITY;
(*
```

ATTRIBUTE DEFINITIONS:

tol_geometry_app	:	**tol_geometry_app** references descriptions of straight lines being the representations of geometry elements that have to be controlled.
tolerance_value	:	The value determines the extent of the tolerance zone. Another factor influencing the tolerance zone is the value of the attribute **material_condition**.
per_unit_length	:	The value of this attribute specifies the linear distance within which the tolerance value applies. Where the value is omitted the linear distance is equal to the represented length of the controlled feature.
circular_tol_zone	:	If the flag is true, the tolerance zone has a circular form and a "ø" precedes the number determined by the attribute **tolerance_value**. A true flag is only admissible, where an axis is controlled. A false flag denotes a tolerance range being limited by two offset lines.
material_condition	:	This attribute references a defined type that specifies the material condition applied by the straightness tolerance. The following values are enumerated: MAXMC (maximum material condition), LEASTMC (least material condition), REGARDLESS (regardless of feature size) and NONE (not applicable).
arrow_position	:	**arrow_position** denotes the terminating point of the arrow of the leader at a represented geometry element or at a projection line being an extension line of a dimension graph.
arrow_direction	:	The direction of the arrow that has to be derived from the representation of the geometry element.

PROPOSITIONS:

a. The **tolerance_value** has to be greater than 0.0 with the exception where a maximum material condition is applied. In the latter case the **tolerance_value** may be equal to 0.0 .

b. The point specified by **arrow_position** either is placed at a curve of the referenced geometry representation or at a dimension graph described by the entity type REPRESENTED_SHAPE_DIMENSION. The dimension graph has to refer to the representation of the controlled geometry element and the direction of the dimension line has to be parallel to the direction specified by the attribute **arrow_direction**.

6.3.7. FLAT FORM TOL

The structure FLAT_FORM_TOL describes the representation of a flatness tolerance that belongs to the type of form tolerances. Form tolerances must not have datum features, because the form of a geometry element does not depend on other geometry appearances.
In the structure the following inherent constraints are considered:

- The flatness tolerance must only be represented in a view, where the controlled geometry element (only planes are controlled by flatness tolerances) is represented by a bounded line.
- A unit area may be specified by two equal numbers separated by an "x" and placed to the right of the tolerance value, separated by a slash.
- Where a maximum material condition is applied, an "M" placed in a circle succeeds the tolerance value and the optional unit area.
- The arrow of the leader of the geometry tolerance frame is perpendicular to the representation of the controlled geometry elements.

```
*)
ENTITY flat_form_tol SUBTYPE OF (shape_loc_tol);
   tol_geometry_app      : straight_geometry_app;
   tolerance_value       : REAL;
   per_unit_area         : OPTIONAL POSITIVE_REAL;
   material_condition    : tol_mlsn;    -- see /1/,
                           4.10.1.2.9
   arrow_position        : reference_term_point;
```

```
DERIVE
   arrow_direction          : direction  :=  perpendicular
                              (tol_geometry_app.
                              dir_of_geometry_app);
WHERE
   (* a *)    (tolerance_value > 0.0)  OR  ( (tolerance_value
   = 0.0)  AND  (material_condition  =  .maxmc.) );
   (* b *)    ( (typeof (arrow_position) =
   point_on_geometry)  AND  (embedded  (tol_geometry_app,
   arrow_position) ) )  OR  (  (TYPEOF  (arrow_position)  =
   point_on_dimension_graph)  AND   (TYPEOF
   (arrow_position.dimension_graph)   =
   represented_shape_dimension)  AND   (is_parallel
   (arrow_direction,
   arrow_position.dimension_graph.next_dir)  )  );
END_ENTITY;
(*
```

ATTRIBUTE DEFINITIONS:

tol_geometry_app	:	**tol_geometry_app** references descriptions of straight lines being the representations of geometry elements that have to be controlled. The controlled geometry elements have to be planar surfaces.
tolerance_value	:	The value determines the extent of the tolerance zone bounded by two parallel planes. Another factor influencing the tolerance zone is the value of the attribute **material_condition.**
per_unit_area	:	The value of this attribute specifies the planar area within which the tolerance value applies. Where the value is omitted the extent of the planar area is equal to the extent of the controlled planes.
material_condition	:	This attribute references a defined type that specifies the material condition applied by the flatness tolerance. The following values are enumerated: MAXMC (maximum

material condition), LEASTMC (least material condition), REGARDLESS (regardless of feature size) and NONE (not applicable).

arrow_position : **arrow_position** denotes the terminating point of the arrow of the leader at a represented geometry element or at a projection line being an extension line of a dimension graph.

arrow_direction : The direction of the arrow that has to be derived from the representation of the geometry element.

PROPOSITIONS:

a. The **tolerance_value** has to be greater than 0.0 with the exception where a maximum material condition is applied. In the latter case the **tolerance_value** may be equal to 0.0 .

b. The point specified by **arrow_position** either is placed at a curve of the referenced geometry representation or at a dimension graph described by the entity type REPRESENTED_SHAPE_DIMENSION. The dimension graph has to refer to the representation of the controlled geometry element and the direction of the dimension line has to be parallel to the direction specified by the attribute **arrow_direction**.

6.3.8. CIRCULAR FORM TOL

CIRCULAR_FORM_TOL is the structure for the description of the representation of a circularity tolerance that belongs to the type of form tolerances. Form tolerances must not have datum features, because the form of a geometry element does not depend on other geometry appearances.

In the structure the following inherent constraints are considered:

- The circularity tolerance symbol may be applied by representations of surfaces of revolution.
- Where a maximum material condition is applied, an "M" placed in a circle succeeds the tolerance value.
- The arrow of the leader of a circularity tolerance may be placed at the representation of the surface of revolution or at an extension line being part of a dimension graph that determines the diameter of the surface.

- Where the leader points to a side projection of the surface of revolution, the direction of the arrow is perpendicular to the represented axis.
- Where the leader points to an up projection of the surface of revolution (in this case a circle with its center is represented), the arrow is directed radially relative to the circle.

```
*)
ENTITY circular_form_tol SUBTYPE OF (shape_loc_tol);
  tol_geometry_app      : surf_of_rev_app;
  tolerance_value       : REAL;
  material_condition    : tol_mlsn;   -- see /1/,
                          4.10.1.2.9
  arrow_position        : reference_term_point;
  arrow_direction       : direction;        --    see   /1/,
                          4.5.3.7
WHERE
  (* a *)   (tolerance_value > 0.0) OR ( (tolerance_value
  = 0.0) AND (material_condition = .maxmc.) );
  (* b *)   ( (typeof (arrow_position) =
  point_on_geometry) AND (embedded (tol_geometry_app,
  arrow_position) ) ) OR ( ( (typeof (arrow_position) =
  point_on_dimension_graph) AND (typeof
  (arrow_position.dimension_graph) =
  side_projected_feature_dim) AND (is_parallel
  (arrow_direction,
  arrow_position.dimension_graph.next_dir) ) ) XOR (
  (typeof (arrow_position.dimension_graph) =
  represented_circle_dimension) AND (embedded
  (tol_geometry_app, arrow_position.dimension_graph.
  geometry_appearance) ) AND (is_parallel
  (arrow_direction,
  arrow_position.dimension_graph.dim_line_dir) ) ) );
  (* c *)   coordinate_space (arrow_direction) = 2;
END_ENTITY;
(*
```

ATTRIBUTE DEFINITIONS:

tol_geometry_app	:	**tol_geometry_app** references representations of surfaces of revolution that have to be controlled. The representations of these surfaces may either be any circles or curves in connection with an axis.
tolerance_value	:	The value determines the extent of the tolerance zone bounded by two concentric circles. Another factor influencing the tolerance zone is the value of the attribute **material_condition**.
material_condition	:	This attribute references a defined type that specifies the material condition applied by the circularity tolerance. The following values are enumerated: MAXMC (maximum material condition), LEASTMC (least material condition), REGARDLESS (regardless of feature size) and NONE (not applicable).
arrow_position	:	**arrow_position** denotes the terminating point of the arrow of the leader at a represented geometry element or at an extension line of a dimension graph dimensioning the diameter of the surface of revolution.
arrow_direction	:	The direction of the arrow of the leader.

PROPOSITIONS:

a. The **tolerance_value** has to be greater than 0.0 with the exception where a maximum material condition is applied. In the latter case the **tolerance_value** may be equal to 0.0 .

b. The leader either terminates at the representation of the geometry element or at a dimension graph being connected with the geometry representation and the arrow of the leader has to be parallel to the dimension line.

c. The dimensionality of **arrow_direction** has to have the value 2.

6.3.9. CYLINDRICAL FORM TOL

CYLINDRICAL_FORM_TOL is the description of the representation of a cylindricity tolerance that belongs to the type of form tolerances. Form tolerances must not have datum features, because the form of a geometry element does not depend on other geometry appearances.
In the structure the following inherent constraints are considered:

- The cylindricity tolerance symbol may be applied by representations of cylinders.
- Where a maximum material condition is applied, an "M" placed in a circle succeeds the tolerance value.
- The arrow of the leader of a cylindricity tolerance may be placed at the representation of the cylinder or at an extension line being part of a dimension graph that determines the diameter of the cylinder.
- Where the leader points to a side projection of the cylinder, the direction of the arrow is perpendicular to the represented axis.
- Where the leader points to an up projection of the cylinder (in this case a circle with its center is represented), the arrow is directed radially relative to the circle.

```
*)
ENTITY cylindrical_form_tol SUBTYPE OF (shape_loc_tol);
   tol_geometry_app      : surf_of_rev_app;
   tolerance_value       : REAL;
   material_condition    : tol_mlsn;   -- see /1/,
                           4.10.1.2.9
   arrow_position        : reference_term_point;
   arrow_direction       : direction;      --   see   /1/,
                           4.5.3.7
WHERE
   (* a *)   (tolerance_value > 0.0) OR ( (tolerance_value
   = 0.0) AND (material_condition = .maxmc.) );
   (* b *)   (typeof (arrow_position = point_on_geometry)
   AND (embedded (tol_geometry_app, arrow_position) ) )
   OR ( ( (typeof (arrow_position =
   point_on_dimension_graph) ) AND (typeof
   (arrow_position.dimension_graph) =
   side_projected_feature_dim) AND (is_parallel
   (arrow_direction,
```

```
   arrow_position.dimension_graph.next_dir) ) ) XOR ( (
   typeof (arrow_position.dimension_graph) =
   represented_circle_dimension) AND (embedded
   (tol_geometry_app, arrow_position.dimension_graph.
   geometry_appearance) ) AND (is_parallel
   (arrow_direction,
   arrow_position.dimension_graph.dim_line_dir) ) ) );
   (* c *) coordinate_space (arrow_direction) = 2;
END_ENTITY;
(*
```

ATTRIBUTE DEFINITIONS:

tol_geometry_app	:	**tol_geometry_app** references representations of the controlled cylinders. The representations of these cylinders can either be any circles or straight lines in connection with an axis.
tolerance_value	:	The value determines the extent of the tolerance zone bounded by two concentric cylinders. Another factor influencing the tolerance zone is the value of the attribute **material_condition**.
material_condition	:	This attribute references a defined type that specifies the material condition applied by the cylindricity tolerance. The following values are enumerated: MAXMC (maximum material condition), LEASTMC (least material condition), REGARDLESS (regardless of feature size) and NONE (not applicable).
arrow_position	:	**arrow_position** denotes the terminating point of the arrow of the leader at a represented geometry element or at an extension line of a dimension graph dimensioning the diameter of the cylinder.
arrow_direction	:	The direction of the arrow of the leader.

PROPOSITIONS:

a. The **tolerance_value** has to be greater than 0.0 with the exception where a maximum material condition is applied. In the latter case the **tolerance_value** may be equal to 0.0 .

b. The leader either terminates at the representation of the geometry element or at a dimension graph being connected with the geometry representation and the arrow of the leader has to be parallel to the dimension line.

c. The dimensionality of **arrow_direction** has to have the value 2.

6.3.10. PROFILE OF LINE

The structure PROFILE_OF_LINE contains the description of the representation of a profile of a line tolerance that belongs to the type of profile tolerances.

In a drawing the profile is determined by points (these points lie on the curve representing the profile), the positions of which are determined by dimension graphs. Where a profile tolerance is applied, the dimensions relevant to the profile have to have the quality of a basic dimension. Thus the profile tolerance is similar to a position tolerance and may be specified relative to certain combinations of datum features. A combination of one optional plane together with either at least two further planes or one axis may be referred to as datum features.

In the structure the following inherent constraints are considered:

- The profile of a line tolerance symbol may be applied by representations of any curves.
- The arrow of the leader of a profile of a line tolerance has to be placed at the representation of a curve.
- The direction of the arrow is perpendicular to the representation of the curve in their intersecting point.
- Where the side of the tolerance zone should be given relative to the represented curve, a short part of an equidistant curve is represented on this side that is relevant to the tolerance zone.

```
*)
ENTITY profile_of_line SUBTYPE OF (shape_loc_tol);
   tol_geometry_app        : curve_app;
   tolerance_value         : POSITIVE_REAL;
```

```
   application_side       : tol_ibo;   -- see /1/,
                            4.10.1.2.8
   offset_curve_length    : OPTIONAL  POSITIVE_REAL;
   arrow_position         : point_on_geometry;
   datum_reference        : OPTIONAL  position_datum;
DERIVE
   arrow_direction        : direction  :=
                            is_perpendicular_to
                            (tol_geometry_app,
                            arrow_position);
WHERE
   (* a *)   embedded (tol_geometry_app, arrow_position);
   (* b *)   ( (application_side = .bilateral.) AND
   (offset_curve_length = NULL) ) OR ( (application_side
   <> .bilateral.) AND (offset_curve_length <> NULL) );
   (* c *)   (datum_reference = NULL) OR (
   (datum_reference <> NULL) AND ( ( (TYPEOF
   (datum_reference) = axis1_plane1_datum) AND
   (datum_reference.axis_reference.
   material_condition = .none.) AND (
   (datum_reference.plane_reference = NULL) OR (
   (datum_reference.plane_reference <> NULL) AND
   (datum_reference.plane_reference.material_condition =
   .none.) ) ) ) ) OR ( (typeof (datum_reference) =
   plane3_datum) AND (datum_reference.primary_plane_ref.
   material_condition = .none.) AND (
   (datum_reference.sec_tert_planes_ref[i] = NULL) OR (
   (datum_reference.sec_tert_planes_ref <> NULL) AND
   (datum_reference.sec_tert_planes_ref[i].material_condi
   tion = .none.) ) ) ) );
END_ENTITY;
(*.
```

ATTRIBUTE DEFINITIONS:

tol_geometry_app	:	**tol_geometry_app** references representations of any curves that have to be controlled. The representations of these curves are again bounded two dimensional curves.
tolerance_value	:	The value determines the extent of the tolerance zone bounded by two curves that are equidistant to the represented curve.
application_side	:	The defined type TOL_IBO that is referred to at this place determines the side of the tolerance zone relative to the represented curve. TOL_IBO may denote INSIDE, BILATERAL, or OUTSIDE.
offset_curve_length	:	This attribute is only applicable, if the attribute **application_side** returns INSIDE or OUTSIDE. Then **offset_curve_length** determines the length of the represented offset curve indicating the side of the tolerance zone. The offset curve is drawn at both sides of the position given by **arrow_position** with half the length specified by **offset_curve_length**. The offset of the curve is a default value.
arrow_position	:	**arrow_position** denotes the terminating point of the arrow of the leader at the represented curve.
datum_reference	:	A combination of datum features may be referenced at this place. One to three planes or one axis and an optional plane can be combined as datum features.
arrow_direction	:	The direction of the arrow of the leader has to be perpendicular to the represented curve at the intersecting point of the arrow and the curve.

PROPOSITIONS:

a. The arrow has to be placed at the represented controlled curve.

b. Where the tolerance zone is placed on only one side of the curve, an offset curve indicating the side has to be represented.

c. No material conditions may be applied by the datum features.

6.3.11. PROFILE OF SURFACE

PROFILE_OF_SURFACE contains the description of the representation of a profile of a surface tolerance that belongs to the type of profile tolerances. The controlled profile is established by a cross section of a surface that is represented in a view of the drawing.
In a drawing the profile is determined by points (these points lie on the curve representing the profile), the positions of which are determined by dimension graphs. Where a profile tolerance is applied, the dimensions relevant to the profile have to have the quality of a basic dimension. Thus the profile tolerance is similar to a position tolerance and may be specified relative to certain combinations of datum features. A combination of one optional plane together with either at least two further planes or one axis may be referred to as datum features.
In the structure the following inherent constraints are considered:

- The profile of a surface tolerance symbol may be applied by representations of any surfaces.
- The arrow of the leader of a profile of a surface tolerance has to be placed at the curve being part of the representation of a surface.
- The direction of the arrow is perpendicular to the representation of the surface in their intersecting point.
- Where the side of the tolerance zone should be given relative to the represented surface, a short part of an equidistant curve is represented on this side that is relevant to the tolerance zone.

```
*)
ENTITY profile_of_surface  SUBTYPE OF (shape_loc_tol);
   tol_geometry_app       : curve_app;
   tolerance_value        : POSITIVE_REAL;
   application_side       : tol_ibo;    -- see /1/,
                            4.10.1.2.8
   offset_curve_length    : OPTIONAL  POSITIVE_REAL;
   arrow_position         : point_on_geometry;
   datum_reference        : OPTIONAL  position_datum;
DERIVE
   arrow_direction        : direction  :=
                            is_perpendicular_to
                            (tol_geometry_app,
                            arrow_position);
```

```
WHERE
   (* a *)   embedded (tol_geometry_app, arrow_position);
   (* b *)   ( (application_side = .bilateral.) AND
   (offset_curve_length = NULL) ) OR ( (application_side
   <> .bilateral.) AND (offset_curve_length <> NULL) );
   (* c *)   (datum_reference = NULL) OR (
   (datum_reference <> NULL) AND ( ( (typeof
   (datum_reference) = axis1_plane1_datum) AND
   (datum_reference.axis_reference.
   material_condition = .none.) AND (
   (datum_reference.plane_reference = NULL) OR (
   (datum_reference.plane_reference <> NULL) AND
   (datum_reference.plane_reference.material_condition =
   .none.) ) ) ) ) OR ( (typeof (datum_reference) =
   plane3_datum) AND (datum_reference.primary_plane_ref.
   material_condition = .none.) AND (
   (datum_reference.sec_tert_planes_ref[i] = NULL) OR (
   (datum_reference.sec_tert_planes_ref <> NULL) AND
   (datum_reference.sec_tert_planes_ref[i].material_condi
   tion = .none.) ) ) ) );
END_ENTITY;
(*
```

ATTRIBUTE DEFINITIONS:

tol_geometry_app	:	**tol_geometry_app** references representations of any surfaces that have to be controlled. The representations of these surfaces are bounded two dimensional curves.
tolerance_value	:	The value determines the extent of the tolerance zone bounded by two curves that are equidistant to the represented curve.
application_side	:	The defined type TOL_IBO that is referred to at this place determines the side of the tolerance zone relative to the represented curve. TOL_IBO may denote INSIDE, BILATERAL, or OUTSIDE.

offset_curve_length : This attribute is only applicable, if the attribute **application_side** returns INSIDE or OUTSIDE. Then **offset_curve_length** determines the length of the represented offset curve indicating the side of the tolerance zone. The offset curve is drawn on both sides of the position given by **arrow_position** with half the length specified by **offset_curve_length**. The offset of the curve is a default value.

arrow_position : **arrow_position** denotes the terminating point of the arrow of the leader at the represented curve.

datum_reference : A combination of datum features may be referenced at this place. One to three planes or one axis and an optional plane can be combined as datum features.

arrow_direction : The direction of the arrow of the leader has to be perpendicular to the represented curve at the intersecting point of the arrow and the curve.

PROPOSITIONS:

a. The arrow has to be placed at the represented curve.

b. Where the tolerance zone is placed on only one side of the curve an offset curve indicating the side has to be represented.

c. No material conditions may be applied by the datum features.

6.3.12. PARALLEL ORIENTATION TOL

PARALLEL_ORIENTATION_TOL is the supertype of the entity types PAR_AXIS_ORIENT_TOL and PAR_PLANE_ORIENT_TOL. Both subtypes describe representations of parallelism tolerances and belong to the type of orientation tolerances.
When applying PAR_AXIS_ORIENT_TOL the controlled represented geometry element is an axis and PAR_PLANE_ORIENT_TOL is the description of a representation of an orientation tolerance controlling a plane.
In the structure the following inherent constraints are considered:

- An unit length may be specified and placed to the right of the tolerance value, separated by a slash.

- Where a maximum material condition is applied, an "M" placed in a circle succeeds the tolerance value and the optional unit length.
- The arrow of the leader of the geometry tolerance frame is perpendicular to the representation of the controlled geometry elements.

```
*)
ENTITY parallel_orientation_tol SUPERTYPE OF
                         (par_axis_orient_tol XOR
                         par_plane_orient_tol)
                         SUBTYPE OF (shape_loc_tol);
   tolerance_value          : REAL;
   per_unit_length          : OPTIONAL POSITIVE_REAL;
   material_condition       : tol_mlsn;    -- see /1/,
                              4.10.1.2.9
   arrow_position           : reference_term_point;
WHERE
   (* a *)   (tolerance_value > 0.0) OR ( (tolerance_value
   = 0.0) AND (material_condition = .maxmc.) );
END_ENTITY;
(*
```

ATTRIBUTE DEFINITIONS:

tolerance_value : The value determines the extent of the tolerance zone. Another factor influencing the tolerance zone is the value of the attribute **material_condition**.

per_unit_length : **per_unit_length** specifies the linear distance within which the tolerance value applies. Where the value is omitted the linear distance is equal to the represented length of the controlled feature.

material_condition : This attribute references a defined type that specifies the material condition applied by the parallelism tolerance. The following values are enumerated: MAXMC (maximum material condition), LEASTMC (least material condition), REGARDLESS (regardless of feature size) and NONE (not applicable).

arrow_position : **arrow_position** denotes the terminating point of the arrow of the leader at a represented geometry element or at a projection line being an extension line of a dimension graph.

PROPOSITIONS:

a. The **tolerance_value** has to be greater than 0.0 with the exception where a maximum material condition is applied. In the latter case the **tolerance_value** may be equal to 0.0 .

6.3.13. PAR AXIS ORIENT TOL

PAR_AXIS_ORIENT_TOL is the description of a representation of a parallelism tolerance controlling the orientation of an axis of a surface of revolution. The tolerance representation may either be combined with an up projection or side projection of an axis.
The tolerance zone has to be described relative to the datum features. Where the tolerance zone of an axis is described relative to a parallel plane, the tolerance zone has one degree of freedom with regard to orientation. A further plane - parallel to the axis and perpendicular to the first plane reduces the degree of freedom. There is no degree of freedom left, where the tolerance zone of an axis is described relative to another parallel axis. Therefore either one representation of an axis or one or two represented planes have to be referenced as datum features.
In the structure the following inherent constraints are considered:

- The controlled geometry elements have to be represented as up or side projections of surfaces of revolution.
- Where an axis is referred to as a datum feature, the tolerance zone has a circular form.
- Where the tolerance zone has a circular form, a "ø" precedes the tolerance value.
- A parallelism tolerance controlling the orientation of an axis may apply to a projection zone. In this case a "P" placed in a circle succeeds the tolerance value and the optional unit length as well as the optional material condition.

```
*)
ENTITY par_axis_orient_tol SUBTYPE OF
                         (parallel_orientation_tol);
   tol_geometry_app       : surf_of_rev_app;
   arrow_direction        : direction;    -- see /1/,
                            4.5.3.7
   datum_reference        : axis1_or_plane2_datum;
   zone_projection        : LOGICAL;
WHERE
   (* a *)  ( (typeof (arrow_position) =
   point_on_geometry) AND (embedded (tol_geometry_app,
   arrow_position) ) AND (is_perpendicular_to
   (tol_geometry_app, arrow_position) = arrow_direction)
   ) OR ( (typeof (arrow_position) =
   point_on_dimension_graph) AND ( ( (typeof
   (arrow_position.dimension_graph) =
   represented_shape_dimension) AND (is_parallel
   (arrow_direction,
   arrow_position.dimension_graph.next_dir) ) ) XOR (
   (typeof (arrow_position.dimension_graph) =
   circular_shape_dimension) AND (embedded
   (tol_geometry_app,
   arrow_position.dimension_graph.geometry_appearance) )
   AND (is_parallel (arrow_direction,
   arrow_position.dimension_graph.dim_line_dir) ) ) ) );
   (* b *)  coordinate_space (arrow_direction) = 2;
END_ENTITY;
(*
```

ATTRIBUTE DEFINITIONS:

tol_geometry_app : **tol_geometry_app** references representations of the controlled geometry elements that are projected surfaces of revolution. An up projection consists of at least one circle and a side projection consists of a bounded curve in connection with a center line being the representation of the axis.

arrow_direction : The direction of the arrow of the leader pointing at the representation of the controlled geometry.

datum_reference : **datum_reference** references the representations of the datum features. The datum features may either be one axis or one or two planes. Where a represented axis is referenced (the referenced entity has to be a subtype of the entity type AXIS1_DATUM), the tolerance zone has a circular form and a "ø" precedes the number determined by the attribute **tolerance_value**. A tolerance zone bounded by two offset planes per datum feature is determined, if one or two represented planes are referenced (the referenced entity has to be of type PLANE2_DATUM).

zone_projection : Where the flag **zone_projection** is true, a tolerance projection zone is applied and a "P" placed in a circle is represented in the geometry tolerance frame.

PROPOSITIONS:

a. If the arrow of the leader is placed at the representation of the controlled geometry, the direction of the arrow is perpendicular to the represented geometry element. If the arrow of the leader is placed on the extension line of a dimension graph, the direction of the arrow is perpendicular to the extension line.

b. The dimensionality of **arrow_direction** has to have the value 2.

6.3.14. PAR PLANE ORIENT TOL

The entity type PAR_PLANE_ORIENT_TOL describes a representation of a parallelism tolerance controlling the orientation of a plane that is represented by a straight line.
The tolerance zone has to be described relative to the datum features. Where the tolerance zone of a plane is described relative to a parallel axis, the tolerance zone has one degree of freedom with regard to orientation. A further axis - not parallel to the first axis, but parallel to the controlled plane reduces the degree of freedom. There is no degree of freedom left, where the tolerance zone of a plane is described relative to another parallel plane. Therefore either one

representation of a plane or one or two represented axes have to be referenced as datum features.

In the structure the following inherent constraints are considered:

- The controlled geometry elements have to be represented planes.
- The direction of the arrow of the leader is perpendicular to the line that is the representation of the plane.

```
*)
ENTITY par_plane_orient_tol SUBTYPE OF
                              (parallel_orientation_tol);
  tol_geometry_app        : straight_geometry_app;
  datum_reference         : axis2_or_plane1_datum;
DERIVE
  arrow_direction         : direction := perpendicular
                            (tol_geometry_app.
                            dir_of_geometry_app);
WHERE
   (* a *)   ( (typeof (arrow_position) =
   point_on_geometry) AND (embedded (tol_geometry_app,
   arrow_position) ) ) OR ( (typeof (arrow_position) =
   point_on_dimension_graph) AND typeofF
   (arrow_position.dimension_graph) =
   represented_shape_dimension) AND (IS_PARALLEL
   (arrow_direction,
   arrow_position.dimension_graph.next_dir) ) );
END_ENTITY;
(*
```

ATTRIBUTE DEFINITIONS:

tol_geometry_app : **tol_geometry_app** references a representation of the controlled geometry element that is either a projected plane or a form feature consisting of two parallel planes.

datum_reference : **datum_reference** references the representations of the datum features. The datum features may either be one or two axes or one plane the description of which is contained in the subtypes of the structure AXIS2_OR_PLANE1_DATUM. The tolerance zone is bounded by two offset planes that are parallel to the datum features.

arrow_direction : The direction of the arrow of the leader being derived from and pointing at the representation of the controlled geometry.

PROPOSITIONS:

a. The arrow of the leader is either placed at the representation of the controlled geometry or perpendicular to and on the extension line of a dimension graph.

6.3.15. PERPENDICULAR ORIENT TOL

PERPENDICULAR_ORIENT_TOL is the structure for the description of representations of perpendicularity tolerances controlling an axis or a plane. An axis is controlled where the subtype PERP_AXIS_ORIENT_TOL is applied and in case of applying the subtype PERP_PLANE_ORIENT_TOL a plane is controlled. Both subtypes belong to the type of orientation tolerances.

In the structure the following inherent constraints are considered:

- An unit length may be specified and placed to the right of the tolerance value, separated by a slash.
- Where a maximum material condition is applied, an "M" placed in a circle succeeds the tolerance value and the optional unit length.
- The arrow of the leader of the geometry tolerance frame is perpendicular to the representation of the controlled geometry elements.

```
*)
ENTITY  perpendicular_orient_tol  SUPERTYPE  OF
                              (perp_axis_orient_tol  XOR
                              perp_plane_orient_tol)
                              SUBTYPE  OF  (shape_loc_tol);
```

```
   tolerance_value          REAL;
   per_unit_length        : OPTIONAL  POSITIVE_REAL;
   material_condition     : tol_mlsn;    -- see /1/,
                            4.10.1.2.9
   arrow_position         : reference_term_point;
WHERE
   (* a *)   (tolerance_value > 0.0)  OR  ( (tolerance_value
   = 0.0)  AND  (material_condition  =  .maxmc.)  );
END_ENTITY;
(*
```

ATTRIBUTE DEFINITIONS:

tolerance_value : The value determines the extent of the tolerance zone. Another factor influencing the tolerance zone is the value of the attribute **material_condition**.

per_unit_length : **per_unit_length** specifies the linear distance within which the tolerance value applies. Where the value is omitted the linear distance is equal to the represented length of the controlled feature.

material_condition : This attribute references a defined type that specifies the material condition applied by the perpendicularity tolerance. The following values are enumerated: MAXMC (maximum material condition), LEASTMC (least material condition), REGARDLESS (regardless of feature size) and NONE (not applicable).

arrow_position : **arrow_position** denotes the terminating point of the arrow of the leader at a represented geometry element or on a projection line being an extension line of a dimension graph.

PROPOSITIONS:

a. The **tolerance_value** has to be greater than 0.0 with the exception where a maximum material condition is applied. In the latter case the **tolerance_value** may be equal to 0.0 .

6.3.16. PERP AXIS ORIENT TOL

PERP_AXIS_ORIENT_TOL is the description of a representation of a perpendicularity tolerance controlling the orientation of an axis of a surface of revolution. The tolerance representation may be combined with either an up projection or side projection of an axis.
The tolerance zone has to be described relative to the datum features. Where the tolerance zone of an axis is described relative to a perpendicular axis, the tolerance zone has one degree of freedom with regard to orientation. A further axis - perpendicular to the controlled axis as well as to the first datum feature reduces the degree of freedom. There is no degree of freedom left, where the tolerance zone of an axis is described relative to a perpendicular plane. Therefore either one representation of a plane or one or two represented axes have to be referenced as datum features.
In the structure the following inherent constraints are considered:

- The controlled geometry elements have to be represented as up or side projections of surfaces of revolution.
- Where a plane is referred to as a datum feature, the tolerance zone has a circular form.
- Where the tolerance zone has a circular form, a "ø" precedes the tolerance value.
- A perpendicularity tolerance controlling the orientation of an axis may apply to a projection zone. In this case a "P" placed in a circle succeeds the tolerance value and the optional unit length as well as the optional material condition.

```
*)
ENTITY  perp_axis_orient_tol  SUBTYPE  OF
                              (perpendicular_orient_tol);
   tol_geometry_app            : surf_of_rev_app;
   arrow_direction             : direction;     --  see  /1/,
                                 4.5.3.7
   datum_reference             : axis2_or_plane1_datum;
   zone_projection             : LOGICAL;
WHERE
   (* a *)    ( (typeof (arrow_position) =
   point_on_geometry)  AND  (embedded  (tol_geometry_app,
   arrow_position)  )  AND  (is_perpendicular_to
   (tol_geometry_app,  arrow_position)  =  arrow_direction)
   )  OR  (  (typeof  (arrow_position)  =
   point_on_dimension_graph)  AND  (  (  (typeof
```

```
    (arrow_position.dimension_graph)  =
    side_projected_feature_dim)  AND  (is_parallel
    (arrow_direction,
    arrow_position.dimension_graph.next_dir) ) )  XOR  (
    (typeof  (arrow_position.dimension_graph)  =
    circular_shape_dimension)  AND  (embedded
    (tol_geometry_app,
    arrow_position.dimension_graph.geometry_appearance) )
    AND  (is_parallel  (arrow_direction,
    arrow_position.dimension_graph.dim_line_dir) ) ) ) );
    (* b *)   coordinate_space (arrow_direction) =2;
END_ENTITY;
(*
```

ATTRIBUTE DEFINITIONS:

tol_geometry_app : **tol_geometry_app** references representations of the controlled geometry that are projected surfaces of revolution. An up projection consists of at least one circle and a side projection consists of a bounded curve in connection with a center line being the representation of the axis.

arrow_direction : The direction of the arrow of the leader pointing at the representation of the controlled geometry.

datum_reference : **datum_reference** references the representations of the datum features. The datum features may either be one plane or one or two axes. Where a represented plane is referenced (the referenced entity has to be a subtype of the entity type PLANE1_DATUM), the tolerance zone has a circular form and a "ø" precedes the number determined by the attribute **tolerance_value**. A tolerance zone bounded by two offset planes per datum feature is determined, if one or two represented axes are referenced (the referenced entity has to be of type AXIS2_DATUM). The offset planes are perpendicular to the axis being referred to as a datum feature.

zone_projection : Where the flag **zone_projection** is true, a tolerance projection zone is applied and a "P" placed in a circle is represented in the geometry tolerance frame.

PROPOSITIONS:

a. If the arrow of the leader is placed at the representation of the controlled geometry, the direction of the arrow is perpendicular to the represented geometry element. If the arrow of the leader is placed on the extension line of a dimension graph, the direction of the arrow is perpendicular.

b. The dimensionality of **arrow_direction** has to have the value 2.

6.3.17. PERP PLANE ORIENT TOL

PERP_PLANE_ORIENT_TOL describes the representation of a perpendicularity tolerance controlling the orientation of a plane that is represented by a straight line.
The tolerance zone has to be described relative to the datum features. Where the tolerance zone of a plane is described relative to a perpendicular plane, the tolerance zone has left one degree of freedom with regard to orientation. A further referenced plane datum - perpendicular to the controlled plane reduces the degree of freedom. There is no degree of freedom left, where the tolerance zone of a plane is described relative to a perpendicular axis. Therefore either one representation of an axis or one or two represented planes have to be referenced as datum features.
In the structure the following inherent constraints are considered:

- The controlled geometry elements have to be represented planes.
- The direction of the arrow of the leader is perpendicular to the line that is the representation of the plane.

```
*)
ENTITY  perp_plane_orient_tol  SUBTYPE  OF
                               (perpendicular_orient_tol);
   tol_geometry_app         : straight_geometry_app;
   datum_reference          : axis1_or_plane2_datum;
DERIVE
```

```
   arrow_direction        : direction  :=  perpendicular
                             (tol_geometry_app);
WHERE
   (* a *)   ( (typeof (arrow_position) =
   point_on_geometry) AND (embedded (tol_geometry_app,
   arrow_position) ) ) OR ( (typeof (arrow_position) =
   point_on_dimension_graph) AND (typpof
   (arrow_position.dimension_graph) =
   represented_shape_dimension) AND (is_parallel
   (arrow_direction,
   arrow_position.dimension_graph.next_dir) ) );
END_ENTITY;
(*
```

ATTRIBUTE DEFINITIONS:

tol_geometry_app : **tol_geometry_app** references a representation of either a geometry element that is a projected plane or a form feature consisting of two parallel planes. Both are representations of the controlled geometry.

datum_reference : **datum_reference** references the representations of the datum features. The datum features may either be one or two planes or one axis the description of which is contained in the subtypes of the structure AXIS1_OR_PLANE2_DATUM. The tolerance zone is bounded by two offset planes that are perpendicular to the datum features.

arrow_direction : The direction of the arrow of the leader being derived from and pointing at the representation of the controlled geometry.

PROPOSITIONS:

a. The arrow of the leader is either placed at the representation of the controlled geometry or perpendicular to and on the extension line of a dimension graph.

6.3.18. ANGULARITY ORIENT TOL

The structure ANGULARITY_ORIENT_TOL describes the representation of an angularity tolerance that belongs to the type of orientation tolerances.

The tolerance zone has to be described relative to the datum features. The datum features may either be one or two planes or one or two axes. Relative to these datum features it is possible to definitely determine the orientation of a plane or axis.

In the structure the following inherent constraints are considered:

- The controlled geometry elements have to be represented axes or planes.
- Where the tolerance zone has a circular form, a "ø" precedes the tolerance value.
- A unit length may be specified and placed to the right of the tolerance value, separated by a slash.
- Where a maximum material condition is applied, an "M" placed in a circle succeeds the tolerance value and the optional unit length.
- An angularity tolerance controlling the orientation of an axis may apply to a projection zone. In this case a "P" placed in a circle succeeds the tolerance value and the optional unit length as well as the optional material condition.

```
*)
ENTITY angularity_orient_tol SUBTYPE OF (shape_loc_tol);
   tol_geometry_app       : surface_app;
   tolerance_value        : REAL;
   per_unit_length        : OPTIONAL POSITIVE_REAL;
   circular_tol_zone      : LOGICAL;
   material_condition     : tol_mlsn;    -- see /1/,
                            4.10.1.2.9
   arrow_position         : reference_term_point;
   arrow_direction        : direction;    -- see /1/,
                            4.5.3.7
   datum_reference        : axis2_or_plane2_datum;
   zone_projection        : LOGICAL;
WHERE
   (* a *)   typeof (tol_geometry_app) <> curve_app;
   (* b *)   (tolerance_value > 0.0) OR ( (tolerance_value
   = 0.0) AND (material_condition = .maxmc.) );
```

```
   (* c *)  (NOT circular_tol_zone) OR (
   (circular_tol_zone) AND ( (typeof (tol_geometry_app) =
   surf_of_rev_app) ) );
   (* d *)  ( (typeof (arrow_position) =
   point_on_geometry) AND (embedded (tol_geometry_app,
   arrow_position) ) AND (is_perpendicular_to
   (tol_geometry_app, arrow_position) = arrow_direction)
   ) OR ( (typeof (arrow_position) =
   point_on_dimension_graph) AND ( ( (typeof
   (arrow_position.dimension_graph) =
   represented_shape_dimension) AND (is_parallel
   (arrow_direction,
   arrow_position.dimension_graph.next_dir) ) ) OR (
   (typeof (arrow_position.dimension_graph) =
   circular_shape_dimension) AND (embedded
   (tol_geometry_app,
   arrow_position.dimension_graph.geometry_appearance) )
   AND (is_parallel (arrow_direction,
   arrow_position.dimension_graph.dim_line_dir) ) ) ) );
   (* e *)  ( (zone_projection) AND (typeof
   (tol_geometry_app) = surf_of_rev_app) ) OR (NOT
   zone_projection);
END_ENTITY;
(*
```

ATTRIBUTE DEFINITIONS:

tol_geometry_app	:	**tol_geometry_app** references a representation of either a controlled geometry element that is a projected plane or a controlled form feature consisting of two parallel planes or a surface of revolution.
tolerance_value	:	The value determines the extent of the tolerance zone. Another factor influencing the tolerance zone is the value of the attribute **material_condition**.

per_unit_length	:	**per_unit_length** specifies the linear distance within which the tolerance value applies. Where the value is omitted the linear distance is equal to the represented length of the controlled feature.
circular_tol_zone	:	If the flag is true, the tolerance zone has a circular form and a "ø" precedes the number determined by the attribute **tolerance_value**. A true flag is only admissible where an axis is controlled. A false flag denotes a tolerance range being limited by two offset planes.
material_condition	:	This attribute references a defined type that specifies the material condition applied by the angularity tolerance. The following values are enumerated: MAXMC (maximum material condition), LEASTMC (least material condition), REGARDLESS (regardless of feature size) and NONE (not applicable).
arrow_position	:	**arrow_position** denotes the terminating point of the arrow of the leader at a represented geometry element or on an extension line of a dimension graph being connected with the represented geometry element.
arrow_direction	:	The direction of the arrow of the leader.
datum_reference	:	**datum_reference** references the representations of the datum features. The datum features may either be one or two planes or one or two axes the description of which is contained in the entity type AXIS2_OR_PLANE2_DATUM.
zone_projection	:	Where the flag **zone_projection** is true, a tolerance projection zone is applied and a "P" placed in a circle is represented in the geometry tolerance frame.

PROPOSITIONS:

a. Only the axes of surfaces of revolutions and planes may be controlled by the angularity tolerance. The subtype BOUNDED_SURF_APP of the entity type SURFACE_APP describes the two dimensional representation of any surface and thus must not be referenced.

b. The **tolerance_value** has to be greater than 0.0 with the exception where a maximum material condition is applied. In the latter case the **tolerance_value** may be equal to 0.0 .

c. A circular form of the tolerance zone is applicable, if an axis of a surface of revolution is controlled.

d. If the arrow of the leader is placed at the representation of the controlled geometry, the direction of the arrow is perpendicular to the represented geometry element. If the arrow of the leader is placed on the extension line of a dimension graph, the direction of the arrow is perpendicular to the extension line.

e. A tolerance projection zone may only be applied, where an axis of a surface of revolution is controlled.

6.3.19. POSITION LOC TOL

The structure POSITION_LOC_TOL describes the representation of a position tolerance that belongs to the type of location tolerances. The subtype POS_POINT_LOC_TOL is applied, if the controlled geometry element is represented as a point, an up projected axis for instance. Where the controlled geometry element is represented as a line (e. g.: A side projected axis), the subtype POS_LINE_LOC_TOL describes the appearance of the position tolerance.
The tolerance zone has to be described relative to the datum features. The datum features may either be one to three planes or one axis and an optional plane.
The following inherent constraints are considered in the structure:

- Where the tolerance zone has a circular form, a "ø" precedes the tolerance value.
- Where a maximum material condition is applied, an "M" placed in a circle succeeds the tolerance value.
- A position tolerance may apply to a projection zone. In this case a "P" placed in a circle succeeds the tolerance value and the optional material condition.

```
*)
ENTITY position_loc_tol SUPERTYPE OF (pos_point_loc_tol
                        XOR pos_line_loc_tol)
                        SUBTYPE OF (shape_loc_tol);
   tolerance_value       : REAL;
   circular_tol_zone     : LOGICAL;
```

```
   material_condition     : tol_mlsn;    -- see /1/,
                            4.10.1.2.9
   arrow_position         : reference_term_point;
   datum_reference        : position_datum;
   zone_projection        : LOGICAL;
WHERE
   (* a *)   (tolerance_value > 0.0) OR ( (tolerance_value
   = 0.0) AND (material_condition = .maxmc.) );
   (* b *)   ( (zone_projection) AND (typeof
   (tol_geometry_app) = surf_of_rev_app) ) OR (NOT
   zone_projection);
END_ENTITY;
(*
```

ATTRIBUTE DEFINITIONS:

tolerance_value : The value determines the extent of the tolerance zone. Another factor influencing the tolerance zone is the value of the attribute **material_condition**.

circular_tol_zone : If the flag is true, the tolerance zone has a circular form and a "ø" precedes the number determined by the attribute **tolerance_value**. A true flag is only admissible, where an axis is controlled.

material_condition : This attribute references a defined type that specifies the material condition applied by the position tolerance. The following values are enumerated: MAXMC (maximum material condition), LEASTMC (least material condition), REGARDLESS (regardless of feature size) and NONE (not applicable).

arrow_position : **arrow_position** denotes the terminating point of the arrow of the leader at a represented geometry element or on a projection line being an extension line of a dimension graph.

datum_reference : **datum_reference** references the representations of the datum features. The datum features may either be one to three planes or one axis together with an optional plane.

zone_projection : Where the flag **zone_projection** is true, a tolerance projection zone is applied and a "P" placed in a circle is represented in the geometry tolerance frame.

PROPOSITIONS:

a. The **tolerance_value** has to be greater than 0.0 with the exception where a maximum material condition is applied. In the latter case the **tolerance_value** may be equal to 0.0 .

b. A tolerance projection zone may only be applied, where an axis of a surface of revolution is controlled.

6.3.20. POS LINE LOC TOL

POS_LINE_LOC_TOL describes the representation of a position tolerance that controls a geometry element represented as a line (e. g.: A side projected axis or plane).
The following inherent constraints are considered in the structure:

- The direction of the arrow of the leader is perpendicular to the representation of the controlled geometry elements.
- A circular form of the tolerance zone is applicable, if an axis of a cylinder or cone is controlled and represented by a side projection.

```
*)
ENTITY pos_line_loc_tol SUBTYPE OF (position_loc_tol);
   tol_geometry_app       : straight_geometry_app;
DERIVE
   arrow_direction        : direction := perpendicular
                            (tol_geometry_app.dir_of_geome
                            try_app);
WHERE
   (* a *)  ( (typeof (arrow_position) =
   point_on_geometry) AND (embedded (tol_geometry_app,
   arrow_position) ) ) OR ( (typeof (arrow_position) =
   point_on_dimension_graph) AND (typeof
   (arrow_position.dimension_graph) =
```

```
   represented_shape_dimension)  AND  (IS_PARALLEL
   (arrow_direction,
   arrow_position.dimension_graph.next_dir)  )  );
END_ENTITY;
(*
```

ATTRIBUTE DEFINITIONS:

tol_geometry_app : **tol_geometry_app** references descriptions of straight lines being the representations of the geometry elements that have to be controlled.

arrow_direction : The direction of the arrow of the leader that has to be derived from the represented lines.

PROPOSITIONS:

a. The point specified by **arrow_position** is placed either on a line of the referenced geometry representation or at a dimension graph described by the entity type REPRESENTED_SHAPE_DIMENSION. The dimension graph has to refer to the representation of the controlled geometry element and the direction of the dimension line has to be parallel to the direction specified by the attribute **arrow_direction**.

6.3.21. POS POINT LOC TOL

POSITION_POINT_LOC_TOL describes the representation of a position tolerance that the position of axes of surfaces of revolution.
The following inherent constraints are considered in the structure:
- The representations of the controlled geometry elements have to be up projections of surfaces of revolution.

```
*)
ENTITY pos_point_loc_tol  SUBTYPE  OF  (position_loc_tol);
   tol_geometry_app      : surf_of_rev_app;
```

```
   arrow_direction        : direction;       --    see   /1/,
                            4.5.3.7
WHERE
   (* a *)   ( (typeof (arrow_position) =
   point_on_geometry) AND (embedded (tol_geometry_app,
   arrow_position) ) ) OR ( (typeof (arrow_position) =
   point_on_dimension_graph) AND (typeof
   (arrow_position.dimension_graph) =
   circular_shape_dimension) AND (embedded
   (tol_geometry_app,
   arrow_position.dimension_graph.geometry_appearance) )
   AND (is_parallel (arrow_direction,
   arrow_position.dimension_graph.dim_line_dir) ) );
   (* b *)   coordinate_space (arrow_direction) = 2;
END_ENTITY;
(*
```

ATTRIBUTE DEFINITIONS:

tol_geometry_app : **tol_geometry_app** references descriptions of up projected surfaces of revolution being the representations of the geometry elements that have to be controlled.

arrow_direction : The direction of the arrow of the leader.

PROPOSITIONS:

a. The point specified by **arrow_position** is either placed on a line of the referenced geometry representation or at a dimension graph described by the entity type CIRCULAR_SHAPE_DIMENSION. The dimension graph has to refer to the representation of the controlled geometry element and the direction of the dimension line has to be parallel to the direction specified by the attribute **arrow_direction**.

b. The dimensionality of **arrow_direction** has to have the value 2.

6.3.22. CONCENTRICITY LOC TOL

The entity type CONCENTRICITY_LOC_TOL describes the representation of a concentricity tolerance that belongs to the type of location tolerances.
The tolerance zone has to be described relative to the datum feature that has to be an axis of a surface of revolution. The controlled axis has to be concentric to the datum feature.
The following inherent constraints are considered in the structure:

- The represented controlled geometry element has to be an axis of a surface of revolution.
- Where the arrow of the leader is placed at a side projection of a surface of revolution, the arrow is directed perpendicular to the represented axis of the controlled geometry.
- Where the arrow of the leader is placed at an up projection of a surface of revolution, the arrow is directed radial with regard to the represented circle.
- The tolerance zone has to have a circular form and a "ø" precedes the tolerance value.
- Where a maximum material condition is applied, an "M" placed in a circle succeeds the tolerance value and the optional unit length.

```
*)
ENTITY  concentricity_loc_tol  SUBTYPE  OF  (shape_loc_tol);
   tol_geometry_app        : surf_of_rev_app;
   tolerance_value         : REAL;
   material_condition      : tol_mlsn;    --  /1/,  4.10.1.2.9
   arrow_position          : reference_term_point;
   arrow_direction         : direction;    --  /1/,  4.5.3.7
   datum_reference         : axis_datum;
WHERE
   (* a *)   (tolerance_value  >  0.0)  OR  (  (tolerance_value
   =  0.0)  AND  (material_condition  =  .maxmc.)  );
   (* b *)   (  (typeof  (arrow_position)  =
   point_on_geometry)  AND  (embedded  (tol_geometry_app,
   arrow_position)  )  )  OR  (  (typeof  (arrow_position)  =
   point_on_dimension_graph)  AND  (  (  (typeof
   (arrow_position.dimension_graph)  =
   circular_shape_dimension)  AND  (embedded
   (tol_geometry_app,
   arrow_position.dimension_graph.geometry_appearance)  )
   AND  (is_parallel  (arrow_direction,
```

```
   arrow_position.dimension_graph.dim_line_dir) ) ) OR (
   (typeof (arrow_position.dimension_graph) =
   side_projected_feature_dim) AND (is_parallel
   (arrow_direction,
   arrow_position.dimension_graph.next_dir) ) ) ) );
END_ENTITY;
(*
```

ATTRIBUTE DEFINITIONS:

tol_geometry_app : The attribute **tol_geometry_app** references a representation of the controlled geometry element that is either a side or up projection of a surface of revolution.

tolerance_value : The value determines the extent of the tolerance zone. Another factor influencing the tolerance zone is the value of the attribute **material_condition**.

material_condition : This attribute references a defined type that specifies the material condition applied by the concentricity tolerance. The following values are enumerated: MAXMC (maximum material condition), LEASTMC (least material condition), REGARDLESS (regardless of feature size) and NONE (not applicable).

arrow_position : **arrow_position** denotes the terminating point of the arrow of the leader at a represented geometry element or on an extension line of a dimension graph.

arrow_direction : The direction of the arrow of the leader.

datum_reference : **datum_reference** references the representations of the datum features. The datum feature has to be an axis of a surface of revolution the description of which is contained in the entity type AXIS_DATUM.

PROPOSITIONS:

a. The **tolerance_value** has to be greater than 0.0 with the exception where a maximum material condition is applied. In the latter case the **tolerance_value** may be equal to 0.0 .

b. The arrow of the leader is placed either at the representation of the controlled geometry or on the extension line of a dimension graph dimensioning the diameter of the controlled geometry. In this case the direction of the arrow is perpendicular to the extension line.

6.3.23. SYMMETRY LOC TOL

The entity type SYMMETRY_LOC_TOL describes the representation of a symmetry tolerance that belongs to the type of location tolerances. The ANSI-Standard does not provide a symmetry tolerance.

The tolerance zone has to be described relative to the datum feature that has to be a plane or a median plane derived from a symmetrical planar geometry.

The following inherent constraints are considered in the structure:

- The represented controlled geometry elements have to be planes or axes which have to be placed symmetrically with regard to the datums.
- Where a maximum material condition is applied, an "M" placed in a circle succeeds the tolerance value and the optional unit length.

```
*)
ENTITY  symmetry_loc_tol  SUBTYPE  OF  (shape_loc_tol);
   tol_geometry_app          : surface_app;
   tolerance_value           : REAL;
   material_condition        : tol_mlsn;    --  see  /1/,
                               4.10.1.2.9
   arrow_position            : reference_term_point;
   arrow_direction           : direction;    --  see  /1/,
                               4.5.3.7
   datum_reference            plane_datum;
WHERE
   (* a *)    (tolerance_value > 0.0) OR ( (tolerance_value
   = 0.0) AND (material_condition = .maxmc.) );
   (* b *)   ( (typeof (arrow_position) =
   point_on_geometry) AND (embedded (tol_geometry_app,
   arrow_position) ) AND (is_perpendicular_to
   (tol_geometry_app, arrow_position) = arrow_direction)
   ) OR ( (typeof (arrow_position) =
```

```
    point_on_dimension_graph) AND ( ( (typeof
    (arrow_position.dimension_graph) =
    represented_shape_dimension) AND (is_parallel
    (arrow_direction,
    arrow_position.dimension_graph.next_dir) ) ) OR (
    (typeof (arrow_position.dimension_graph) =
    circular_shape_dimension) AND (embedded
    (tol_geometry_app,
    arrow_position.dimension_graph.geometry_appearance) )
    AND (is_parallel (arrow_direction,
    arrow_position.dimension_graph.dim_line_dir) ) ) ) );
END_ENTITY;
(*
```

ATTRIBUTE DEFINITIONS:

tol_geometry_app	:	**tol_geometry_app** references a representation of the controlled geometry element that is a projected plane or a form feature consisting of two parallel planes or a surface of revolution.
tolerance_value	:	The value determines the extent of the tolerance zone. Another factor influencing the tolerance zone is the value of the attribute **material_condition**.
material_condition	:	This attribute references a defined type that specifies the material condition applied by the symmetry tolerance. The following values are enumerated: MAXMC (maximum material condition), LEASTMC (least material condition), REGARDLESS (regardless of feature size) and NONE (not applicable).
arrow_position	:	**arrow_position** denotes the terminating point of the arrow of the leader at a represented geometry element or on an extension line of a dimension graph being connected with the represented geometry element.
arrow_direction	:	The direction of the arrow of the leader.

datum_reference : **datum_reference** references the representations of a datum feature. The datum feature has to be a plane, the description of which is contained in the entity type PLANE_DATUM.

PROPOSITIONS:

a. The **tolerance_value** has to be greater than 0.0 with the exception where a maximum material condition is applied. In the latter case the **tolerance_value** may be equal to 0.0 .

b. If the arrow of the leader is placed at the representation of the controlled geometry, the direction of the arrow is perpendicular to the represented geometry element. If the arrow of the leader is placed on the extension line of a dimension graph, the direction of the arrow is perpendicular to the extension line.

6.3.24. CIRCULAR RUNOUT TOL

The structure CIRCULAR_RUNOUT_TOL describes the representation of a circular runout tolerance that belongs to the type of runout tolerances.

The tolerance zone has to be described relative to the datum feature that has to be an axis. The direction of the tolerance zone is perpendicular to every point of the rotational surface with the exception, where the direction of the leader is dimensioned relative to the referenced datum feature (see figure 6.4.1 and 6.4.2). In this case the represented angle determines the direction of the tolerance zone.

The following inherent constraints are considered in the structure:

- The represented controlled geometry elements have to be surfaces of revolution.
- The datum feature has to be established by one or two axes and the optional second axis has to be aligned to the first one.
- Where two aligned axes serve as datum features their identifying letters are placed in the same compartment of the geometry tolerance frame.
- Where the direction of the tolerance zone is not perpendicular to every point of the rotational surface an angular dimension is applied to determine the direction of the arrow of the leader.
- An angular dimension for determining the direction of the arrow of the leader may only be applied, where the controlled geometry is represented in a side projection.

```
*)
ENTITY  circular_runout_tol  SUBTYPE  OF  (shape_loc_tol);
   tol_geometry_app        : surf_of_rev_app;
   tolerance_value         : POSITIVE_REAL;
   arrow_position          : point_on_geometry;
   arrow_direction         : direction;   -- see /1/,
                             4.5.3.7
   datum_reference         : axis_datum;
   co_datum_ref            : OPTIONAL  axis_datum;
   angle_indicator         : OPTIONAL
                             chain_angle_combination;
WHERE
   (* a *)   embedded (tol_geometry_app, arrow_position);
   (* b *)   ( (angle_indicator = NULL) AND
   (is_perpendicular_to  (tol_geometry_app,
   arrow_position) = arrow_direction) ) OR (
   (angle_indicator <> NULL) AND (typeof
   (angle_indicator.first_attribute) =
   initial_dim_attributes) AND (perpendicular
   (arrow_direction) =
   angle_indicator.first_attribute.next_dir ) AND
   (tol_geometry_app.first_attribute.determinator  =
   arrow_position) );
END_ENTITY;
(*
```

ATTRIBUTE DEFINITIONS:

tol_geometry_app	:	**tol_geometry_app** references a representation of a surface of revolution that has to be controlled.
tolerance_value	:	The value determines the extent of the tolerance zone.
arrow_position	:	**arrow_position** denotes the terminating point of the arrow of the leader at a represented geometry element referenced by the attribute **tol_geometry_app**.
arrow_direction	:	The direction of the arrow of the leader.

datum_reference : **datum_reference** references the representations of a datum feature. The datum feature has to be an axis, the description of which is contained in the entity type AXIS_DATUM.

co_datum_ref : Together with the represented axis referred to by **datum_reference** the represented axis optionally referenced by **co_datum_ref** may establish a datum feature. Both axes have to be aligned.

angle_indicator : The direction of the arrow may be explicitely dimensioned by an angular dimension graph of entity type CHAIN_ANGLE_COMBINATION. The direction of one extension line of the dimension graph is identical to the direction of the arrow of the leader. The other extension line is parallel to the represented axis of the controlled geometry element.

PROPOSITIONS:

a. Where no angular dimension for determining the direction of the arrow of the leader is applied, the arrow is directed perpendicular to the represented surface of revolution.

b. The arrow of the leader has to be placed at the represented controlled surface.

6.3.25. TOTAL RUNOUT TOL

TOTAL_RUNOUT_TOL is the description for the representation of a total runout tolerance that belongs to the type of runout tolerances.
The tolerance zone has to be described relative to the datum feature that has to be an axis.
The following inherent constraints are considered in the structure:

- The represented controlled geometry elements have to be cylindrical surfaces or faces of cylinders.
- The datum feature has to be established by one or two axes and the optional second axis has to be aligned to the first one.
- Where two aligned axes serve as datum features their identifying letters are placed in the same compartment of the geometry tolerance frame.

```
*)
ENTITY total_runout_tol SUBTYPE OF (shape_loc_tol);
   tol_geometry_app       : surf_of_rev_app;
   tolerance_value        : POSITIVE_REAL;
   arrow_position         : reference_term_point;
   arrow_direction        : direction;      --   see   /1/,
                            4.5.3.7
   datum_reference        : axis_datum;
   co_datum_ref           : OPTIONAL axis_datum;
WHERE
   (* a *)   ( (typeof (arrow_position) =
   point_on_geometry) AND (embedded (tol_geometry_app,
   arrow_position) ) AND (is_perpendicular_to
   (tol_geometry_app, arrow_position) = arrow_direction)
   ) OR ( (typeof (arrow_position) =
   point_on_dimension_graph) AND ( ( (typeof
   (arrow_position.dimension_graph) =
   side_projected_feature_dim) AND (is_parallel
   (arrow_direction,
   arrow_position.dimension_graph.next_dir) ) ) OR (
   (typeof (arrow_position.dimension_graph) =
   represented_circle_dimension) ) AND (embedded
   (tol_geometry_app, arrow_position.dimension_graph.
   geometry_appearance) ) AND (is_parallel
   (arrow_direction,
   arrow_position.dimension_graph.dim_line_dir) ) ) );
END_ENTITY;
(*
```

ATTRIBUTE DEFINITIONS:

tol_geometry_app	:	**tol_geometry_app** references a representation of a cylindrical surface or face of a cylinder that has to be controlled.
tolerance_value	:	The value determines the extent of the tolerance zone.

arrow_position : **arrow_position** denotes the terminating point of the arrow of the leader at a represented geometry element referenced by the attribute **tol_geometry_app**.

arrow_direction : The direction of the arrow of the leader.

datum_reference : **datum_reference** references the representations of a datum feature. The datum feature has to be an axis, the description of which is contained in the entity type AXIS_DATUM.

co_datum_ref : Together with the represented axis referred to by **datum_reference** the represented axis optionally referenced by **co_datum_ref** may establish a datum feature. Both axes have to be aligned.

PROPOSITIONS:

a. Where the arrow of the leader is placed at the represented controlled geometry, the arrow is directed perpendicular to it. Where the arrow is placed at a dimension graph dimensioning the diameter of the controlled geometry, the arrow is aligned to the dimension line.

6.3.26. AXIS DATUM

AXIS_DATUM is the structure of the description of a representation of a datum feature. The represented feature has to be either an up or a side projection of an axis of a surface of revolution described in one of the two subtypes SIDE_AXIS_DATUM and UP_AXIS_DATUM.

There are two possibilities to represent the link between the datum feature representation and the geometry tolerance frame:

The first one is to place a letter identifying the datum feature (the so-called datum reference letter) in a compartment of the geometry tolerance frame as well as in the datum feature symbol and optionally in several datum target symbols. It depends on the importance - primary, secondary or tertiary - of the datum, where the letter is placed in the geometry tolerance frame. The datum reference letter of a primary datum is placed in the third compartment, the letter of the secondary is placed in the fourth compartment and the letter of the tertiary datum is placed in the fifth compartment of the geometry tolerance frame.

The second possibility is to link the geometry tolerance frame with the representation of the datum feature by several connected lines ending with a triangle at either the datum feature or a dimension graph dimensioning it. In this case only one datum feature may be applied by the shape and location tolerance and no material condition as well as no datum targets may be specified.

The following inherent constraints are considered in the structure:

- The geometry tolerance frame may be linked with the represented datum feature either by datum reference letters or several connected lines.
- Three points may be specified at the represented datum feature as datum targets.
- Where three points are specified as datum targets at a side projection of a surface of revolution, the points have to be placed on an imaginary line that is perpendicular to the represented axis of the surface of revolution.
- Where three points are specified as datum targets at an up projection of a surface of revolution, the distance between each point has to be the same.

```
*)
ENTITY  axis_datum;
   axis_representation        : surf_of_rev_app;
   rep_of_ref                 : tol_datum_linkage;
   target_identification      : OPTIONAL  LIST  [3:3]  OF
                                target_point;
WHERE
   (* a *)   (target_identification = NULL) OR (
   (target_identification <> NULL) AND (typeof
   (rep_of_ref) = indirect_link);
   (* b *)   ( (typeof (rep_of_ref.pos_of_triangle) =
   point_on_geometry) AND (embedded
   (rep_of_ref.pos_of_triangle,  axis_representation)  )  )
   OR ( ( (typeof (rep_of_ref.pos_of_triangle) =
   point_on_dimension_graph) AND (typeof
   (rep_of_ref.pos_of_triangle.dimension_graph) =
   side_projected_feature_dim) AND (is_parallel
   (rep_of_ref.pos_of_triangle.dimension_graph.next_dir,
   rep_of_ref.dir_of_triangle) ) ) OR ( (typeof
   (rep_of_ref.pos_of_triangle.dimension_graph) =
```

```
    circular_shape_dimension)  AND  (embedded
    (rep_of_ref.pos_of_triangle.dimension_graph.geometry_a
    ppearance,  axis_representation) )  AND  (is_parallel
    (rep_of_ref.pos_of_triangle.dimension_graph.dim_line_d
    ir,  rep_of_ref.dir_of_triangle) ) ) );
END_ENTITY;
(*
```

ATTRIBUTE DEFINITIONS:

axis_representation	:	The attribute **axis_representation** references the description of a representation of a surface of revolution the axis of which serves as a datum feature.
rep_of_ref	:	The attribute **rep_of_ref** references the entity type TOL_DATUM_LINKAGE the subtypes of which describe the linkage of the geometry tolerance frame with the datum feature by either a datum reference letter or several connected lines.
target_identification	:	Exactly three points may be referenced as target points. They have to be placed on the representation of the surface of revolution to which the datum axis belongs.

PROPOSITIONS:

a. Where target points are specified, the geometry tolerance frame has to be linked with the representation of the datum feature by a datum reference letter.

b. The triangle is either placed at the represenation of the datum feature or at a dimension graph dimensioning the diameter of the feature and the direction of the triangle has to be parallel to the dimension line.

6.3.27. PLANE DATUM

The structure PLANE_DATUM describes a representation of a datum feature. The represented feature has to be a side projection of a plane.

There are two possibilities to represent the link between the datum feature representation and the geometry tolerance frame:

The first one is to place a datum reference letter in a compartment of the geometry tolerance frame as well as in either the datum feature symbol or in several datum target symbols. It depends on the importance - primary, secondary or tertiary - of the datum, where the letter is placed in the geometry tolerance frame. The datum reference letter of a primary datum is placed in the third compartment, the letter of the secondary is placed in the fourth compartment and the letter of the tertiary datum is placed in the fifth compartment of the geometry tolerance frame.

The second possibility is to link the geometry tolerance frame with the representation of the datum feature by several connected lines ending with a triangle at either the datum feature or a dimension graph dimensioning it. In this case only one datum feature may be applied by the shape and location tolerance and no material condition as well as no datum targets may be specified.

The following inherent constraints are considered in the structure:

- The geometry tolerance frame may be linked with the represented datum feature either by datum reference letters or several connected lines.
- At least three points or areas or one or two lines may be specified at the represented datum feature as datum targets.

```
*)
ENTITY  plane_datum;
   plane_representation   : straight_geometry_app;
   rep_of_ref             : tol_datum_linkage;
   target_identification  : OPTIONAL  LIST  [1:3]  OF
                            target_datum;
WHERE
   (*  a  *)    perpendicular  (rep_of_ref.dir_of_triangle)  =
   direction_fun   (plane_representation);
   (*  b  *)    (  (typeof  (rep_of_ref.pos_of_triangle)  =
   point_on_geometry)  AND  (embedded
   (rep_of_ref.pos_of_triangle,  plane_representation)  )
   OR  (  (typeof  (rep_of_ref.pos_of_triangle)  =
   point_on_dimension_graph)  AND  (typeof
   (rep_of_ref.pos_of_triangle.dimension_graph)  =
   represented_shape_dimension)  AND  (is_paralell
```

```
   (rep_of_ref.pos_of_triangle.dimension_graph.next_dir,
   rep_of_ref.dir_of_triangle) ) );
   (* c *)  (target_identification = NULL) OR (
   (target_identification <> NULL) AND (typeof
   (target_identification[i]) = typeof
   (target_identification[i+1]) ) AND ( ( (typeof
   (target_identification[i]) = target_line) AND (sizeof
   (target_identification) <= 2) ) OR (typeof
   (target_identification[i]) <> target_line) ) AND
   (typeof (rep_of_ref) = indirect_link) );
END_ENTITY;
(*
```

ATTRIBUTE DEFINITIONS:

plane_representation : **plane_representation** references the description of a side projection of a plane serving as a datum feature.

rep_of_ref : The attribute **rep_of_ref** references the entity type TOL_DATUM_LINKAGE the subtypes of which describe the linkage of the geometry tolerance frame with the datum feature by either a datum reference letter or several connected lines.

target_identification : Either one to three points or one to three areas or one or two lines may be referenced as target datums. They have to be placed on a representation of the datum feature.

PROPOSITIONS:

a. The direction of the triangle placed at the terminating point of either the datum feature symbol or of the connected lines indicating the datum feature has to be perpendicular to the side projected plane.

b. The triangle is placed at either the represenation of the datum feature or at a dimension graph dimensioning the feature and the direction of the triangle has to be parallel to the dimension line.

c. Where datum targets are specified, the geometry tolerance frame has to be linked with the representation of the datum feature by a datum reference letter and at least two lines may be specified as datum targets.

6.3.28. AXIS2 OR PLANE2 DATUM

The structure AXIS2_OR_PLANE2_DATUM is referenced where representations of either one or two axes or planes are indicated as datum features.

```
*)
ENTITY  axis2_or_plane2_datum  SUPERTYPE  OF  (axis2_datum
                                XOR  plane2_datum);
END_ENTITY;
(*
```

6.3.29. AXIS1 OR PLANE2 DATUM

The structure AXIS1_OR_PLANE2_DATUM is referenced where representations of either one axis or at least two planes are indicated as datum features.

```
*)
ENTITY  axis1_or_plane2_datum  SUPERTYPE  OF  (axis1_datum
                                XOR  plane2_datum);
END_ENTITY;
(*
```

6.3.30. AXIS2 OR PLANE1 DATUM

The structure AXIS2_OR_PLANE1_DATUM is referenced where representations of either at least two axes or one plane are indicated as datum features.

```
*)
ENTITY axis2_or_plane1_datum SUPERTYPE OF (axis2_datum
                         XOR plane1_datum);
END_ENTITY;
(*
```

6.3.31. AXIS1 DATUM

AXIS1_DATUM references the description of a represented surface of revolution.

```
*)
ENTITY axis1_datum SUBTYPE OF (axis1_or_plane2_datum);
   axis_reference          : axis_datum;
END_ENTITY;
(*
```

ATTRIBUTE DEFINITIONS:

axis_reference : **axis_reference** is the attribute referencing the description of a represented surface of revolution, the axis of which serves as a datum feature.

6.3.32. AXIS2 DATUM

AXIS2_DATUM is the entity type referring to one or two axes that serve as a primary or secondary datum feature.

```
*)
ENTITY axis2_datum SUBTYPE OF (axis2_or_plane1_datum AND
                         axis2_or_plane2_datum);
   prim_sec_axis_ref     : LIST [1:2] OF UNIQUE
                           axis_datum;
```

```
WHERE
   (* a *)   (prim_sec_axis_ref[2] = NULL) XOR (
   (prim_sec_axis_ref[2] <> NULL) AND (typeof
   (prim_sec_axis_ref[1].rep_of_ref) = indirect_link) AND
   (typeof (prim_sec_axis_ref[2].rep_of_ref) =
   indirect_link) );
END_ENTITY;
(*
```

ATTRIBUTE DEFINITIONS:

prim_sec_axis_ref : This attribute references descriptions of one or two datum axes. **prim_sec_axis_ref**[1] is the description of the primary datum axis and **prim_sec_axis_ref**[2] is the description of the secondary datum axis.

PROPOSITIONS:

a. Where two axes are referenced, the link between the geometry tolerance frame and the datum feature has to be established by datum reference letters.

6.3.33. PLANE1 DATUM

PLANE1_DATUM references the description of a side projected plane serving as a datum feature.

```
*)
ENTITY plane1_datum SUBTYPE OF (axis2_or_plane1_datum);
   plane_reference       : plane_datum;
END_ENTITY;
(*
```

ATTRIBUTE DEFINITIONS:

plane_reference : **plane_reference** is the attribute referencing the description of a side projected plane which serves as a datum feature.

6.3.34. PLANE2 DATUM

PLANE2_DATUM is the entity type referring to one or two planes that serve as a primary or secondary datum feature.

```
*)
ENTITY plane2_datum SUBTYPE OF (axis1_or_plane2_datum
                              AND axis2_or_plane2_datum);
   prim_sec_planes_ref    : LIST [1:2] OF UNIQUE
                              plane_datum;
WHERE
   (* a *)    (prim_sec_planes_ref[2] = NULL) OR (
   (prim_sec_planes_ref[2] <> NULL) AND (typeof
   (prim_sec_planes_ref[1].rep_of_ref) = indirect_link)
   AND (typeof (prim_sec_planes_ref[2].rep_of_ref) =
   indirect_link) );
END_ENTITY;
(*
```

ATTRIBUTE DEFINITIONS:

prim_sec_planes_ref : This attribute references descriptions of one or two datum planes. **prim_sec_planes_ref**[1] is the description of the primary datum plane and **prim_sec_planes_ref**[2] is the description of the secondary datum plane.

PROPOSITIONS:

a. Where two planes are referenced, the link between the geometry tolerance frame and the datum feature has to be established by datum reference letters.

6.3.35. POSITION DATUM

The structure POSITION_DATUM is referenced by the descriptions of representations of position tolerances where representations of either at least three planes or one axis and one optional plane are indicated as datum features.

```
*)
ENTITY  position_datum  SUPERTYPE  OF  (axis1_plane1_datum
                                         XOR  plane3_datum);
END_ENTITY;
(*
```

6.3.2.36. AXIS1 PLANE1 DATUM

AXIS1_PLANE1_DATUM is the subtype of POSITION_DATUM that describes the combination of one axis and an optional plane referred to as datum features by a position tolerance.

```
*)
ENTITY  axis1_plane1_datum  SUBTYPE  OF  (position_datum);
   axis_reference         : axis_datum;
   rank_of_axis           : axis_datum_valence;
   plane_reference        : OPTIONAL  plane_datum;
WHERE
   (* a *)   ( (plane_reference = NULL) AND (rank_of_axis
   = .primary.) ) XOR ( (plane_reference <> NULL) AND
   (typeof  (axis_reference.rep_of_ref)  =  indirect_link)
```

```
   AND  (typeof  (plane_reference.rep_of_ref)  =
   indirect_link)  );
END_ENTITY;
(*
```

ATTRIBUTE DEFINITIONS:

axis_reference	:	This attribute references the description of one datum axis.
rank_of_axis	:	The defined type AXIS_DATUM_VALENCE determines the importance of the datum axis referred to by **axis_reference**. Where the axis is determined as primary datum, the optional datum plane referred to by **plane_reference** may only be a secondary datum and vice versa.
plane_reference	:	This attribute references the description of one optional datum plane. If the axis is a primary datum the plane is a secondary datum and vice versa.

PROPOSITIONS:

a. Where an axis datum as well as a plane datum are referenced, the link between the geometry tolerance frame and the datum features has to be established by datum reference letters. Only in this case the axis datum may be a secondary datum.

6.3.37. PLANE3 DATUM

PLANE3_DATUM is the subtype of POSITION_DATUM that describes the combination of one to three planes referred to as datum features by a position tolerance.

```
*)
ENTITY plane3_datum  SUBTYPE  OF  (position_datum);
   planes_ref             : LIST  [1:3]  OF  UNIQUE
                               plane_datum;
```

```
WHERE
   (* a *)   (sizeof (planes_ref) = 1) XOR ( (sizeof
   (planes_ref) > 1) AND (typeof
   (planes_ref.rep_of_ref[i])  =  indirect_link)  );
END_ENTITY;
(*
```

ATTRIBUTE DEFINITIONS:

planes_ref : This attribute references the description of one to three datum planes. **planes_ref**[1] refers to the primary datum, **planes_ref**[2] refers to the secondary datum and **planes_ref**[3] refers to the primary datum.

PROPOSITIONS:

a. Where more than one plane datum is referenced, the link between the geometry tolerance frame and the datum features has to be established by datum reference letters.

6.3.38. TARGET DATUM

The structure TARGET_DATUM describes the representation of points, lines or areas identifying datum targets that are placed at represented datum features.
The following inherent constraints are considered in the structure:

- The datum target symbols are placed horizontally with regard to the orientation of the drawing sheet.
- The symbol consists of a circle, a leader and an horizontal line dividing the circle in an upper and lower part (see figure 6.8).
- The datum reference letter and a succeeding number are placed in the lower part of the circle.
- The line connecting the symbol with the datum target terminates at the datum target with an arrow and is radial to the circle of the symbol.

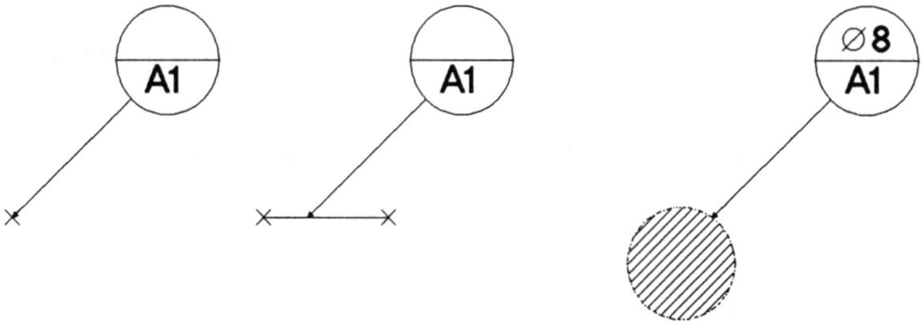

Fig. 6.8: Datum target symbols with the representation of datum targets

```
*)
ENTITY target_datum SUPERTYPE OF (target_point XOR
                        target_area XOR target_line);
   pos_of_symbol            : view_position;
END_ENTITY;
(*
```

ATTRIBUTE DEFINITIONS:

pos_of_symbol : This attribute determines the position of the center of the circle of the datum target symbol.

6.3.39. TARGET POINT

TARGET_POINT being a subtype of TARGET_DATUM describes the representation of a target point.
The following inherent constraints are considered in the structure:

- The target point is represented by an "X".

```
*)
ENTITY target_point SUBTYPE OF (target_datum);
   location                 : view_position;
END_ENTITY;
(*
```

ATTRIBUTE DEFINITIONS:

location : **location** describes the position of the target point at the represented datum feature. The line connecting the symbol with the datum target terminates at this position with an arrow.

6.3.40. TARGET AREA

The subtype TARGET_AREA of the supertype TARGET_DATUM specifies the representation of a target area at the datum feature.

The following inherent constraints are considered in the structure:

- The target area is represented by either a square or a circle bounded by a chain thin line and filled with hatching.
- A note specifying the dimensions of the area is added to the datum target symbol.
- Where the target area is a circle, the note consists of a number and a preceding "ø" dimensioning the diameter of the circle. The note is placed in the upper part of the circle of the datum target symbol.
- Where the target area is a square, the note consists of two equal numbers separated by an "x" dimensioning the extent of the square. The note is placed outside the circle of the datum target symbol, but with a leader pointing in the upper part of the circle and ending with a small filled circle.

```
*)
ENTITY target_area SUBTYPE OF (target_datum);
   location                : view_position;
   circular_zone           : LOGICAL;
   char_length             : POSITIVE_REAL;
   note_position           : OPTIONAL view_position;
WHERE
   (* a *)   ( (circular_zone = .T.) AND (note_position =
   NULL) ) OR (circular_zone = .F.);
END_ENTITY;
(*
```

ATTRIBUTE DEFINITIONS:

location	:	**location** describes the position of the center or middle of the target area at the datum feature. The line connecting the symbol with the datum target points at this position and terminates at the border of the area with an arrow.
circular_zone	:	Where the flag **circular_zone** is true the target area is a circle. A false flag denotes a square as target area.
char_length	:	Either the diameter of the circular target area or the length and width of the square.
note_position	:	The position of the number dimensioning the extent of the target area. Where the attribute value is omitted, the note is placed in the upper part of the circle of the datum target symbol.

PROPOSITIONS:

a. Where the target area is a circle, the note is placed in the upper part of the datum target symbol. Where the target area is a square, the note is placed outside the datum target symbol and a leader points from the note to the datum target symbol.

6.3.41. TARGET LINE

TARGET_LINE is the subtype of TARGET_DATUM that specifies the representation of a target line at the datum feature.

The following inherent constraints are considered in the structure:

- The target area is represented by a line connecting two points marked with an "X".

```
*)
ENTITY  target_line  SUBTYPE  OF  (target_datum);
   start_point          : view_position;
   end_point            : view_position;
   arrow_position       : POSITIVE_REAL;
```

```
WHERE
   (* a *)   start_point <> end_point;
END_ENTITY;
(*
```

ATTRIBUTE DEFINITIONS:

start_point	:	**start_point** describes the starting point of the target line marked with an "X".
end_point	:	The terminating point of the target line.
arrow_position	:	This attribute determines the position of the arrow of the line connecting the datum target symbol with the target line. The position is given by a parameter of the line starting at **start_point** and ending at **end_point**.

PROPOSITIONS:

a. The start and the end point may not be identical.

6.3.42. REF TO GEOMETRY

REF_TO GEOMETRY is the structure of the description of the representation of the leader between the compound of geometry tolerance frames and the represented controlled geometry. Two possibilities for the appearance of the leader are described by the subtypes of REF_TO_GEOMETRY: The first one describes the lines connecting the compound of geometry tolerance frames with the representation of the geometry (see figure 6.9). The second possibility is to place the arrow(s) together with an index letter at the geometry appearances and an identical index at the line starting at the compound (see figure 6.10).

ATTRIBUTE DEFINITIONS:

start_point : **start_point** describes the starting point of the target line marked with an "X".

end_point : The terminating point of the target line.

arrow_position : This attribute determines the position of the arrow of the line connecting the datum target symbol with the target line. The position is given by a parameter of the line starting at **start_point** and ending at **end_point**.

PROPOSITIONS:

a. The start and the end point may not be identical.

6.3.2.39. REF TO GEOMETRY

REF_TO GEOMETRY is the structure of the description of the representation of the leader between the compound of geometry tolerance frames and the represented controlled geometry. Two possibilities for the appearance of the leader are described by the subtypes of REF_TO_GEOMETRY: The first one describes the lines connecting the compound of geometry tolerance frames with the representation of the geometry (see figure 6.9). The second possibility is to place the arrow(s) together with an index letter at the geometry appearances and an identical index at the line starting at the compound (see figure 6.10).

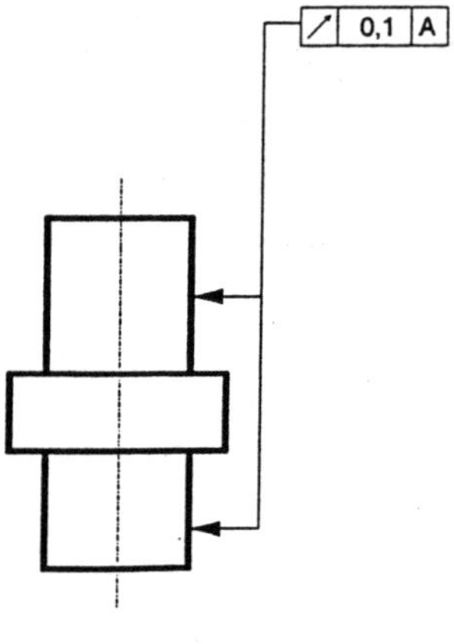

Fig. 6.9: Leader with lines

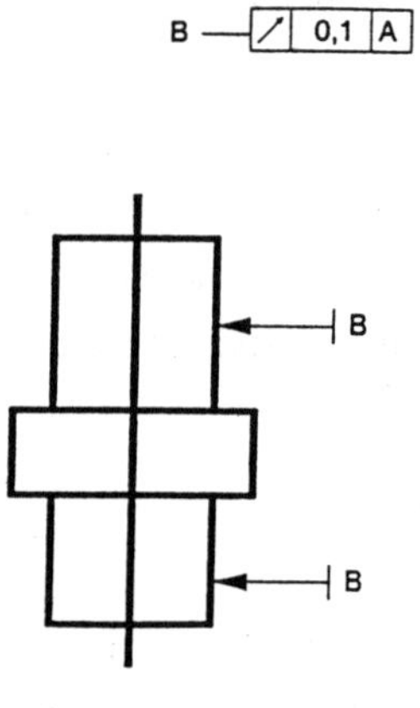

Fig. 6.10: Leader with index letters

```
*)
ENTITY  reference_line  SUBTYPE  OF  (ref_to_geometry);
   connection_polyline     : SET  [1:#]  OF  view_position;
END_ENTITY;
(*
```

ATTRIBUTE DEFINITIONS:

connection_polyline : This attribute contains the descriptions of the lines connecting the compound of geometry tolerance frames with its arrows. The listed positions represent ATTRIBUTE DEFINITIONS:

connection_polyline : This attribute contains the descriptions of the lines connecting the compound of geometry tolerance frames with its arrows. The listed positions represent the bends of the polyline.

6.3.44. REFERENCE SIGN

The subtype REFERENCE_SIGN describes the linkage of the compound of geometry tolerance frames with the representation of the geometry by index letters.
The following inherent constraints are considered in the structure:

- The index letter is placed at the arrow(s) at the geometry appearances and an identical index letter is attached to the line starting at the compound.

```
*)
ENTITY  reference_sign  SUBTYPE  OF  (ref_to_geometry);
   id_sign               : CHARACTER;
   length_of_arrow       : POSITIVE_REAL;
END_ENTITY;
(*
```

ATTRIBUTE DEFINITIONS:

id_sign : The index letter of the leader.

length_of_arrow : The length of the line that terminates with an arrow at the representation of the controlled geometry or at a dimension graph.

6.3.45. TOL DATUM LINKAGE

The structure TOL_DATUM_LINKAGE is the supertype of INDIRECT_LINK describing the linkage of a geometry tolerance frame with the represented datum feature by datum reference letters and DIRECT_LINK describing the linkage by several lines ending with a triangle at the represented datum feature or at a dimension graph dimensioning the feature (see figures 6.11 and 6.12).

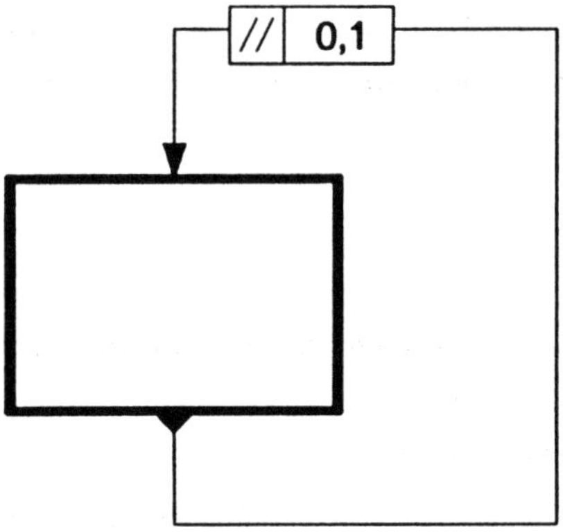

Fig. 6.11: Direct link

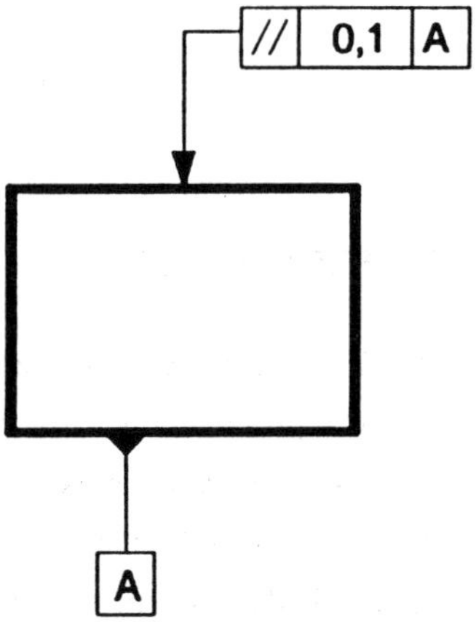

Fig. 6.12: Indirect link with datum feature symbol

```
*)
ENTITY tol_datum_linkage SUPERTYPE OF (indirect_link XOR
                              direct_link);
   pos_of_triangle        : reference_term_point;
   dir_of_triangle        : direction;    -- see /1/,
                              4.5.3.7
END_ENTITY;
(*
```

ATTRIBUTE DEFINITIONS:

pos_of_triangle	:	The position of the triangle at either the representation of the datum feature or a dimension graph dimensioning the datum feature.
dir_of_triangle	:	The direction of the triangle.

6.3.46. INDIRECT LINK

INDIRECT_LINK describes the linkage of a geometry tolerance frame with the represented datum feature by datum reference letters.
The following inherent constraints are considered in the structure:

- Where a maximum material condition is applied, an "M" placed in a circle succeeds the datum reference letter.
- The line of the datum feature symbol has the same direction as the triangle.

```
*)
ENTITY indirect_link SUBTYPE OF (tol_datum_linkage);
   id_sign              : CHARACTER;
   material_condition   : tol_mlsn;    -- see /1/,
                          4.10.1.2.9
   length_of_symbol     : POSITIVE_REAL;
END_ENTITY;
(*
```

ATTRIBUTE DEFINITIONS:

id_sign	:	The datum reference letter.
material_condition	:	This attribute references a defined type that specifies the material conditions applied by the datum feature. The following values are enumerated: MAXMC (maximum material condition), LEASTMC (least material condition), REGARDLESS (regardless of feature size) and NONE (not applicable).

length_of_symbol : The length of the line of the datum feature symbol.

6.3.47. DIRECT LINK

DIRECT_LINK describes the linkage of a geometry tolerance frame with the represented datum feature by several lines.

The following inherent constraints are considered in the structure:

- The line terminating at the datum feature or dimension graph has the same direction as the triangle.

```
*)
ENTITY direct_link SUBTYPE OF (tol_datum_linkage);
   linkage_polyline       : LIST [2:#] OF UNIQUE
                            view_position;
END_ENTITY;
(*
```

ATTRIBUTE DEFINITIONS:

linkage_polyline : The definition of the polyline linking the geometry tolerance frame with the represented datum feature or dimension graph.

```
*)
END_SCHEMA;          -- end TOLERANCE_REPRESENTATION_SCHEMA
(*
```

7. Shape Attributes Representation

```
*)
SCHEMA  shape_attributes_representation_schema;
   EXPORT  EVERYTHING;
   ASSUME  (drafting_resources_schema,
   dimensioning_schema);
(*
```

7.1. Introduction

In this schema the descriptions of representations of product information concerning the condition of surfaces and edges as well as general information associated with the geometry appearances by leaders are contained. The described symbols are attached to the representations of the surfaces and edges.

7.2. Shape Attributes Representation TYPE Definitions

7.2.1. ROUGHNESS TYPE

The defined type ROUGHNESS_TYPE describes methods for the measuring of the roughness of a surface that differs from the default method "arithmetical mean deviation" or "average peak-to-valley height" (R_a). Enumerated are: R_t (total peak-to-valley height), R_p (smoothness).

```
*)
TYPE  roughness_type  =  ENUMERATION  OF  (rt,  rp);
END_TYPE;
(*
```

7.2.2. GROOVES DIRECTION

The defined type GROOVES_DIRECTION - applied by the structure describing the surface finish symbol - specifies the direction of the grooves on a surface resulting from a manufacturing process. The direction of the grooves partially is given relative to the projection plane of the view in which the surface finish symbol is represented. The following possibilities are enumerated:
PAR (parallel to the projection plane of the view where the surface finish symbol is applied), PERP (perpendicular to the projection plane), CROSS (crossed and oblique to the projection plane), VAR (various directions), CONCENTR (concentric to the center of the specified surface) and RAD (radial to the center of the specified surface).

```
*)
TYPE grooves_direction = ENUMERATION OF (par, perp,
                          cross, var, concentr, rad);
END_TYPE;
(*
```

7.2.3. HARDNESS TYPE

HARDNESS_TYPE specifies the method of hardness test. The following methods are enumerated:
HV (Vickers), HB (Brinell) and HRC (Rockwell).

```
*)
TYPE hardness_type = ENUMERATION OF (hv, hb, hrc);
END_TYPE;
(*
```

7.2.4. CORNER ORIENTATION

The defined type CORNER_ORIENTATION describes the orientation of the specified corner with regard to the orientation of the corner symbol.

```
*)
TYPE  corner_orientation  =  ENUMERATION  OF  (horizontal,
                                   vertical,  neutral);
END_TYPE;
(*
```

7.2.5. CORNER GENERALIZATION

CORNER_GENERALIZATION describes the kind of corners the corner symbol is applied to. It may be either internal or external or both kinds of corners.

```
*)
TYPE  corner_generalization  =  ENUMERATION  OF  (internal,
                                   external,  both);
END_TYPE;
(*
```

7.3. Shape Attributes Representation ENTITY Definitions

7.3.1. GENERAL SURF FINISH

GENERAL_SURF_FINISH is the structure for the description of the appearance and placement of all surface finish symbols on a drawing sheet.
A represented surface finish symbol may contain information about the roughness of the surface, the hardness, the grooves, the surface coat and where a further cutting process is necessary.
In a technical drawing a general surface finish symbol that is valid for most of the represented surfaces is placed next to the information field. All applied surface finish symbols - or a substitute for all of them - differing from the general symbol are placed behind it within brackets. Additional to that the represented surfaces which differ from the description of the general surface finish symbol, are marked with the symbols that are valid for them (see figures 7.2 and 7.3). In the designed data structure there is no associativity preserved between the

general surface symbol and all the represented surfaces it is valid for.
The relations of the entity types comprised within this structure are shown in figure 7.1.

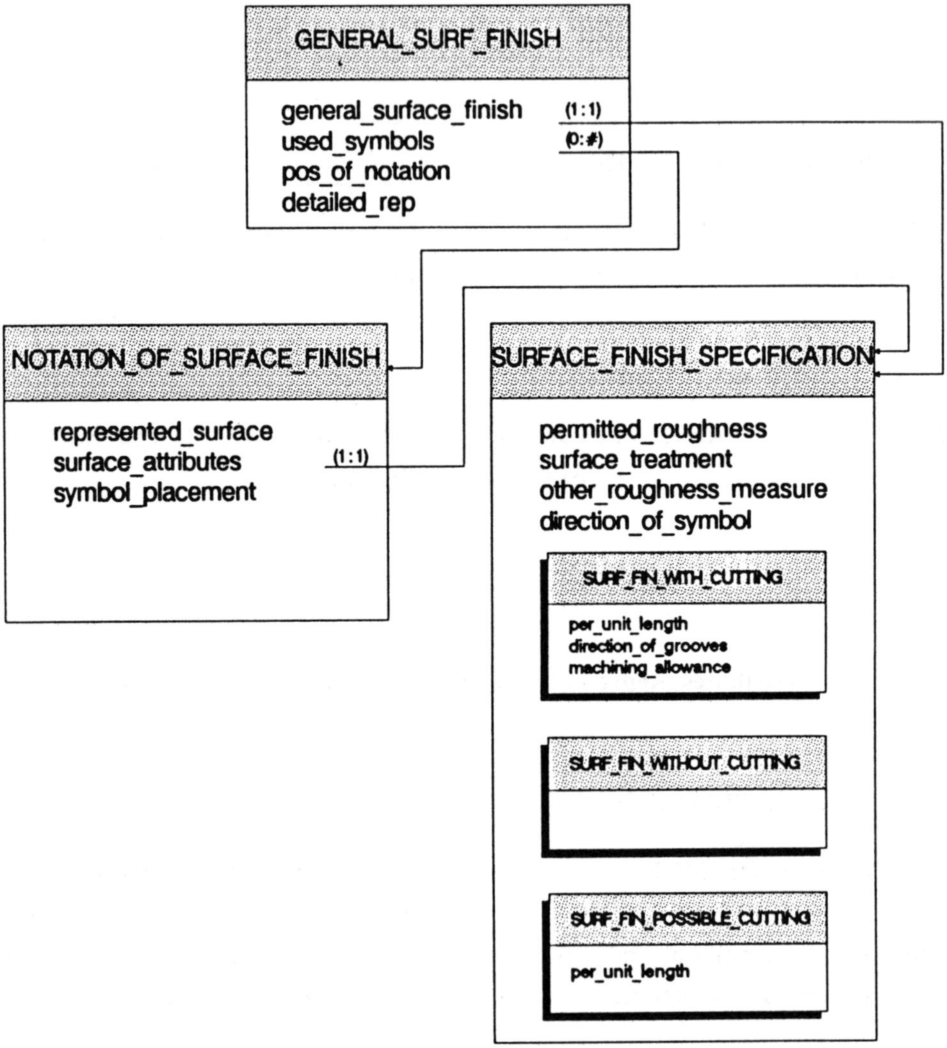

Fig. 7.1: The structure for the description of surface finish symbol representations

Concerning surface finish symbols the following statement has to be considered and is integrated in the structure:

- The general surface symbol and the symbols being placed behind it within brackets are orientated horizontally with regard to orientation of the drawing sheet.

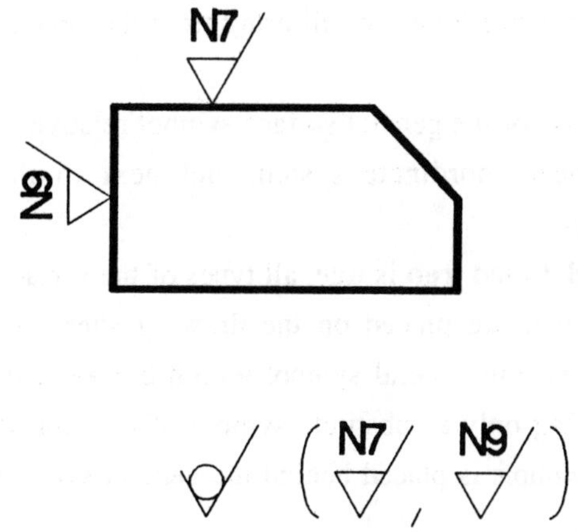

Fig. 7.2: Arrangement of surface finish symbols

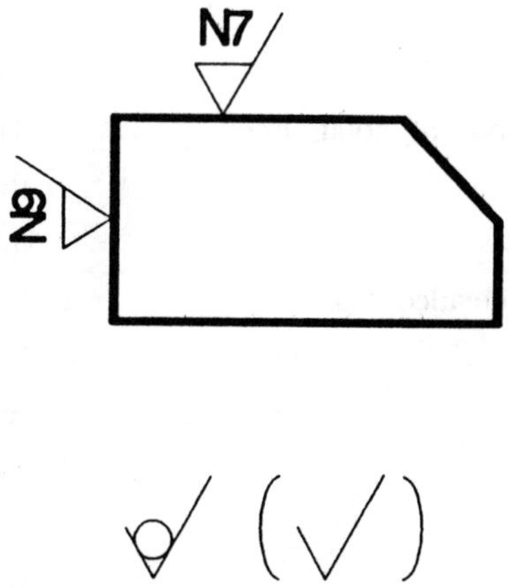

Fig. 7.3: Arrangement of surface finish symbols with a substitute behind the general symbol

```
*)
ENTITY  general_surf_finish;
   general_surface_finish: surface_finish_specification;
   used_symbols           : OPTIONAL  LIST  [1:#]  OF
                            notation_of_surface_finish;
   pos_of_notation        : sheet_position;
   detailed_rep           : LOGICAL;
END_ENTITY;
(*
```

ATTRIBUTE DEFINITIONS:

general_surface_finish : **general_surface_finish** references the description of the surface finish symbol that is valid for most of the represented

		surfaces on a drawing sheet.
used_symbols	:	The description of all different appearances and their associativities of the surface finish symbols of a drawing sheet except the general surface finish symbol. Where the list is omitted, no surface finish symbol differing from the general symbol exists.
pos_of_notation	:	This is the position of the general surface symbol relative to the drawing sheet coordinate system and next to the information field.
detailed_rep	:	Where the flag **detailed_rep** is true, all types of the surface finish symbols that are placed on the drawing sheet are represented behind the general symbol within brackets. In case of a false flag only a substitute symbol of all applied surface finish symbols is placed behind the general symbol within brackets.

7.3.2. NOTATION OF SURFACE FINISH

The entity type NOTATION_OF_SURFACE_FINISH describes the associativity of a surface finish symbol to at least one represented surface. Even the placement of the symbol at the surface representation(s) is described. Within this structure it is impossible to guarantee that either the surface finish symbols or their leaders point from "outside" to the surface representations, because up to now there is no possibility to decide unequivocally where the material lies in a geometry representation.

Concerning the associativity and placement of the surface finish symbols the following statements have to be considered:

- A surface finish symbol may be placed either at a curve that is the representation of the surface or at a leader pointing at the surface representation or on an extension line of a dimension graph that is aligned with the surface representation.
- A surface finish symbol placed at the represented surface is perpendicular to the surface representation in their intersecting points.
- A surface finish symbol placed at a leader is oriented horizontally with regard to the drawing sheet and the leader starts with a horizontal line at the symbol and terminates perpendicular to the surface representation with an arrow.
- A surface finish symbol placed on an extension line of a dimension line is orientated perpendicular to the extension line.

```
*)
ENTITY  notation_of_surface_finish;
   represented_surface   : LIST  [1:#]  OF  surface_app;
   surface_attributes    : surface_finish_specification;
   symbol_placement      : LIST  [1:#]  OF  symbol_position;
WHERE
   (* a *)   coordinated_lists  (represented_surface,
   symbol_placement);
   (* b *)   (sizeof  (represented_surface) = 1)  OR  (
   (sizeof  (represented_surface)  >  1)  AND  (typeof
   (symbol_placement[i])  =  symbol_at_leader)  );
   (* c *)   (  (typeof  (symbol_placement)  =
   symbol_at_leader)  AND  (embedded
   (symbol_placement[i].pos_at_reference,
   represented_surface[i])  )  )  OR  (  (typeof
   (symbol_placement)  =  point_on_dimension_graph)  AND  (  (
   (typeof  (symbol_placement.dimension_graph)  =
   represented_shape_dimension)  AND  (embedded
   (symbol_placement.dimension_graph.determinator,
   represented_surface)  AND  (is_parallel
   (surface_attributes.direction_of_symbol,
   symbol_placement.dimension_graph.next_dir)  )  )  OR  (
   (typeof  (symbol_placement.dimension_graph)  =
   circular_shape_dimension)  AND  (embedded
   (symbol_placement.dimension_graph.geometry_appearance,
   represented_surface)  )  AND  (is_parallel
   (surface_attributes.direction_of_symbol,
   symbol_placement.dimension_graph.dim_line_dir)  )  )  )  )
   OR  (  (typeof  (symbol_placement)  =  point_on_geometry)
   AND  (embedded  (symbol_placement.position,
   represented_surface)  )  AND
   (surface_attributes.direction_of_symbol  =
   is_perpendicular_to  (represented_surface.
   appearance_of_geometry,  symbol_placement.position)  ));
```

```
   (* d *)    typeof  (symbol_placement.dimension_graph)  <>
   thread_dimensioning;
END_ENTITY;
(*
```

ATTRIBUTE DEFINITIONS:

represented_surface : All the listed representations of the surfaces are pointed at by the surface finish symbol specified by the attribute **surface_attributes**.

surface_attributes : The specification of the surface finish symbol that points to the referenced represented surfaces.

symbol_placement : The placement of the symbol at either a surface representation or on an extension line of a dimension graph or at leader(s), where more than one surface representation is referenced by the attribute **represented_surface**. It has to be mentioned that the entries of both lists determined by the attributes **represented_surface** and **symbol_placement** have to be in a one to one correspondence. That means: At every surface representation a position for the linkage with a surface finish symbol has to be provided.

PROPOSITIONS:

a. The entries of both the attributes of LIST-type - namely **represented_surface** and **symbol_placement** - must be in a one to one correspondence.
b. Where the number of entries in the list established by the attribute **represented_surface** is greater than one, the entries of the list **symbol_placement** have to be of entity type SYMBOL_AT_LEADER.
c. The surface finish symbol may either be placed i) at a leader that is connected with the surface representation or ii) at a dimension graph being connected with the specified surface representation and the direction of the dimension line and the symbol have to be identical or iii) at the surface representation and the symbol has to be perpendicular to the surface representation in the intersecting point.
d. The surface finish symbol must not be placed at a thread dimension.

7.3.3. SURFACE FINISH SPECIFICATION

SURFACE_FINISH_SPECIFICATION is the structure of the description of the surface properties. The surface properties have an influence on the appearance of the surface finish symbol: The symbols denoting a cutting process, no cutting process and an optional cutting process have to be destinguished (see figure 7.4) and are described in the subtypes of SURFACE_FINISH_SPECIFICATION.

Concerning the surface finish symbol appearance the following statement has to be considered:

- The dimensions of the surface finish symbols depend on the chosen line width.

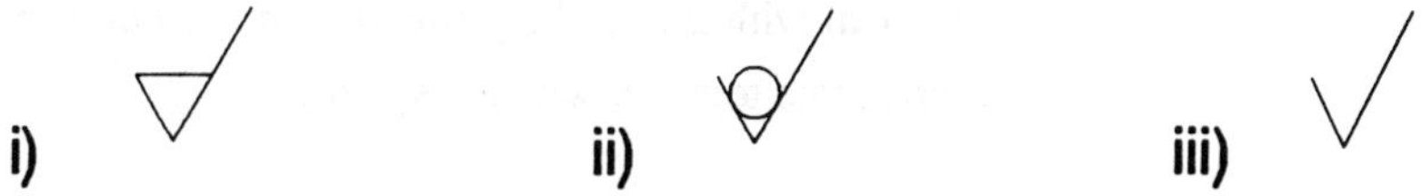

Fig. 7.4: Surface finish symbols for i) a cutting procedure, ii) no cutting procedure, iii) an optional cutting procedure

```
*)
ENTITY  surface_finish_specification  SUPERTYPE  OF
                            (surf_fin_with_cutting  XOR
                            surf_fin_without_cutting  XOR
                            surf_fin_possible_cutting);
   permitted_roughness    : OPTIONAL  surface_quality;
   surface_treatment      : OPTIONAL  STRING;
   other_roughness_measure : OPTIONAL  roughness_type;
   direction_of_symbol    : direction;    -- see /1/,
                                 4.5.3.7
WHERE
   (* a *)   coordinate_space (direction_of_symbol) = 2;
END_ENTITY;
(*
```

ATTRIBUTE DEFINITIONS:

permitted_roughness	:	The specification of the quality of the surface. It may be specified by representing the applied category of the roughness or a value determining the roughness. Both alternatives provide a mandatory upper limit and an optional lower limit.
surface_treatment	:	The optional description of a special treatment of the surface.
other_roughness_measure	:	The method for measuring the roughness is determined by this attribute, where another method as "average peak-to-valley height" is applied.
direction_of_symbol	:	The direction of the represented surface finish symbol identical with the reading direction of the numbers or letters represented together with the symbol.

PROPOSITIONS:

a. The dimensionality of **arrow_direction** has to have the value 2.

7.3.4. SURF FIN WITH CUTTING

SURF_FIN_WITH_CUTTING is the structure for the description of a surface finish symbol, where a cutting process is mandatory.

```
*)
ENTITY  surf_fin_with_cutting  SUBTYPE  OF
                          (surface_finish_specification);
   per_unit_length         : OPTIONAL  POSITIVE_REAL;
   direction_of_grooves    : OPTIONAL  grooves_direction;
   machining_allowance     : OPTIONAL  POSITIVE_REAL;
END_ENTITY;
(*
```

ATTRIBUTE DEFINITIONS:

per_unit_length	:	The specified length within which the roughness value is determined.
direction_of_grooves	:	The direction of the grooves resulting from the cutting process.
machining_allowance	:	The value of the machining allowance.

7.3.5. SURF FIN WITHOUT CUTTING

SURF_FIN_WITHOUT_CUTTING is the structure of the description of a surface finish symbol, where no further cutting process is admissible.

```
*)
ENTITY  surf_fin_without_cutting  SUBTYPE  OF
                              (surface_finish_specification);
END_ENTITY;
(*
```

7.3.6. SURF FIN POSSIBLE CUTTING

The entity type SURF_FIN_POSSIBLE_CUTTING describes a surface finish symbol, where a further cutting process is admissible but not mandatory.

```
*)
ENTITY  surf_fin_possible_cutting  SUBTYPE  OF
                              (surface_finish_specification);
   per_unit_length           : OPTIONAL  POSITIVE_REAL;
END_ENTITY;
(*
```

ATTRIBUTE DEFINITIONS:

per_unit_length : The specified length within which the roughness value is determined.

7.3.7. SURFACE QUALITY

The entity type SURFACE_QUALITY is the supertype of the subtypes ROUGHNESS_CATEGORY and ROUGHNESS_VALUE. Thus it is possible to determine the roughness of the surface by either roughness categories as defined in ISO-Standards (ISO 1302) or by a roughness value.

```
*)
ENTITY surface_quality SUPERTYPE OF (roughness_category
                                XOR roughness_value);
END_ENTITY;
(*
```

7.3.8. ROUGHNESS CATEGORY

ROUGHNESS_CATEGORY is the subtype describing the roughness of a surface by categories.
In the structure the following constraints have to be considered:

- The category number has to be less than or equal to 12 and greater than or equal to 1.
- The number determining the upper limit of the roughness is placed above the number of the lower limit, if a lower limit is specified.
- The number of the category is preceded by an "N".

```
*)
ENTITY roughness_category SUBTYPE OF (surface_quality);
   upper_limit            : CHARACTER;
   lower_limit            : OPTIONAL CHARACTER;
END_ENTITY;
(*
```

ATTRIBUTE DEFINITIONS:

upper_limit : The category of the roughness that must not be exceeded by the surface.

lower_limit : Where **lower_limit** is not omitted, the attribute specifies the roughness category that must not be remained under by the surface.

7.3.9. ROUGHNESS VALUE

ROUGHNESS_VALUE is the subtype describing the value of the roughness of a surface.
In the structure the following constraint has to be considered:

- The value determining the upper limit of the roughness is placed above the number of the lower limit, if a lower limit is specified.

```
*)
ENTITY roughness_value SUBTYPE OF (surface_quality);
   upper_limit              : POSITIVE_REAL;
   lower_limit              : OPTIONAL POSITIVE_REAL;
WHERE
   (* a *)  ( (lower_limit <> NULL) AND (upper_limit >
   lower_limit) ) OR (lower_limit = NULL);
END_ENTITY;
(*
```

ATTRIBUTE DEFINITIONS:

upper_limit : The roughness value, that must not be exceeded by the surface.

lower_limit : Where **lower_limit** is not omitted, the attribute specifies the roughness value that must not be remained under by the surface.

PROPOSITIONS:

a. The upper limit of the roughness has to be greater than the lower limit.

7.3.10. SURFACE TREATMENT

SURFACE_TREATMENT is the structure of the description of either a surface hardness information (subtype SURFACE_HARDENING) or a surface coat (subtype SURFACE_COAT). A representation of surface treatment information is shown in figure 7.5. In the structure the following constraints have to be considered:

- The surface treatment information is placed next to the information field.
- Where not all represented surfaces are subject to the surface treatment specification, the indicated surfaces are marked by a chain thin line being represented as an offset curve of the surface representation. In this case a chain thin line also precedes the surface treatment information.
- The information is represented in sequential lines that are oriented horizontally with regard to the drawing format.

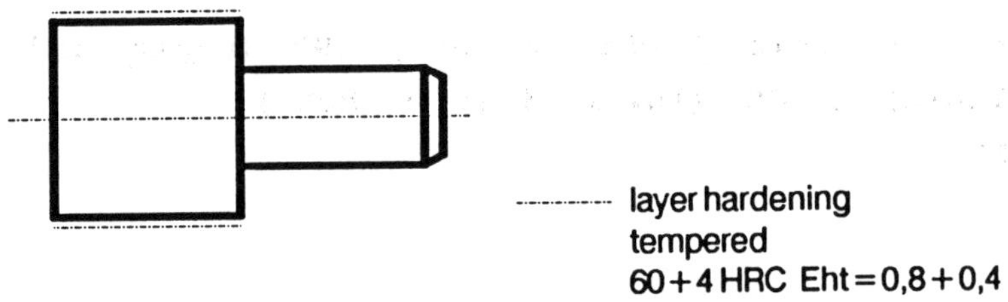

Fig. 7.5: Surface treatment information

```
*)
ENTITY  surface_treatment  SUPERTYPE  OF  (surface_hardening
                                XOR  surface_coat);
   application_area        : surface_indication;
```

```
   position_of_note        : sheet_position;
END_ENTITY;
(*
```

ATTRIBUTE DEFINITIONS:

application_area	:	The reference to the representations of the surfaces, that are subject to the surface treatment.
position_of_note	:	The position of the represented information.

7.3.11. SURFACE HARDENING

The entity type SURFACE_HARDENING being a subtype of SURFACE_TREATMENT describes the hardening procedure applied to a surface.
In the structure the following constraint has to be considered:

- In the lines the information is placed as follows: In the first line the procedure of hardening, in the second line the method of certifying the hardness and the hardness value together with its tolerance and in the third line the inspection tool and force are described.

```
*)
ENTITY surface_hardening SUBTYPE OF (surface_treatment);
   procedure              : hardening_technology;
   hardening_measurement : hardness_type;
   hardness_value         : POSITIVE_REAL;
   hardness_tolerance     : POSITIVE_REAL;
   inspection_tool_dim    : OPTIONAL POSITIVE_REAL;
   inspection_force       : OPTIONAL POSITIVE_REAL;
WHERE
   (* a *)  ( (inspection_force = NULL) AND
   (inspection_tool_dim = NULL) ) OR (
   (inspection_tool_dim <> NULL) AND ( (
   (hardening_measurement = .hb.) AND (inspection_force
   <> NULL) ) OR ( (hardening_measurement = .hv.) AND
   (inspection_force = NULL) ) ) );
END_ENTITY;
(*
```

ATTRIBUTE DEFINITIONS:

procedure : The referenced entity type HARRDENING_TECHNOLOGY is the supertype of entities describing several hardening procedures, i. e. carbonizing, layer hardening, nitrifying and the common hardening procedure.

hardening_measurement : This attribute denotes the type of hardness test. Enumerated are "HV", "HB" and "HRC".

hardness_value : The value of the hardness.

hardness_tolerance : The upper tolerance of the admissible hardness.

inspection_tool_dim : The dimension of the tool used for the inspection of the hardness. Where a hardness test according to "HRC" is applied, the attribute **inspection_tool_dim** has to be omitted.

inspection_force : The force applied for inspection that has to be determined, where a hardening test according to "HV" is defined.

PROPOSITIONS:

a. Only where a hardness test according to "HB" or "HV" is applied, a dimension of the inspection tool is required. Additional to that the definition of a inspection force is necessary in case of a hardness test according to "HB".

7.3.12. SURFACE COAT

The entity type SURFACE_HARDENING describes the coat of a surface.

```
*)
ENTITY  surface_coat  SUBTYPE  OF  (surface_treatment);
   covering_material      : STRING;
   comment                : OPTIONAL  STRING;
   material_thickness     : OPTIONAL  POSITIVE_REAL;
END_ENTITY;
(*
```

ATTRIBUTE DEFINITIONS:

covering_material	:	The material of the coat.
comment	:	A further specification of the coat, where necessary.
material_thickness	:	The coating thickness.

7.3.13. SURFACE INDICATION

The structure SURFACE_INDICATION establishes the associativity of the description of the surface treatment with the surface representations.
In the structure the following constraint has to be considered:

- The represented surfaces may be marked by a chain thin line.

```
*)
ENTITY  surface_indication;
   represented_surface    : LIST  [1:#]  OF  surface_app;
   start_point            : OPTIONAL  view_position;
   end_point              : OPTIONAL  view_position;
   offset_value           : POSITIVE_REAL;
WHERE
   (* a *)   (sizeof  (represented_surface)  =  1)  OR  (
   (sizeof  (represented_surface)  >  1)  AND  (connected
   (represented_surface[i].appearance_of_geometry,
   represented_surface[i+1].appearance_of_geometry)  );
   (* b *)   (  (start_point  =  NULL)  AND  (end_point  =  NULL)
   )  OR  (  (start_point  <>  NULL)  AND  (end_point  <>  NULL)
   AND  (embedded  (start_point,  represented_surface)  )  AND
   (embedded  (end_point,  represented_surface)  )  AND
   (start_point  <>  end_point)  );
END_ENTITY;
(*
```

ATTRIBUTE DEFINITIONS:

represented_surface	:	The reference to the representations of the surfaces to which a specified surface treatment has to be applied to.
start_point	:	A position at a surface representation where the chain thin line starts. If both the values of **start_point start_point** are omitted, the indicated surfaces are not marked.
end_point	:	The position at a surface representation where the chain thin line terminates.
offset_value	:	The offset of the chain thin line to the surface representation.

PROPOSITIONS:

a. The indicated surface representations have to be connected.

b. Where a start and terminating point of the chain thin line are specified, they have to be different and have to lie on the surface representations.

7.3.14. HARDENING TECHNOLOGY

HARDENING_TECHNOLOGY is the structure of the description of the technology applied for the hardening process. The following alternatives are supported: Hardening, carbonizing, layer hardening and nitrifying.

```
*)
ENTITY hardening_technology SUPERTYPE OF (hardening XOR
                          carbonizing XOR layer_hardening
                          XOR nitrifying);
   tempering                   : LOGICAL;
END_ENTITY;
(*
```

ATTRIBUTE DEFINITIONS:

tempering : This flag denotes whether a further tempering process is applied or not.

7.3.15. HARDENING

This entity type describes a common hardening process.

```
*)
ENTITY hardening SUBTYPE OF (hardening_technology);
   annealing                    : LOGICAL;
END_ENTITY;
(*
```

ATTRIBUTE DEFINITIONS:

annealing : This flag denotes whether an annealing process is applied or not.

7.3.16. CARBONIZING

This entity type is applied, where a carbonizing process has to be specified.

```
*)
ENTITY carbonizing SUPERTYPE OF (hardening_technology);
   annealing              : LOGICAL;
   layer_thickness        : POSITIVE_REAL;
   thickness_tolerance    : POSITIVE_REAL;
END_ENTITY;
(*
```

ATTRIBUTE DEFINITIONS:

annealing	:	This flag denotes whether an annealing process is applied or not.
layer_thickness	:	The thickness of the layer that has to be hardened.
thickness_tolerance	:	The tolerance value for the thickness of the hardened layer.

7.3.17. LAYER HARDENING

This entity type is applied, where a layer hardening process has to be specified.

```
*)
ENTITY  layer_hardening  SUPERTYPE  OF
                         (hardening_technology);
   annealing                : LOGICAL;
   layer_thickness          : POSITIVE_REAL;
   thickness_tolerance      : POSITIVE_REAL;
END_ENTITY;
(*
```

ATTRIBUTE DEFINITIONS:

annealing	:	This flag denotes whether an annealing process is applied or not.
layer_thickness	:	The thickness of the layer that has to be hardened.
thickness_tolerance	:	The tolerance value for the thickness of the hardened layer.

7.3.18. NITRIFYING

This entity type is applied, where a layer nitrifying has to be specified.

```
*)
ENTITY nitrifying SUPERTYPE OF (hardening_technology);
   layer_thickness          : POSITIVE_REAL;
   thickness_tolerance      : POSITIVE_REAL;
END_ENTITY;
(*
```

ATTRIBUTE DEFINITIONS:

annealing	:	This flag denotes whether an annealing process is applied or not.
layer_thickness	:	The thickness of the layer that has to be hardened.
thickness_tolerance	:	The tolerance value for the thickness of the hardened layer.

7.3.19. DIMENSION OF CORNER

IMENSION_OF_CORNER is the structure for dimensioning corners. It is possible to dimension several specified corners by a general symbol (supported by the subtype GENERAL_CORNER_DIM) or to dimension single corners by attaching a corner dimension symbol to each of them (subtype SELECTED_CORNER_DIM). Representations of the symbol are shown in figure 7.6.

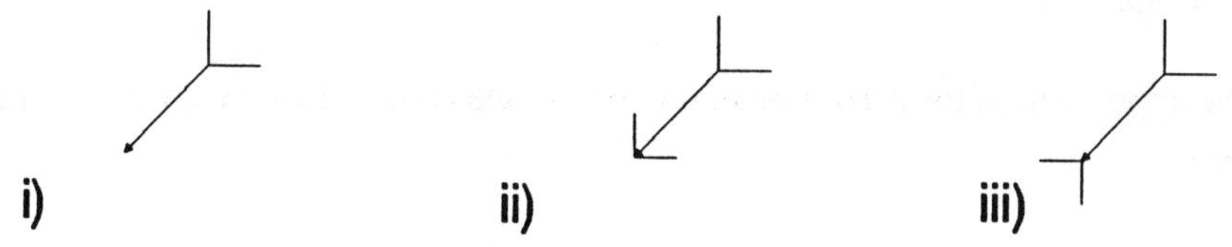

Fig. 7.6: The corner dimension symbol: i) Basic symbol, ii) symbol for internal corners, iii) symbol for external corners

In the structure the following constraints have to be considered:

- Where a general corner symbol is applied, it is placed horizontally next to the information field.
- Where a single corner is specified, the symbol points at the corner representation.

```
*)
ENTITY  dimension_of_corner  SUPERTYPE  OF
                             (selected_corner_dim  XOR
                             general_corner_dim);
   upper_corner_limit       : REAL;
   lower_corner_limit       : REAL;
   spec_placement_at_symb  : corner_orientation;
WHERE
   (* a *)   upper_corner_limit  >  lower_corner_limit;
END_ENTITY;
(*
```

ATTRIBUTE DEFINITIONS:

upper_corner_limit	:	The upper limit of the derivation of the form of the corner.
lower_corner_limit	:	The lower limit of the derivation of the form of the corner.
spec_placement_at_symb	:	The placement of the limit specifications within the symbol that denotes whether the corner has a horizontal, vertical or neutral orientation with regard to the orientation of the represented symbol.

PROPOSITIONS:

a. The upper limit of the derivation of the form of the corner has to be greater than the lower limit.

7.3.20. SELECTED CORNER DIM

SELECTED_CORNER_DIM is the description of a corner dimension symbol specifying a single corner and pointing at the representation of the corner.

```
*)
ENTITY  selected_corner_dim  SUBTYPE  OF
                             (dimension_of_corner);
```

```
   position_of_symbol     : view_position;
   referenced_corner      : corner_rep;
END_ENTITY;
(*
```

ATTRIBUTE DEFINITIONS:

position_of_symbol	:	The position of the intersecting points of the three lines of the symbol.
referenced_corner	:	The reference to the representation of the specified corner.

7.3.21. GENERAL CORNER DIM

GENERAL_CORNER_DIM is the description of a corner dimension symbol specifying several corners. A special type of corner (either internal or external) may be specified. The symbol is placed next to the information field.

```
*)
ENTITY  general_corner_dim  SUBTYPE  OF
                           (dimension_of_corner);
   position_of_symbol     : sheet_position;
   internal_external      : corner_generalization;
END_ENTITY;
(*
```

ATTRIBUTE DEFINITIONS:

position_of_symbol	:	The position of the intersecting points of the three lines of the symbol relative to the drawing coordinate system.
internal_external	:	The type of corners that are subject to the symbol (internal, external or both).

7.3.22. LEADER WITH NOTE

The entity type LEADER_WITH_NOTE describes the appearance of a leader associating a textual information to a geometry representation on a drawing sheet.

In the structure the following constraints have to be considered:

- The textual information is connected with the geometry representation by a polyline, the so-called leader line.
- The leader line terminates with an arrow at a geometry line, with a point on a surface and without a termination symbol at a dimension graph.

```
*)
ENTITY  leader_with_note;
   terminator_position      : view_position;
   text_position            : view_position;
   text_direction           : direction;    -- see /1/,
                              4.5.3.6
   polyline_points          : OPTIONAL LIST [1:#] OF
                              view_position;
   text                     : STRING;
WHERE
   (* a *)   coordinate_space (text_direction) = 2;
END_ENTITY;
(*
```

ATTRIBUTE DEFINITIONS:

terminator_position	:	The position of the termination symbol at a represented geometry line or on a represented surface or a dimension graph. The type of the termination symbol depends on the position of the symbol: The leader terminates with an arrow on a geometry line, with a point on a surface and witout a termination symbol at a dimension graph.
text_position	:	The placement of the text.
text_direction	:	The reading direction of the text.

polyline_points	:	The leader line starts at **text_position** and terminates at **terminator_position**. The positions determined by **polyline_points** define the polyline connecting **text_position** with **terminator_position**. Where **polyline_points** is omitted the leader line is a straight line.
text	:	The represented information content is specified by the attribute **text**.

PROPOSITIONS:

a. The dimensionality of text_direction has to have the value 2.

```
*)
END_SCHEMA;          -- end
   SHAPE_ATTRIBUTES_REPRESENTATION_SCHEMA;
(*
*)
END_SCHEMA;           -- end DRAFTING_SCHEMA;
(*
```

8. Additional Remarks

8.1. Associativity Between Annotation Graphs and the Geometry Descriptions

The intention of the submitted Drafting Model is to support a consistent set of data describing technical drawings. In this context "consistent" stands for lacking of contradictory information content and redundancies. Another fact taken into consideration is that the representation of annotation described by the data within the Drafting Model depends on the representation of the geometry. For achieving these goals it is necessary to distinguish between different sets of data:

- Data describing the representation of product information.
- Data containing the product information.

Transformed to the data within the Drafting Model describing annotation:

- Data describing the pictorial representation of annotation graphs, e. g.: The representation of extension lines, dimension lines, termination symbols, geometry tolerance frames, surface finish symbols, etc.
- Data containing product information. For example the dimensional value, tolerance value, etc. To avoid redundancies these data are derived from the Geometry or Tolerance Model etc., where they are either listed explicitely or they have to be calculated.

The distinction between data describing the three dimensional geometry of the product and those describing its two dimensional representation is the result of an analogous procedure.
In the current version of the presentation model of STEP/IPIM two possibilities for describing the representation of the geometry are enumerated:

a) Presentations of geometry may be described by the existing ISO standard for computer graphics metafiles (CGM, ISO 8632). Because there is no associativity preserved between product information and its representation, many disadvatages occur when transmitting presentation data with this solution: The transmitted data are partially redundant and therefore a further manipulation of the transmitted product model would result in a contradictory set of data. (E. g.: The overall dimensions of a product are inhered in the description of the product model. The lines and curves representing a view at the product model also inhere these dimensions. A manipulation of the original product model has no consequences on the presentation of the view, because there are no links between both the data describing the product model and the data describing its representation.)

b) More importance is attached to the concept of describing a representation of geometry by defining projection rules, the positioning of views and the paths and extent of the section areas (so-called "viewing-pipeline"). So the representation of geometry can be generated from the geometry model by applying these rules. This concept is obviously supporting the associativity between the product information and its representation.

As mentioned before the representation of annotation deeply depends on the representation of the geometry. So it is a logical conclusion to support associativity between annotation and geometry by describing the links between the represented annotation and the represented geometry. In case b) an indirect associativity of annotation to the geometry model is guaranteed. In case a) both annotation and geometry representation lack associativity to the geometry model. Another imaginable possibility would be the description of links between annotation and geometry model. The realization of this idea is very laboriously with regard to the various classes of geometry modeller of the CAD-Systems. A further problem would arise when trying to guarantee a valid representation of "view with annotation", e. g.: Where the description of a dimension graph is only linked with the geometry model, it is definetely not sure that the representation of the dimension graph is due to the representation of the geometry.

The proposed concept of the CAD*I Drafting Model supports links of the annotation representations to the representation of geometry. When establishing the links between the representation of both annotation and geometry, the two possibilities of describing the geometry representations as explained above have to be taken into consideration:

a) The data structures of a CGM file describing lines and curves of the geometry appearance can be easily transformed into data structures being proposed in chapter 3.4. After that these listed entities can be referenced by the entities describing graphical representations of annotation. But for several applications of annotation representations it is definetely not enough to represent lines and curves derived from the geometry model without any further semantic, e. g.: The diameter of a side projected cylinder has to be dimensioned by a diameter dimension in order to guarantee a valid "view with annotation". Up to now a side projection of a cylinder supported by the current presentation model would create a rectangle. Without any further information it is impossible to identify this representation as a side projected cylinder, because it might also be a projection of a rectangular plane or something like that. Even if the semantic "projected cylinder" would be attached to the rectangle, it would be difficult to interprete the picture in a right way, because the orientation of the cylinder might only be determined by a complicated reference to a second projection, assumed there is one (See figure 8.1). An additional representation of a center line would cause less expenses than referring to a second projection.

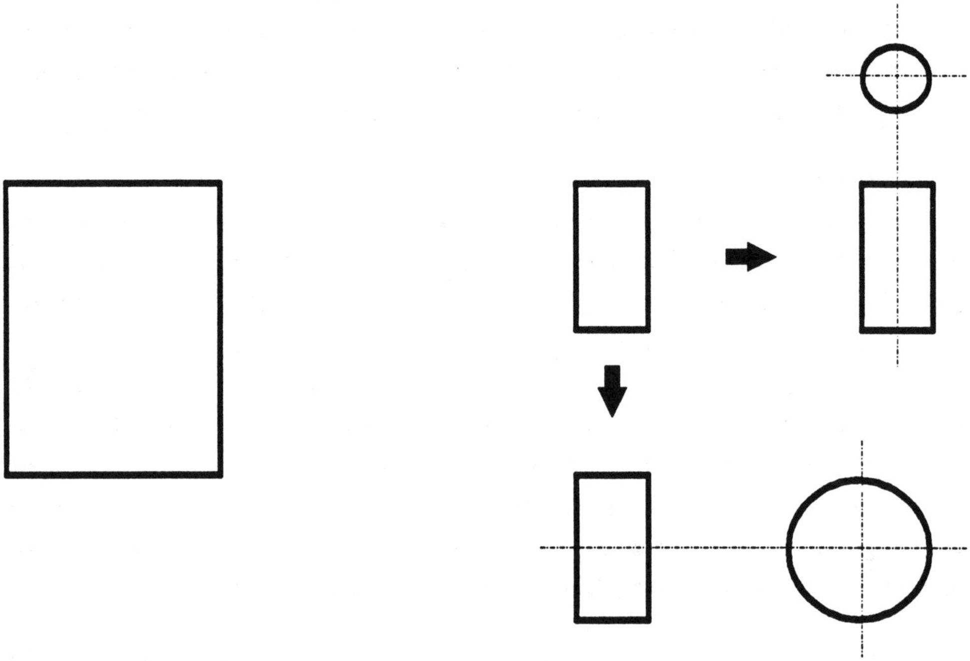

Fig. 8.1: Side projected cylinder and its possible orientations

Another solution would be the design of a capability of attaching attributes to all elements being a part of a geometry representation. In this example two parallel lines would carry the message "derived from a rotational surface" and "derived from two planes parallel to the direction of the projection" would be attached to the other two parallel lines. In this case also a description of a center line could be realized by drafting data.

b) Nearly the same problems arise, when considering the lines and curves that have to be derived from the transmitted Geometry Model as well as the presentation rules (i. e.: Projection rules, positioning of views, etc.). The only difference is that only the rules for generating those elements and not the descriptions of the lines and curves - as in case a) - are transmitted. So the projection rules have to be designed in such a way, that further semantics may be attached to the generated elements.

Up to now no solution is proposed for the associativity of annotation being attached to geometry that has no identifiable representation, e. g.: Where a note is directed to a represented surface by a leader and only the boundaries of the surface are represented, the termination symbol of the leader is placed within these boundaries, but there exists no description of the represented surface that could be referred to by the description of the leader.
A possibility to define areas bounded by represented curves and attaching the semantic "projected surface" would help overcoming this problem.

8.2. Example

The gradual proceeding when deriving a technical drawing from a product model is shown in figure 8.2.

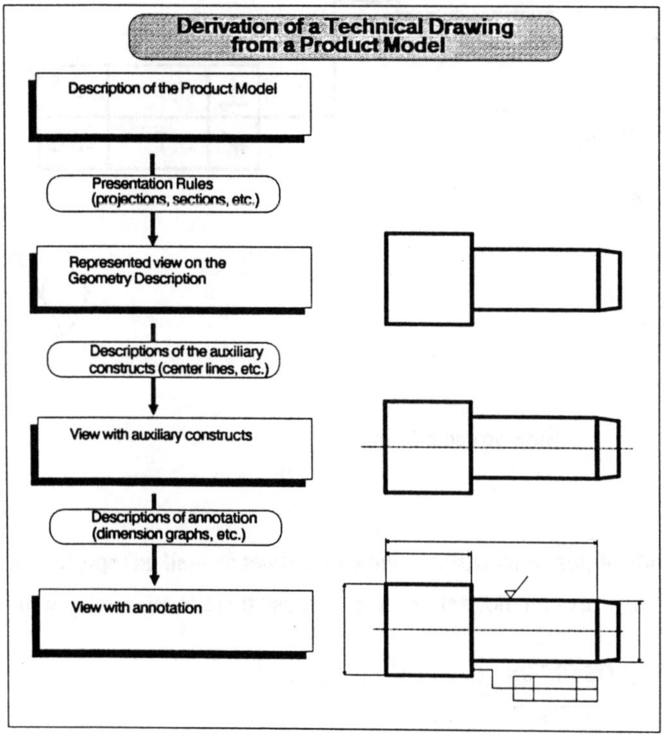

Fig. 8.2: Derivation of a technical drawing from a product model

Figure 8.3 shows the representation of a side projected pin described by the synthetic physical file listed below.

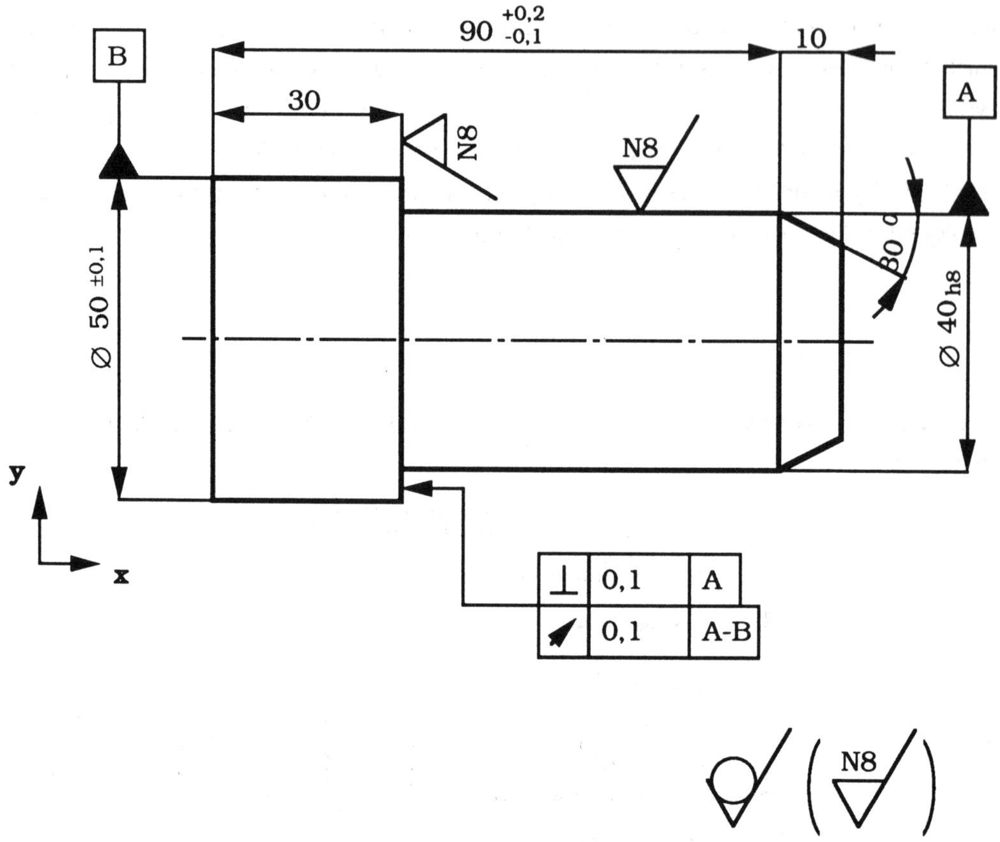

Fig. 8.3: Side projected pin

-- descriptions of positions within a view or a sheet as well as representations of geometry (the data structures are not defined yet, because there is an overlap with presentation data):

```
@1  = VIEW_POSITION (...);
@2  = VIEW_POSITION (...);
@3  = VIEW_POSITION (...);
@4  = VIEW_POSITION (...);
@5  = VIEW_POSITION (...);
@6  = VIEW_POSITION (...);
@7  = VIEW_POSITION (...);
@8  = VIEW_POSITION (...);
```

```
@9  = VIEW_POSITION (...);
@10 = VIEW_POSITION (...);
@15 = POINT_ON_GEOMETRY (...);
@16 = POINT_ON_GEOMETRY (...);
@20 = CENTER_LINE (...);
@21 = STRAIGHT_GEOMETRY_APP (...);
@22 = SURF_OF_REV_APP (...);
@23 = SURF_OF_REV_APP (...);
```

-- descriptions of the dimension graphs:

```
@50 = LIN_DIM (LIN_DIM (LIN_DIM (INITIAL_DIM_ATTRIBUTES
      (DIRECTION (1.0, 0,0,), #1), LINEAR_LENGTH_NOTATION
      (TOLERANCED_DIMENSION_APP (),,1,), DIM_NOTE_WITHOUT_LEADER
      (0.5), .T., 10.0, #2, .F.), LINEAR_LENGTH_NOTATION
      (TOLERANCED_DIMENSION_APP (SIZE_TOL_RANGE (+0.2, -0.1)
      ),,1,), DIM_NOTE_WITHOUT_LEADER (O.5), .T., 10.0, #3,
      .T.), LINEAR_LENGTH_NOTATION (TOLERANCED_DIMENSION_APP
      (),,1,), DIM_NOTE_WITHOUT_LEADER (0.5), .F.,, #4, .T.);
@51 = SIDE_DIA_DIM ((#20, #1, LINEAR_LENGTH_NOTATION
      (TOLERANCED_DIMENSION_APP (SIZE_TOL_RANGE (+0.1, -0.1)),,
      1,), DIM_NOTE_WITHOUT_LEADER (0.5), 15.0, .T.);
@52 = SIDE_DIA_DIM (#20, #3, LINEAR_LENGTH_NOTATION
      (TOLERANCED_DIMENSION_APP (FIT_CLASS_SPEC ('H', '8',
      .T.)),, 1,), DIM_NOTE_WITHOUT_LEADER (0.5), -30.0, .T.);
@53 = ROTATIONAL_CHAMFER_DIMENSION (PLANAR_ANGLE_NOTATION
      (TOLERANCED_DIMENSION_APP (),, 1,
      .DEGREE.),DIM_NOTE_WITHOUT_LEADER (0.5),
      .COUNTERCLOCKWISE., .F., +10.0, #4, DIRECTION (-0.5, -
      0.866,), #52);
```

-- descriptions of the geometry tolerance representations:

```
@60 = AXIS_DATUM (#22, INDIRECT_LINK (POINT_ON_DIMENSION_GRAPH
      (#5, #52), DIRECTION (0.0, 1.0), 'A', .NONE., 20.0),);
```

```
@61 = AXIS_DATUM (#23, INDIRECT_LINK (POINT_ON_DIMENSION_GRAPH
      (#9, #51), DIRECTION (0.0, 1.0), 'B', .NONE., 20.0),);
@70 = SHAPE_LOC_TOL_COMPOUND ((PERP_PLANE_ORIENT_TOL (0.1,,
      .NONE., #15, #21, AXIS1_DATUM (#60), .F.),
      CIRCULAR_RUNOUT_TOL (#21, 0.1, #15, DIRECTION (-1.0, 0.0),
      #60, #61,)), #6, REFERENCE_LINE ((#7, #8)),);
```

-- descriptions of the surface finish symbols:

```
@75 = NOTATION_OF_SURFACE_FINISH ((#22), SURF_FIN_WITH_CUTTING
      (SURFACE_QUALITY ('8',),,, DIRECTION (0.0, 1.0,),,,),
      (#11));
@76 = NOTATION_OF_SURFACE_FINISH ((#21), SURF_FIN_WITH_CUTTING
      (SURFACE_QUALITY ('8',),,, DIRECTION (1.0, 0.0,),,,),
      (POINT_ON_DIMENSION_GRAPH (#10, #50));
@77 = GENERAL_SURF_FINISH (SURF_FIN_WITHOUT_CUTTING (,,,
      DIRECTION (0.0, 1.0,)), (#75, #76), SHEET_POSITION (100.0,
      20.0), .T.);
```

References

/1/ ISO STEP Baseline Requirements Document (IPIM)
ISO TC184/SC4/WG1 Document Number N 284
Owner: P.R. Wilson and P.R. Kennicott
October 27, 1988

/2/ Information Modeling Language EXPRESS
ISO TC184/SC4/WG1 Document Number N 307
Owner: Douglas Schenck
December 19, 1988

/3/ Mapping from EXPRESS to Physical File Structure
ISO TC184/SC4/WG1 Document Number N 280
Owner: Jeff Altemueller
September, 1988

/4/ Drafting Facts and Thoughts
ISO TC184/SC4/WG1 Document Number N 197
Owner: R. Korff and M. Endres
January, 1988

/5/ German Contribution to Drafting Model Standardization
ISO TC184/SC4/WG1 Document
Owner: R. Korff etal.
July 1, 1988

/6/ EXPRESS Style Rules
ISO TC184/SC4/WG1 Document Number N 325
Owner: J. Owen and N. Shaw
November 24, 1988

/7/ Initial Graphics Exchange Specification (IGES) Version 4.0
U.S. Department of Commerce
June 1988

/8/ A Guide to Reading an IDEF1X Model
ISO TC184/SC4/WG1 Document Number N 273
Owner: Anne Williams
August 2, 1988

/9/ EXPRESSAM - A Graphical EXPRESS Notation
ISO TC184/SC4/WG1 Document Number N 294
Owner: Bruce E. Lownsbery
October 14, 1988

/10/ Michael Endres, Definition eines CAD-Datenmodells für den Austausch von technischer Information im Anwendungsgebiet "Mechanische Konstruktion" des Automobilbaus"
Thesis at the Technical University of Munich, April 1989

/11/ R. Schuster, D. Trippner, Erfahrungen beim CAD/CAM-Datentransfer mit der IGES-Schnittstelle
CAD/CAM No.4/85, 58-64

/12/ D. Trippner, Experience Gained Using the IGES Interface for CAD/CAM Data Transfer
in: J. Encarnação, R. Schuster, E. Vöge, "Product Data Interfaces in CAD/CAM Applications", 126-141, Springer-Verlag 1986

/13/ K. M. Mittelstaedt, D. Trippner, CAD Data Exchange - Standards, Techniques and Applications
in: M.M. Ruiter (editor), "Advances in Computer Graphics III", 241-292, Springer Verlag 1988

/14/ R. Schuster, D. Trippner, K. Griesbach, Datenmodelle für den Austausch von Produkt- und Fertigungsdaten
Informatik - Forschung und Entwicklung 3 (3), 139-146, 1988

Index

Functions

Defined Types

Entity Types